BLACKBEARD
THE PIRATE

BLACKBEARD THE PIRATE

A Reappraisal of His Life and Times

✦ ✦ ✦

By Robert E. Lee

Dean and Professor of Law Emeritus
Wake Forest University

JOHN F. BLAIR, *Publisher*
Winston-Salem, North Carolina

Eighth Printing, 1995

Copyright © 1974 by Robert E. Lee
Library of Congress Catalog Card Number: 74–75752
Printed in the United States of America
All Rights Reserved

ISBN 0–89587–032–0

Preface

THIS IS A HISTORY of the marauding adventures of Captain Edward Teach, a picturesque colonial pirate. His incredible daredevil feats were a part of the very fabric of the times in which he lived. This history is intended for those who desire to read, against a historical background, true accounts of daring deeds of personal courage.

I have aimed at exhibiting in microcosm the character and spirit of a vanished age and at reclaiming those fragments of truth which many historians either have never discovered or have scornfully rejected, and which novelists have only in part appropriated. I have attempted to segregate fiction and legends from the historical facts. To this end, I have analyzed critically all available source materials. I have tried to scrutinize all extant records, both published and unpublished, including those of the Public Record Office of Great Britain and the state archives and historical societies in this country, as well as contemporary books of the early eighteenth century and letters and documents not available to early writers. Because many readers do not want their eyes distracted by footnotes, the source materials have been placed in the back of the book.

Edward Teach, better known as Blackbeard, is a historical figure. In telling of his epic actions, I narrate something of the laws, customs, and problems of the society in which, even if peripherally, he lived. A period's history can probably best be told through the biography of one of its leading characters, be he a hero or a villain.

It is a common error of mankind to judge the historical figures of a past age by the moral standards of the present. One cannot understand history if one takes men and events out of their moral context and attempts to interpret them by present-day values. The colonial pirates of the early 1700's and those with whom they dealt should be fairly judged in terms of their own milieu, which was not that of a Victorian drawing room.

The author wishes to acknowledge gratefully the valuable assistance rendered by the following persons, who have read the entire manuscript and made suggestions while the work was in progress: the Hon. R. Hunt Parker, late Chief Justice of the Supreme Court of North Carolina; Dr. Harold W. Tribble, President Emeritus of Wake Forest University; C. F. W. Coker, Assistant State Archivist of the North Carolina Department of Archives and History; Harold B. Gill, Jr., Research Associate at Colonial Williamsburg, Inc.; Lucien W. Emerson, a boyhood friend who, under the pseudonym Peter Field, has written more than forty books; and William C. Myers, of the Winston-Salem Bar.

ROBERT E. LEE

Winston-Salem, N.C.
February 19, 1974

Contents

BLACKBEARD
THE PIRATE

Chapter 1

Early Life of Blackbeard

*B*LACKBEARD was the boldest and most notorious of the sea rovers who infested the coastal waters of the English southern colonies in the New World in the early 1700's. His activities, and those of his contemporaries, are an integral part of the colonial history of the United States. Occurring during a period frequently called "the golden age of piracy," their daring exploits ushered in the beginning of the end of piracy on the high seas.

Few authentic records of Blackbeard's life have come to light for any period other than the two or three years before his death. But his deeds during this brief span were meteoric, shooting across the maritime skies of two continents and causing his name to be remembered forever. Aside from appearing in hundreds of history books, his name may be found, in one form or another, in the archives of Great Britain and among the public records of the early governments of Pennsylvania, Virginia, North Carolina, and South Carolina. We know the exact details surrounding his melodramatic death but little about his life prior to 1716, except that he was born in Bristol, England,[1] and that he served as a seaman out of Jamaica on board the ships of privateers during Queen Anne's War.[2] In 1900, Thomas T. Upshur claimed that Teach came from Virginia, but there is no evidence to substantiate his claim.[3]

Customarily, very little can be learned of the childhood and youth of even the best-known pirates. Pirates rarely wrote about themselves and their families. Each hoped to acquire a vast fortune and return to his former home without having tarnished his family name. Historians, therefore, can pinpoint documented records of the capture of ships, "with details of longitude and latitude, inventories of looted cargo, and minute particulars relating to atrocious conduct"; but they can discover little or nothing about the pirates' personal lives before they committed acts of piracy.[4] If a buccaneer was killed in battle, or captured and put on trial, details are not lacking. In this respect, Edward Teach's life follows the pattern of that of most other pirate captains.

It is commonly believed, however, that at the time of his death Blackbeard was a man somewhere between thirty-five and forty years of age.[5] This would place his birth at some time around the year 1680.

There is no absolute certainty as to Blackbeard's real surname. It was the custom of pirates to adopt one or more fictitious surnames while engaging in piracy. In all the records made during the period in which he was committing his sea robberies, he is identified as either Blackbeard or Edward Teach. There are numerous spellings of the latter name, such as Thatch, Thach, Thache, Thack, Tack, Thatche, and Theach. Teach is the form most commonly encountered, and for this reason most historians have identified him by that name. Long after his death the claim was made that Blackbeard's surname in Bristol was Drummond, but this assertion, unsupported by any documented proof, has not been generally accepted by historians. Very likely we shall never know what name Blackbeard bore in his native Bristol.[6]

There are some indications that Edward Teach was born into an intelligent, respectable, well-to-do family, and, if so, he had all the more reason to abandon his real name and assume an alias. Apparently he was an educated man, for there is no doubt that he could read and write. He corresponded with merchants, and, at the time of his death, he had a letter in his possession addressed to him by the Chief Justice and Secretary of the Province of North Carolina, Tobias Knight. Furthermore, he seemed at ease not only in the company of villainous ruffians but also with governors, as if he were accustomed to moving in high circles and to the easy assumption of leadership.

It is hardly surprising that Blackbeard, being a native of Bristol, chose to follow the sea. Located in southwestern England at the confluence of the rivers Avon and Frome, and about eight miles from the Bristol Channel, Bristol was one of the best examples of English towns owing their early growth entirely to sea trade, principally with foreign countries. The Society of Merchant Adventurers was organized there in the 1400's, and by 1500 the Society regulated all the foreign trade of the city and held a lease on port dues. With the colonization of America, the Bristol merchants constructed ships that carried African slaves to the West Indies and obtained, in exchange, sugar and other items from those islands. By the time Edward Teach lived there, Bristol had grown until it was the second-largest city in England.[7]

It was the merchants of Bristol who, shortly after the discovery of America, financed the voyages of John and Sebastian Cabot in the hope of finding a short route to Asia by sailing westward across the Atlantic.[8] William Hawkins and his son John, from Plymouth, were among the many who made further voyages from this area of England. This was the seedtime for the heroic age that was to follow.

But it was the pirates who made England rich and great in her dawn of overseas expansion. Francis Drake, born in Devonshire about 1545, sailed from Plymouth in 1577 on his round-the-world plundering expedition. Upon his return in September, 1580, Queen Elizabeth ordered the royal barge rowed down the Thames so that she might knight the "master thief of the known world on the deck of his *Golden Hind*."[9] The loot Drake brought back to England has been moderately valued at £1,500,000.[10]

Later, in June, 1586, homeward bound from his great raid in the West Indies, Drake luckily appeared off the coast of North Carolina with twenty-three vessels and rescued the survivors of Sir Walter Raleigh's first Roanoke Island colony.[11]

A recent English authority on pirates has written:

If Elizabeth was on the whole severe with pirates operating in home waters, she was more than indulgent with those who ventured further afield. As the national hostility to Spain increased she not only shut her eyes to their aggressions against the Spaniards but even took a financial interest in their ventures. Piracy in wartime had always been more or less sanctioned by the state, but under Elizabeth it was connived at while England was at peace with all the world. As a result of this unofficial encouragement not only was much wealth brought into a poor country but, a matter of far greater importance, a race of tough seamen was evolved which was to save England in her need, bring about the downfall of her principal enemy, and make her the proud mistress of the seas.[12]

In keeping with the precedents established under Elizabeth and other earlier sovereigns, a syndicate of Bristol merchants, in 1708, provided financial support for a plundering expedition around the world. They equipped two vessels under the command of Woodes Rogers, a highly competent officer and navigator from Bristol, who was later to play a small part in Blackbeard's career.

Rogers was a man about thirty years of age and had himself made the original proposal and drafted the plans for the expedition. His family had been prominent in the affairs of Bristol for several generations, and his father before him had followed a career at sea. Strengthening Rogers' ties to the sea was his marriage three years earlier to the eighteen-year-old daughter of Rear Admiral Sir William Whetstone of Bristol, who was the Commander-in-Chief of the West Indies.

Associated with Rogers on the voyage were Captains William Campier, Edward Cooke, Stephen Courtney, and Thomas

Dover. Dover was a successful Bristol physician who could not resist the temptation to take sea voyages. There was a crew of about 334 men, and the two ships, the *Duke* and the *Duchess*, had been especially designed for the planned circumnavigation of the globe. They sailed from Bristol on August 2, 1708, flying the Union Jack and the Red Jack of the privateer, and returned to England on October 14, 1711, with a fabulous net profit that was estimated to range from £200,000 to £800,000.[13]

This expedition led also to the discovery of Alexander Selkirk, the man on whom Daniel Defoe is supposed to have based *Robinson Crusoe*. Selkirk was a buccaneer who, in 1704, had had differences with his captain and had been put ashore on the island of Juan Fernández, located in the Pacific Ocean off the coast of South America, where he lived alone for more than four years. The Rogers expedition found him and brought him back to England.[14] Rogers' book, *A Cruising Voyage Round the World*, has a clear and concise account of Selkirk's experiences on Juan Fernández.

The financial promoters of Rogers' business venture had been influential in obtaining the enactment by Parliament of a new Prize Act in 1708. At one time the Crown had received a fifth of the profits from all privateering enterprises. Later, that was reduced to a tenth. But under the new Prize Act, the Crown received nothing at all. The owners of the vessels and the private investors who had financed a particular voyage received the largest share. A smaller share went to the officers of the expedition, and a still smaller share to the crews.[15] Woodes Rogers became for a time one of the wealthiest men in Bristol, purchasing a fine residence on Queen's Square, then the most fashionable section of the city.[16]

Edward Teach was undoubtedly swayed by Bristol's maritime heritage and traditions, its reliance on sea trade and privateering. But there must have been other influences at work,

too, though these can only be surmised. If he was an educated
boy, it is quite possible that he had read many of the books on
sea travel, exploration, and buccaneering that were available to
the members of the upper classes in the late seventeenth century.
Richard Hakluyt had published, in 1582, *Divers Voyages
Touching the Discovery of America*, and, in 1589, his greatest
work, *Principall Navigations, Voiages and Discoveries of the
English Nation*. A. O. Esquemeling's *Bucaniers of America*
was first published in Amsterdam in 1679, and its English trans-
lation was published in London in 1684. William Dampier published the first volume of his *Voyages* in 1697, other accounts
being issued in 1699 and 1707. And John Lawson's *A New
Voyage to Carolina* first appeared in 1709, although by this
time Teach had probably left Bristol on his own adventures.

The very times in which he lived may have had their impact
on the young Teach. During this period, England was almost
continually at war, the principal battles of which were fought
at sea. King William III's War was fought with France between
1689 and 1697. In 1702, there broke out the renewal of conflict
with Spain, which was to last eleven years. Formally known as
the War of the Spanish Succession, though in America it was
generally called Queen Anne's War, the hostilities ended in
1713 with the Utrecht Treaty.

The scant information available on Teach's early life suggests
that he did, indeed, go to war. There is, however, no record of
when he left his native Bristol and took to the sea. But Captain
Charles Johnson, a recognized authority on the pirates of the
era, states emphatically in his volume, *A General History of the
Robberies and Murders of the Most Notorious Pirates*,* that

*Nothing is known about the identity of the author who signed his
name Captain Charles Johnson. The name may very well be an assumed
one. There are some who believe that the author was Daniel Defoe. Captain Johnson's volume, originally published in 1724, has provided the

Edward Teach sailed for some time out of Jamaica on the ships of privateers during Queen Anne's War, and that "he had often distinguished himself for his uncommon boldness and personal courage."[17] But whether he joined the fighting when the war broke out in 1702 or toward the end in 1713 or sometime in the intervening years is not known.

It was natural enough that a sailor born and reared in Bristol should find his way to the West Indies. This was the scene of perhaps the greatest number of maritime incidents of the seventeenth and early eighteenth centuries. And here were to be found the "Brethren of the Coast," men who at first were privateers and later became pirates.

The Brethren of the Coast were a strange fraternity, united in a spirit of adventure, a love of gold, and a hatred of Spain. They exchanged tales of experiences on tropical islands, where they ate well, tasted delicious fruits, drank intoxicating beverages, fought, and enjoyed the companionship of the unsophisticated daughters of Africa and the Indies. One would suppose that the successful pirate lived a wild and exciting life that was, to him, most satisfactory.

The Bahama Islands, because of their position at the head of the Caribbean and near the shipping lanes to and from Europe, became at about this time the corner of the world where piracy flourished most.[18] New Providence Island, especially, was well placed for piracy. Many of the ablest and best-known pirates used this island as their base of operations. It was ideal, both offensively and defensively, for their business. The Atlantic Ocean has, in that region, currents, shoals, and surfs that make navigation extremely hazardous, particularly for large merchant

---

framework for many books on piracy in subsequent years. Whoever wrote the volume must have had some access to the official correspondence of the times, for much of the information, even conversation, is corroborated in both personal and official dispatches.

ships. The small craft generally used by pirates, however, could be navigated safely through the treacherous waters, for the local seamen knew well the dangers of the area.

The present-day beautiful city of Nassau bears no resemblance to the principal town of New Providence in the early 1700's. In Blackbeard's time, it was nothing more than a mariner's resort, a place where the ordinary sailor or pirate could go for a few days to whoop it up and let off steam. For nearly every dozen pirates there was a bar with entertainment. And if a sailor wanted a woman—and few men of the sea did not—there was an ample supply of all ages, shapes, and tints. The half-breed prostitute was in greatest demand.

It [New Providence] was no city of homes; it was a place of temporary sojourn and refreshment for a literally floating population. The only permanent residents were the piratical camp followers, the traders, and the hangers-on; all others were transient. The shanty town of improvised tents and palm-leaf shelters would have been squalid had it not been for the almost incredible beauty of the island.[19]

Apparently by common consent, whatever system of law and order existed depended upon a council of the captains and quartermasters who happened to be ashore at any particular time.[20]

The pirates were definitely the aristocracy of this colony, then came the traders, the smugglers, and hangers-on. All of this motley band lived well, if somewhat turbulently. They were free of any but self-imposed restraints, they had plenty to eat and more to drink, and they had as much social security as any of them had ever enjoyed before.[21]

Michael Craton, in *A History of the Bahamas*, states that, after Queen Anne's War, "all semblance of organized government broke down and . . . the pirates were in undisputed control."[22]

It was easy for the pirates to take over New Providence for use as their base. Nassau had been sacked and plundered by a combined Spanish and French expedition from Havana in October, 1703; in October, 1706, the Spanish had returned and destroyed what they had left standing three years earlier. The land on New Providence and the other Bahama Islands was owned by six Lords Proprietors. These six, along with two others, were also Lords Proprietors of Carolina. Apparently, they did not consider it profitable to maintain law and order in their province. Consequently, the pirates simply moved in. What the Bahamas needed was a strong Royal Governor, backed up by military and naval forces of the English Crown. Such a man was not forthcoming until June, 1718.

The irresistible allurements of New Providence were not to be denied to Edward Teach, a man destined to possess all the romantic qualifications requisite to fame as a pirate. Probably shortly after Queen Anne's War, he transferred the base of his operations from Jamaica to New Providence.[23] And, as with most of those who had been privateers during the war, it was inevitable that he should turn to piracy. It was a common and a customary way of life for men in the West Indies who were out of work and a long way from home. Robberies, whether on land or sea, have always increased after a war.

It was in New Providence that Edward Teach met and formed a friendship with Captain Benjamin Hornigold. According to Captain Johnson, Teach joined Hornigold's crew sometime late in 1716.[24] Benjamin Hornigold was the fiercest and ablest of all the pirates who regularly operated out of the island, and no one, at the time, was held in higher esteem by the Brethren of the Coast. The whole of the West Indies was a spawning and training area for pirates, and if any one person could have been called the dean of this school of pirates it was Hornigold. Teach served his apprenticeship under a master of the art.

From the harbor of Nassau, Captain Hornigold and his pupil

made their sorties to capture ships of all nations upon the trackless seas. "As an eager young hand aboard Hornigold's pirate ship, Teach showed that he had a marksman's eye, an ability at dirty infighting and a thirst for blood unmatched by any pirate of his time. Hornigold recognized this early and made the young man his protegé."[25]

Sometime in 1716, Captain Hornigold put Edward Teach in charge of a sloop that Teach had taken as a prize after fierce fighting. Teach equipped the sloop with six cannons and a complement of seventy men, after which he continued his alliance with Hornigold.[26]

Teach's daring exploits at sea were discussed and embellished in the taverns of Nassau. His reputation spread alike among seamen who were pirates and those who were not. When he strode into a tavern and demanded a drink, all eyes were upon him. He had, it seems, an amazing tolerance for liquor. Rum was never his master. He could handle it as could no other man of his day, and he was never known to pass out from an excess. "His drinking powers were unmatched."[27] There was never a time in his life when he could not stand up straight and meet the emergency of the occasion. On one occasion, being the showman that he was, Teach impressed those in the tavern "by mixing gunpowder in his rum, setting it on fire and guzzling the explosive mixture."[28]

After taking up pirating, Teach rarely stayed long in New Providence, but moved constantly in and out of its harbor on some new adventure. He did not waste his time in idleness at the bars of the town.

But instead of setting up shore quarters in the town, he established himself at the foot of a hill east of what is now the center of Nassau. Atop the hill he built himself an impressive watchtower; the remains of it are there today. From it he could see far out across the blue-green waters of the Bahamas. It was also an idyllic hideout from dunning tavern keepers and women. Occasionally Blackbeard would descend the tower steps and the steep, narrow trail to the pathway below, where he and some of his favorites from among the crew had set up a few tents. There, under a huge tree, he held court—trading loot, interviewing volunteers for his next cruise, planning its itinerary, and drinking more rum.[29]

Craton states: "In Nassau he is remembered by a tavern, a well, and a lookout tower. Hundreds of tales are still told of his exploits and he is probably the best known of all Bahamian 'historical' characters."[30]

With the coming of spring in 1717, Hornigold and Teach, each captaining a sloop, sailed forth from New Providence for the mainland of America. This was probably the last time Teach was seen on that island. Out upon the high seas they had little difficulty in capturing a sloop from Havana with 120 barrels of flour. Shortly thereafter they stopped a sloop from Bermuda, with one Thurbar as her master, relieved the vessel of several hundred barrels of her cargo of wine, and permitted her to proceed on her way.[31]

Several days later they sighted a large ship sailing from Madeira to Charleston, South Carolina.[32] At sundown the two sloops of Hornigold and Teach, flying their black flags, came upon the scene so suddenly that the master became terrified and offered no resistance whatsoever. From this ship they removed considerable plunder of great value. There are no located historical records of where Hornigold and Teach disposed of their stolen merchandise after this particular voyage.

In the summer or early fall of 1717, the two pirates were seen on the eastern shore of Virginia with their ships careened for the purpose of cleaning the hulls.[33]

On September 29, 1717, near Cape Charles, Virginia, Teach was reported to have attacked and taken into custody the sloop *Betty* of Virginia and to have taken goods therefrom, including some Madeira wine.[34] Having no use for the sloop, the pirates scuttled her with her remaining cargo.

In the Bay of Delaware, on October 22, 1717, Teach's pirates captured the sloop *Robert* of Philadelphia and the sloop *Good Intent* of Dublin, as both headed up the Delaware River for the port of Philadelphia.[35] Everything of any value was removed by the pirates from the two sloops.

Probably during the latter part of 1717, Hornigold and Teach, having returned to the West Indies, sighted off the island of St. Vincent, near latitude 24, a large merchantman flying the French flag.[36] They ran the black flags up their masts and instantly went in pursuit. They came with such speed upon the merchantman that her captain was unable to maneuver her into battle position. Hornigold's sloop closed in on one quarter, Teach's sloop on the other. Before the merchantman's captain could decide what procedure to take, both pirate ships fired a broadside across his bulwarks that killed half his men and terrified the remainder into surrender.

The prize turned out to be the *Concord* of St. Malo, a large French guineaman, commanded by a Captain D'Ocier and carrying a rich cargo of gold dust, money, plate, jewels, and other goods.[37] The ship had been engaging in commerce between the French island of Martinique and the African coast. She was a Dutch-built vessel, well constructed and fast. The two broadsides had done practically no damage to her hull. Teach admired the mighty ship and asked Hornigold whether he could claim her as a prize and be placed in command. Hornigold granted the request, for Teach had demonstrated his ability to handle such a ship.

At about this time, Hornigold had decided on a change of careers. He intended to retire from piracy and take up the honest life of a planter on New Providence. He had been highly successful as a freebooter and had been able to amass a sizable fortune from his well-executed plunderings. He could afford to follow an honest trade. Consequently, he had no need of the *Concord*.

The two pirates shook hands and said their farewells. Neither was ever to see the other again.

Hornigold made his decision at the right moment, for on February 6, 1718, Woodes Rogers, who ten years earlier had himself been engaged in plundering, was commissioned "Captain-General and Governor-in-Chief in and over our Bahama Islands."[38] He sailed from England aboard the *Delicia* on April 11, 1718, accompanied by four warships of the Royal Navy, the frigates *Rose* and *Milford* and the sloops *Buck* and *Shark*, a force sufficient to eliminate piracy in the West Indies.[39] Rogers was to establish headquarters at New Providence. Along with his military contingent, the new Governor brought the King's proclamation, pardoning all pirates of their crimes if they surrendered before September 5, 1718, and if they took an oath not to return to their former enterprise.

Woodes Rogers, following his profitable 1708–1711 trip around the world, had formed a stock company with a group of Bristol merchants for the purpose of colonizing the Bahamas and eliminating piracy in the West Indies. The Lords Proprietors of the Bahamas surrendered the civil and military government of the islands to the Crown and leased the quitrents and royalties to Woodes Rogers and his company for twenty-one years.[40]

Benjamin Hornigold took full advantage of the King's Pardon. News of the amnesty had preceded Rogers, and when the Governor went ashore at New Providence on the morning of July 27, 1718, the principal persons in charge of the island's government—namely the pirates—were there to welcome him. Captain Hornigold and a considerable number of other pirate captains had their men drawn up in two lines, stretching from the water's edge to the fort, and the new Governor and several other dignitaries passed between them. Still armed, the pirates fired shots over Governor Rogers' head as he passed. There were about three hundred pirates in this unusual guard of honor, and more than a thousand on the island.⁴¹ Edward Teach, however, was not among them.

Captain Hornigold received his certificate of pardon and became one of the few who never breached his oath to keep the peace.⁴² In fact, Rogers used his services, as well as those of a number of other pardoned pirates, to track down his former colleagues, perhaps on the theory that "it takes a thief to catch a thief."

Captain Hornigold was sent out sometime in September, 1718, to capture Captain Charles Vane, a notorious pirate who had had the impudence to threaten Governor Rogers. This was the same Captain Vane whom Governor Johnson of South Carolina was so anxiously seeking to capture. Having heard nothing from Hornigold for three weeks, Governor Rogers feared either that Hornigold had been captured by Vane or that he had recommenced pirating, the latter being the general opinion in Nassau at the time. But Hornigold had been spending most of his time concealed, spying on Vane and hoping to take him by surprise. Although he was unsuccessful in capturing the elusive Vane, he was able to seize the sloop *Woolfe*, with Nickolas Woodall master, which had traded with Vane.⁴³ Governor Rogers, receiving the sloop from Hornigold, confiscated her and imprisoned Woodall. Reporting to the Council of Trade and Plantations, in a letter dated October 31, 1718, Governor Rogers stated: "Captain Hornigold having proved honest, disobliged his old friends by seizing this vessel and it divides the people here and makes me stronger than I had expected."⁴⁴

Subsequently, Governor Rogers sent Captain Hornigold out to capture Captain John Auger and a group of pirates who had been pardoned but had later backslidden into piracy. They were captured and returned to Nassau, where they were tried. Nine of the group, by a written judgment dated October 10, 1718, were sentenced "to be hanged by the neck till you shall be dead, dead, dead." One of the nine was William Cunningham, age 45, who had at one time been a gunner with Teach.

Auger, who had been entrusted after his pardon with a vessel and a cargo for a trading trip on behalf of the government, was the first to be hanged. He was penitent at his hanging, asking for a small glass of wine and drinking it "with wishes for the good success of the Bahama Islands and the Governor." Another pulled off his shoes and kicked them over the parapet of the fort, saying "he had always promised not to die with his shoes on." A third, who said he always had wanted to die drunk, was permitted to achieve his ambition.[45]

In making a report to Secretary Craggs, of the Council of Trade and Plantations, dated December 24, 1718, Governor Rogers wrote: "I am glad of this new proof that Captain Hornigold has given to the world to wipe off the infamous name he has hitherto been known by, tho in the very acts of piracy he committed most people spoke well of his generosity."[46]

Chapter 2

Creation of an Image

EDWARD TEACH'S immediate task, after his parting with Benjamin Hornigold, was to convert his prize, the French ship *Concord*, into a pirate ship of his own design. This he did, renaming her the *Queen Anne's Revenge* and mounting upon her forty guns.[1] Later, the vessel was manned by a crew of three hundred, some of whom were members of her crew when she sailed under the French flag. Justly proud of his mighty sea fortress, Captain Teach sailed southward to test her in battle. He did not have long to wait.

While his ship was cruising near the island of St. Vincent, the lookout in the crow's nest sighted a tall ship sailing westward. She turned out to be the *Great Allen*, a large and strongly armed merchant ship, Christopher Taylor, commander, bound from Barbados to Jamaica with a valuable cargo. After a lengthy engagement, Captain Taylor struck his colors and surrendered.[2]

Teach ordered Captain Taylor to move his vessel closer to the shore of St. Vincent so that the crew could be landed. The cargo was transferred from the *Great Allen* to the *Queen Anne's Revenge*. The pirates appropriated for themselves anything they desired; Captain Teach selected, among other things, a very fine silver cup. The ship was then burned and sunk. That night, the sounds of merrymaking on board the pirate craft could be heard by the vanquished and others on shore.

News of the fate of the *Great Allen* spread throughout the West Indies, and with it spread the fame of Edward Teach. He had learned well the lessons taught by Captain Benjamin Hornigold. It must have been at about this time that Captain Horni-gold "boasted as his chief distinction that he had been the one to discover and train the great Blackbeard."[3]

A few days later Teach sighted the *Scarborough*, a British man-of-war of thirty guns, sent out from her station on Barbados with instructions to seek out and destroy the *Queen Anne's Revenge*. With the speed of his ship, the pirate could easily have escaped an encounter. But Edward Teach was never known to shirk a fight. The *Scarborough* opened fire at long range and then closed in for the kill. Teach held his fire as the *Scarborough* drew nearer; then he let her have a broadside that tore great holes in her sails. The crews of both vessels, each testing the strength and capabilities of the other, engaged in a running battle for several hours. Teach's gunners at length proved their superiority. The commander of the now crippled *Scarborough* ordered his crew to withdraw from the conflict and to proceed to its station on Barbados Island.

Teach did not pursue. He was not going to risk the lives of his men and damage to the *Queen Anne's Revenge* in a fight with a vessel that had no cargo. There were plenty of merchant ships in the Caribbean. With a mighty roar of laughter and a final salute of guns, he let the King's warship go her way and turned toward the rich Spanish settlements of South America.[4]

There is no doubt that Captain Teach's reputation as a bold and fearless commander of pirates was greatly enhanced as a consequence of his victory in the battle with the *Scarborough*. Any pirate captain who had both the courage to wage a running battle with a warship of the Royal Navy and the capacity to come out the winner was surely a sea pirate to be avoided. It was an incident much discussed in the bars of the West Indies.

Edward Teach at about this time became convinced, however, that courage and know-how were not sufficient if he was to become a successful pirate with the minimum of risk to his crew and ship. He needed an image. He was a student of psychological warfare far ahead of his time.

Most persons of this period did not wear beards. Captain Teach discovered that, without effort, he could grow a coarse, coal-black beard that covered the whole of his face. Its breadth extended to his ears and its height almost to his eyes. He allowed his monstrous mane to grow to an extravagant length, and he was accustomed to braiding it into little pigtails, tied with ribbons of various colors. With his beard he created an image that has lingered through the centuries. He himself assumed the cognomen Blackbeard. Captain Johnson, writing in 1724, said that Teach was appropriately called Blackbeard "from that large quantity of hair which, like a frightful meteor, covered his whole face and frightened America more than any comet that has appeared there [in] a long time."[5] Hugh Rankin has commented: "It was good business for a pirate to cultivate such a name and make it as fearsome as possible. An evil reputation was a great aid in persuading prospective victims to surrender quickly with a minimum of resistance. With this in mind, he deliberately attempted to emphasize the evil side of his character."[6]

Teach was a tall man, robust and broad-shouldered, with a body sinewed with strength. His eyebrows were phenomenally bushy and bristly. His apparel was as true to his calling as was his physical make-up. His broad hat and outer regalia were frequently all black, and he usually wore knee boots. He dressed for the particular occasion. Sometimes he wore a long-skirted coat of brightly colored silk or velvet, with huge cuffs turned back to the elbows, knee breeches of a gaudy hue, and low shoes with huge buckles. Apparently a firm believer in the value of first impressions, Blackbeard made himself as daring and as horrifying in appearance as in deeds.

In time of battle he wore across his shoulders a sling, in which were fixed two or three pistols, hanging in holsters, like a bandolier. In the broad belt strapped around his waist was an assortment of pistols, daggers, and an oversized cutlass. He was an ambulatory display of weapons. For a finishing touch, he tucked under the brim of his hat, on each side, fuses made of hemp cord about the thickness of a pencil and dipped in a solution of saltpeter and lime water. These burned slowly, at the rate of about twelve inches an hour, and were the same as those used to touch off the cannons on board ship. When set afire, the curling wisps of smoke added to the frightfulness of his appearance.[7]

Teach's deliberately awesome appearance in battle array had its effect. When ferociously attacked, the crews of many merchant ships threw up their hands in surrender to Blackbeard without any pretense of a fight. The poorly paid seamen, upon discovering that they were being attacked by a pirate known as a terror, could not be depended on to resist. Sailors during the early eighteenth century were almost universally superstitious. Both victims and fellow pirates believed Blackbeard to be the Devil incarnate. Among the Brethren of the Coast, one who went to "the greatest length of wickedness" was looked upon with a kind of envy, as a person of "extraordinary gallantry"; and if such a person did in fact have courage, he must certainly be a great man.[8]

There are no records of Blackbeard's having murdered or maimed his captives if they submitted to his authority. If, when he took over a vessel, everyone did exactly as he ordered, there was nothing more to fear than theft of property.

But the slightest resistance, or even an argument, moved Blackbeard to set an example. If a victim did not voluntarily offer up a diamond ring, Blackbeard chopped it off, finger and all. This nearly always impressed the victim, who could be counted on to impress all to whom he related his experience. These tactics also saved time, but their most important function was to help spread the word that, while Blackbeard could be merciful to those who co-operated, woe to those who did not.[9]

All the seventeenth- and eighteenth-century writers on piracy felt morally bound to picture pirates as atrocious, despicable, cruel, and barbarian. Pirates and all who had anything to do with them were automatically sentenced to damnation. "The public must be forever reminded that crime does not pay, although there are sometimes implications that it might be partly good fun."[10] Puritan ministers and legitimate sea captains, with the aid of contemporary writers, are largely responsible for the popular conception of pirates. If a captain lost his ship to a pirate crew, he could be depended upon to exaggerate the depravity and wickedness of the pirates, and any embellishments would enhance his own reputation and make it easier for him to gain command of another ship.[11]

Even the fiction writers of the twentieth century, perhaps because they feel their readers prefer it, have gone to great lengths to picture Blackbeard as a cruel and wicked monster. For example, one novelist has Blackbeard bellowing to Governor Charles Eden, of North Carolina:

I kill where I choose—whom I choose; I slay when offended; I slay sometimes for pleasure and when not at all offended . . . Listen, damn you! Two weeks since I took a Portuguese mulletta, off the Virginia Capes. He had not offended me. Do you know what I did to him? I sliced off his nose, both ears, both lips, and my cook fried them, and I made the Portuguese captain eat his own ears and nose and lips, and then shot him in the bowels because I ordered him to smack his lips, but he had none to smack.[12]

There is no doubt that Blackbeard was conscious of the public image he had created, and, like a good actor, on occasions lived up to it. There were times when he engaged in frolics with members of his own crew solely for the purpose of impressing them with the idea of his superiority. Johnson, his contemporary, tells this story:

For being one day at sea, and little flushed with drink, 'Come,' says he, 'let us make a hell of our own, and try how long we can bear it.' Accordingly he, with two or three others, went down into the hole [sic], and closing up all the hatches, filled several pots full of brimstone and other combustible matter, and set it on fire, and so continued until they were almost suffocated, when some of the men cried out for air. At length, he opened the hatches, not a little pleased that he had held out the longest.[13]

One of his pirates on this occasion jokingly said, "Why Captain, you look as if you were coming straight from the gallows."

"My lad," roared Blackbeard, "that's a brilliant idea. The next time we shall play the game of gallows and see who can swing the longest on the rope without being throttled."[14]

There is no account of anyone's ever expressing a desire to play this particular game with their invincible captain.

Only shortly before the end, Blackbeard impulsively turned the last of those evil tricks that created his image. One night Israel Hands, who had been in command of the *Adventure* when Teach blockaded Charleston, was drinking with Teach and another man at a table in the captain's cabin. Without provocation, Blackbeard drew out a pair of pistols and cocked them under the table. The third man, aware of what was happening, hastily excused himself and stepped out on deck. Blackbeard blew out the candle, crossed his arms beneath the table, and pulled the triggers of both pistols. One misfired, but the slug from the other tore through Hands' knee and crippled him for life. When the pirates on board asked for an explanation, Teach's only answer was a curse and the statement that, "if he did not now and then kill one of them, they would forget who he was."[15]

Yet Blackbeard's image as a fierce and reckless pirate portrayed only one side of his nature. There was a group of persons whom Blackbeard treated differently from all others—they were women. Few pirates treated women or girls with greater respect than he. Whenever Captain Teach entered a tavern, groups of girls usually could be seen arriving shortly afterwards. The males of the tavern who had been patronizing the bar staggered out, and the females sauntered in. He would not let a girl serve him a drink; he preferred to serve the drink to the girl.

Blackbeard would customarily drink with many of the girls, pinch or squeeze some of them, and cheer and applaud them all during their dancing and entertainment. There were, often enough, a few who danced on the top of the bar and the tables, with or without clothes. He would watch and enjoy them all, but nearly always there was one girl more alluring and enticing than the others who would become his favorite, not for just the party of the evening but for the remainder of his stay in the town. This was the girl with whom he would fall in love. Having picked out the girl he wanted, he became a fast worker, as successful in love as he was in the scuttling of ships.

Teach had no power of resistance to the charms of an attractive trollop. Having grown fond of her, he was so much putty in her hands, until the girl became convinced that she had found the Achilles' heel in this outwardly invulnerable pirate. The great Blackbeard, terror of the seas, was temporarily at the mercy of his new-found love, and often actually proposed marriage. Such was Blackbeard's nature, infatuated with every harbor-town girl who caught his fancy.[16]

As a consequence, he more than once found the girl and himself aboard the *Queen Anne's Revenge*, standing before his first mate, who solemnly conducted a marriage ceremony and pronounced them husband and wife. It is doubtful if any of these brides actually considered themselves married to Captain Teach. To them it was an adventure in port with the notorious

Blackbeard, carried through to the finish as a lark. In any event it helped them financially in their business dealings with other men of the sea. To be known as "Blackbeard's wife" accorded them prestige and enhanced the value of their services. "To Blackbeard's crew, especially the mate who performed all the marriage ceremonies, it was a running joke. To Blackbeard it was apparently a source of annoyance when he got to sea and realized he had been taken again by a doxy whom he could have had for a few doubloons. But he never learned."[17]

After several days at sea, Blackbeard himself forgot all about the bride he had left behind. In the next port he was only too likely to go through the same routine with another girl. On the high seas a ruthless pursuer, on land he was the pursued. Each affair was like a haunting first love.

What there was about Blackbeard that fascinated and emotionally aroused the women of this period has never been determined. All the pictures we have of him were painted by artists who never saw him. It could very well be that he had a devilish twinkle in his eye, a tone of voice that modulated on occasion to charm, and a manner of carrying his handsome body that rarely failed to attract a woman.

It has been said that, prior to his formalized wedding of 1718 in North Carolina, he had been married on at least thirteen occasions and even had a wife living in London.[18] The latter assertion might have been based upon the claim of some woman who had married Captain Teach on board his ship in the harbor of one of the West Indies islands and had later returned to England. If she had a child by him or some other person, it would be understandable for her to say that she had been married to Captain Teach.

Under the law it would have been impossible for Blackbeard to have had more than one lawful living wife. Any attempted marriages entered into during the existence of any prior valid marriage would have been bigamous and absolutely void.[19]

In England prior to 1857 the ecclesiastical courts had complete control over divorce, except in rare instances when the very rich or influential were able to procure an absolute divorce by a private act of Parliament. In canon law a valid marriage was, and is, a sacrament, by divine injunction indissoluble. The ecclesiastical courts would grant only divorces *a mensa et thoro* ("from bed and board"), which did not dissolve the marital relation. Such divorces only authorized the separation of the parties. It did not entitle either party to remarry, nor furnish an excuse for unchaste conduct. The ecclesiastical courts had no power to pronounce an absolute divorce if there had in fact been a valid marriage. Ecclesiastical courts, however, were never established in any of the American colonies.[20]

There is no record or any historical intimation that Blackbeard ever caused the termination of a marriage by bringing about the death of one of his so-called wives. He is not to be confused with the fictitious Bluebeard, the monster of Charles Perrault's tale *Barbe Bleue*, who murdered his wives and hid their bodies in a locked room.

There is ample evidence that Blackbeard was not the worst pirate who ever lived. This was simply the image that he had created. It was his beard, and especially his beard in times of battle, that struck terror to the hearts of the less courageous. To awe his followers and to subordinate them, he proclaimed himself the Devil and played the Devil's role at every opportunity. He and others publicized and embellished his infamous acts on the high seas. Only the ladies knew that Blackbeard was not all bad, and much of the devilry they saw in his actions was to their liking.

Chapter 3

Searching for Prizes

*T*HE SEQUENCE OF Blackbeard's nefarious activities on the high seas cannot always be determined with accuracy, their exact dates in some instances never having been recorded. All of those mentioned in this and the following chapters, both dated and undated, occurred within the last year or fifteen months preceding his death on November 22, 1718.

On December 5, 1717, Captain Teach stopped the merchant ship *Margaret* off the coast of Crab Island, and ordered her master, Captain Henry Bostock, on board the *Queen Anne's Revenge*. Blackbeard removed from the *Margaret* her arms, her cargo, which consisted of cattle and hogs, and her books and instruments. No harm was done to either Bostock or the members of his crew, except that Blackbeard forced two members of the crew to join up with him as pirates, and "one Robert Bibby voluntarily took on with him." The *Margaret* was permitted to proceed on her course unharmed, though disarmed.[1]

When Captain Bostock returned to St. Christopher's Island, the base of his operations, he reported the encounter with Blackbeard to Governor Walter Hamilton, who requested Bostock to sign a deposition as to what had transpired. This affidavit, accompanied by a letter signed by Governor Hamilton and addressed to the Council of Trade and Plantations, may today be found in England's Public Record Office.[2] This is the reason there are more details available about this incident than in the case of other ships captured by Blackbeard.

In Bostock's deposition we find the statement that Blackbeard had in command at this time a large ship and a sloop, the ship being a French guineaman, Dutch-built, with thirty-six cannon and three hundred men. Bostock believed the ship to be carrying gold dust of great value, and he had personally observed a great deal of silver plate on board, including a "very fine cup" which he was told was taken from Captain Taylor. Blackbeard's crew told Bostock that they had burnt several other vessels, including two or three operating out of St. Christopher's Island—one in particular, owned by Robert McGill, a native of Antigua, only the day before. The crew said they intended to go to Hispaniola to careen and lie in wait for a Spanish armada expected to sail out of Havana for Hispaniola and Puerto Rico immediately after Christmas with money to pay the garrisons. Blackbeard himself questioned Bostock concerning the going and coming of other ships. Bostock told the pirates of an Act of Grace, or pardon, expected shortly to be sent out from London for all pirates, but they seemed not the slightest interested in this.

Nevertheless, it has been recorded in several places that Blackbeard did sail to the Town of Bath, North Carolina, in January, 1717/1718,* where he surrendered, took the oath to give up piracy, and received a certificate of pardon on the basis of the previously issued proclamation of King George I.[3]

It had long been the custom of the English sovereigns to issue proclamations granting a "gracious pardon" to pirates who

*England followed the Julian Calendar, rather than the Gregorian, prior to 1752. All dates between January 1 and March 24, inclusive, belonged to the old year, March being reckoned the first month of the year, which made February the twelfth. New Year's Day was March 25 under the Julian Calendar. It has become customary for most historians to assign the date of the new year to all old style dates falling between January 1 and March 24, inclusive. Thus, if the date of January 5, 1717, appears in a document prior to 1752, in terms of our current dating it would be January 5, 1718. To remove the doubt, some writers today give the date in one of the following forms: January 5, 1717/1718 or January 5, 1717 [1718].

would voluntarily surrender prior to a designated date and take an oath not to engage in acts of piracy thereafter. These proclamations, known as "Acts of Grace," often resulted in many pirates' surrendering. Most of them used the pardons for the purpose of canceling out prior criminal acts, hoping not to be caught in any subsequent acts of piracy.

These offers of pardon were usually made while England was on the threshold of another war. She needed the pirates in her wars with France and Spain. By offering their services to whichever combatant promised more plunder, the pirates, on more than one occasion, influenced the balance of power in the naval struggle. Each of the great powers wanted the pirates kept on a leash, as it were, at a safe distance from her own commerce and in equal readiness to pounce upon the enemy's ships.

During the reign of Henry VIII, England instituted the policy of issuing letters of marque to privateers. Privateering was a cheap way of waging war. It gave the privateer a legal right to attack and rob the ships of an enemy country, under the cloak of patriotism. England was not too much concerned with the abuse of privateering commissions.

Privateers and pirates furnished England with experienced and hearty seamen. They were daring and skillful in the handling of their ships, and capable of performing incredible feats. They knew the winds and currents. Without the experience and the nautical skills acquired by Englishmen as privateers and pirates, it is doubtful whether England could have controlled the seas and thereby built an empire. In due course of time, England would control her pirates. It is believed that in January, 1717/1718, the knowledgeable Blackbeard realized this.

Under a royal proclamation of the King of England,[4] dated September 5, 1717, pirates were required voluntarily to surrender on or before September 5, 1718, the pardon extending only to those acts of piracy committed before January 5, 1717/

1718. This act was construed by the Attorney General and by the Solicitor General of England as including a pardon for any murder committed during an act of piracy and, furthermore, as not requiring a forfeiture of the goods of the pirates themselves, but providing that persons who had been robbed could by legal process recover their property from the pirates.[5] As a consequence, upon his voluntary surrender, Blackbeard had the legal right, as against the Crown, to the loot he had stolen. In addition, the proclamation was loaded with fat rewards to persons who captured pirates refusing to surrender. It was this proclamation under which hundreds of pirates surrendered.

If Blackbeard did surrender, he must have left the *Queen Anne's Revenge* anchored within Ocracoke Inlet and proceeded to Bath, a distance of about fifty miles, by means of a smaller vessel. The shifting sands in the shallow channel of Pamlico Sound would not have permitted a ship of the size of the *Queen Anne's Revenge* to reach Bath.

Blackbeard undoubtedly had been to Bath before. He may have been there earlier as a privateer, while sailing under Captain Hornigold, or as a captain on one of his own pirate ships. In any event, he knew the waters of the coastal rivers and the sounds of North Carolina. He was acquainted with the colonists of that section.

Blackbeard may have relaxed and rested for a while in and about Bath. Soon, however, the allurements of the free life of the trackless seas proved too strong. He set off on a cruise to the Bay of Honduras, a favorite rendezvous of the Brethren of the Coast. En route, apparently sometime in early March, 1717/ 1718, Teach's lookout in the crow's nest sighted a pirate sloop of ten guns, which turned out to be commanded by Major Stede Bonnet, "lately a gentleman of good reputation and estate" on Barbados Island.[6] Major Bonnet, a round little man in bright waistcoat and trim breeches, clean-shaven and periwigged, boldly came alongside the *Queen Anne's Revenge* and shouted through his speaking trumpet, inquiring to whom he had the honor of speaking.

Blackbeard, scarcely believing his eyes, collapsed into a roar of laughter. Getting control of himself, he thrust his hairy face over the side and bellowed: "A Brother of the Coast; come on up topside, Captain!" Though laying his eyes on Blackbeard for the first time, Bonnet had no doubt as to whom he was addressing. Major Bonnet accepted Captain Teach's invitation and came aboard the *Queen Anne's Revenge* for a social visit.[7]

Stede Bonnet was a retired army officer of the King's Guards who owned a large sugar plantation near Bridgetown, on the island of Barbados. Sometimes referred to as the "gentleman pirate," he was a military officer from a good family, educated and cultured, and he owned a substantial amount of land on the island where he had settled. He was highly respected by his neighbors, and they were greatly surprised when, in 1717, he suddenly decided to become a pirate. There were even those who said he had done so to get away from a nagging wife. Purchasing with his own funds a sloop, naming it the *Revenge*—a favorite name for ships among pirates—he equipped it with ten guns. It was customary to steal the vessel in which one intended to operate as a pirate. Major Bonnet recruited a crew of seventy men, some of whom were experienced pirates, and departed one night without saying good-bye to Mrs. Bonnet.

Although Bonnet had been either adroit or lucky in the capture of a number of prizes, his crew had little confidence in his leadership. There had been talk aboard ship of disposing of him, with which talk he was acquainted.

What happened in the captain's quarters of the *Queen Anne's Revenge* is not known. But the two men with such different backgrounds apparently proved congenial, since great laughter was soon heard. Captain Teach later visited Major Bonnet's

Revenge, and the two decided to cruise together as partners, or joint adventurers. However, within a few days Teach became convinced that Bonnet knew nothing whatsoever about maritime life. With the consent of the crew of the *Revenge*, Teach calmly took over the sloop, placing his second-in-command, Lieutenant Richards, an old-time pirate, in charge.

Teach, as always the diplomat and the leader of men, was able to persuade Bonnet of the wisdom of this action, urging that "as he had not been used to the fatigues and care of such a post, it would be better for him to decline it and live easy, at his pleasure, in such a ship as his, where he should not be obliged to perform duty, but follow his own inclinations."[8] Considering the fact that his own crew was discontented with his command, Major Bonnet was in no position to bargain.

Observing Blackbeard in action during the weeks that followed, Bonnet himself began to experience genuine doubts about being a pirate. He would give up piracy completely, he is said to have muttered to anyone who would listen, and retire to a peaceful life in some port controlled by the Portuguese or the Spanish. He swore he would never return to his plantation on Barbados, because he could never look an Englishman in the eye again.[9]

At Turneffe Island, off the coast of what is now British Honduras and about ten leagues short of the Bay of Honduras, the combined crews of Teach and Bonnet anchored to take on fresh water. The morning following their arrival, a pirate assigned as a lookout on the masthead of one of the vessels yelled that a sloop on the high seas had turned and was heading for the harbor. The pirates hurriedly became activated for battle. Lieutenant Richards, in command of the *Revenge*, was the first to raise the anchor of his sloop and to sail out to challenge the newcomer. The other pirate vessels were close behind, all flying high the black flag. The commander of the incoming sloop had no choice.

He struck the sails of his sloop and came under the stern of the pirate flagship, the *Queen Anne's Revenge*. The sloop was identified as the *Adventure* from Jamaica, with David Harriot as master.[10] She was entering the harbor to fill her own water casks with a fresh supply of water.

A rope-constructed ladder was tossed over the sides of the *Queen Anne's Revenge*, and Captain Harriot was ordered aboard to talk with Captain Teach. Harriot and his crew prudently accepted Blackbeard's invitation to join the freebooters. Half of the *Adventure's* crew were ordered to serve on the flagship, and the remainder to man their own sloop for the "piratical account." Blackbeard's first mate, Israel Hands (sometimes called Hezekiah or Basilica Hands) was placed in command of the *Adventure*.

The now combined crews of Teach, Bonnet, and Harriot, under the overall command of Blackbeard, spent a week of frolicsome merriment on the beach of Turneffe. It was for them a spring vacation on a Caribbean island.

It was a custom of the crew, while cruising the Caribbean, to seek out a secluded island or a mainland cove for a relaxing vacation on shore. Pirates welcomed the comforts and pleasures permissible only on land. The warm and balmy beaches, along with a change of food, were luxuries that few persons of their time could otherwise afford.

Reasons of health and sanitation made these shore parties almost a necessity. Fresh water, carried in casks, was reserved for drinking and cooking only. There was no water for washing and personal hygiene, except during a rainstorm. As a consequence, after a few weeks at sea pirates usually acquired a bronzed tint. "Suntan, plus salt spray and a general accretion, rendered them a rich mahogany color." [11]

Old or spare sails were pressed into service as tents for those who wanted to sleep on land. They usually sought out a campsite near trees. The ideal spot included a source of good water and available firewood. Outdoor barbecues of fresh meats, not to be enjoyed on board ship, were a favorite. The pirates, being on vacation, took readily to fishing or to hunting for wild game. Wild hogs and cattle were often to be had. If there were natives, they usually produced fresh vegetables to exchange for merchandise carried on the ships. But English pirates did not, as a general rule, readily take to the variety of exotic vegetables and fruits in abundant supply on the Caribbean islands. Adhering to a conservatism traditional with the English, they preferred the old stand-bys of beef, pork, fish, and rum for their "belly timber." The green turtle, however, became an exception to the general rule.

The pirates, like most persons visiting the Caribbean, learned quickly to enjoy green turtle soup. Laced with sherry wine, it is an adventure in the culinary arts that few persons have been able to resist. Although these turtles have since become extremely rare in the West Indies, in the days of piracy they were abundant. "Perhaps more than any other article of diet the green turtle made the West Indies a happier place for mankind."[12] It has even been claimed that the green turtle was a factor "responsible for the concentration of piratical activity in this part of the world."[13]

One of the chief advantages of green turtles to pirates was that they could be kept alive on board ship for weeks without any attention. The turtles held on tenaciously to life for long periods without food. If fresh meat was desired during a voyage, all that the cook needed do was to go into the hold and butcher a turtle.[14]

The pleasures of pirates during their Caribbean carousings were relatively simple. They probably paid scant attention to the beautiful flowers growing wild, unless these happened to adorn the body of some native girl. The unusual and gay-plumaged birds very likely interested them. Various freebooters occasionally captured parrots and taught them to curse like a sailor. The pirates saw their tropical paradise while it was still possessed of a natural grandeur unmarred by modern civilization.

Feasting and drinking on a large scale were the basic joys of these island picnics. The pirates simply took it easy, with nothing in particular to do. There was always the punch bowl, replenished from time to time. Various concoctions, then as well as now, in the Caribbean, were mixed in the punch bowl. The pirates drank from a ladle or dipper.

If there was a dearth of natives to amuse the pirates, they could entertain themselves. Songs and music have had an important place in the life of all seafaring men. Pirates in this respect were not exceptional. The few pirate songs that have come down to us are just as ribald as the ballads popular among sailors today. Every pirate craft had its musician. When there were girls available, the men were fond of the informal folk dances with which they were familiar at home.[15]

The mock trial was also a favorite diversion. Captain Johnson tells of an English actor who, upon conviction of a crime, was transported as a felon to work on a Jamaica plantation, escaped, and joined the pirate crew of Captain Bellamy on board the *Whidaw* in 1717.[16]

This whimsical fellow made a play whilst he was on board, which he called *The Royal Pirate*; and this (which to see once would make a cynic laugh) was acted on the quarter-deck with great applause, both of the actors and poet; but an accident which turned the farce into tragedy, occasioned an order of council to forbid its being played a second time. The case was thus: Alexander the Great, environed by his guards, was examining a pirate brought before him. The gunner who was drunk, took this to be in earnest, and that his messmate was in danger, and hearing Alexander say,

Know'st thou that Death attends thy mighty crimes,
And thou shall'st hang tomorrow morn betimes,

Swore *by G-d he'd try that*, and running into the gun room, where he left three companions over a bowl of rum punch as drunk as himself, told them, *They were going to hang honest Jack Spinckes, and if they suffered it, they should all be hanged one after another, but, by G-d, they should not hang him, for he'd clear the decks,* and taking a grenade with a lighted match, followed by his comrades with their cutlass, he set fire to the fuse and threw it among the actors.[17]

The blast not only put an abrupt end to the production, but seriously injured Spinckes and several other players. The gunner and his companions were put in irons and the illusion of the theatre was explained to them. "The Royal Pirate" was not produced again.

On April 9, 1718, Teach's now enlarged fleet weighed anchor and set sail northward for the Bay of Honduras, where they found harbored a large ship and four sloops. The ship was the *Protestant Caesar* of Boston, with a Captain Wyar in command. Three of the sloops belonged to Captain Jonathan Bernard, of Jamaica, and the fourth, to a Captain James.[18]

The pirate vessels, all flying the black flag, brazenly sailed into the bay. Blackbeard upset the quietness of the scene by firing a cannon. This so frightened Captain Wyar and all the members of his crew that they scurried into small boats and rowed to safety on shore. All the vessels surrendered without resistance. Blackbeard dispatched his quartermaster and eight members of his crew to take possession of the large abandoned ship. They plundered the *Protestant Caesar* of her cargo, and then the ship was set on fire, because it was owned by persons in Boston, where some pirates had recently been tried and hanged. Teach assigned Richards and Hands to take over the four sloops. The three owned by Bernard were later released, but the fourth, the one owned by Captain James, was burnt because James ventured to raise a protest.

Upon leaving the Bay of Honduras, Blackbeard's fleet sailed to the Grand Cayman, a small island about thirty leagues to the west of Jamaica, where they took a small turtler. They probably seized other sloops near Cuba, including a Spanish sloop. They put into the port of Havana, as was the custom of pirates from time to time, to dispose of their loot and to replenish stores. They spent several days hunting for valuables in the hulls of ships wrecked on the rocks of the Bahama Islands, a pastime particularly intriguing to Bonnet. From the Bahama wrecks they proceeded northward, capturing as they cruised two sloops and an English brigantine, bound from Guinea to South Carolina.[19]

Found on Blackbeard's vessel when he was slain at Ocracoke Inlet were several memoranda, written by his own hand in the ship's log: "Such a day, rum all out:—Our company somewhat sober:—A damned confusion amongst us!—Rogues a-plotting: —Great talk of separation—so I looked sharp for a prize:—Such a day took one, with a great deal of liquor on board, so kept the company hot, damned hot; then all things went well again."[20]

Edward Teach was unquestionably an unusual leader among men to become the master pirate of a quality that won him universal recognition. Captains of other ships were impressed with the discipline among his men and the deference shown Captain Teach by his officers. To handle his ship in all kinds of weather and in sea fights, to make his way disabled to sheltered and friendly harbors for repairs, and to control and care for his unruly ruffians through disease and discontent was little more than the average sea captain was called on to perform. Teach did more, employing the arts of the diplomat in dealing with his partners (as in the case of Major Stede Bonnet) and in providing himself with a safe market for his stolen merchandise. He knew how to inspire his men with confidence, how to teach them to accept discipline and to obey commands under stress, and how to train his crew to use the sails and arms of the ship with proficiency. He was a superb organizer of both the men and the materials of his trade.

Not only a skillful navigator, a thoroughly competent naval tactician, and an adroit leader of men, Edward Teach had a flair for dramatic show well calculated to impress the captains of the vessels he attacked. Blackbeard was a swashbuckling, fierce-visaged pirate who became the model for countless blood-and-thunder tales of the sea rovers, and his reputation as an invincible freebooter soon spread up and down the Atlantic coastline. A mere rumor of his presence was often enough to panic and demoralize his enemies. It was a part of his stock in trade to cause some to hate and fear him, and others to respect and be loyal to him. With his ability, determination, and masterful personality, Edward Teach could have risen to prominence in any profession he selected, for within two years from the time he became a sea robber, he reached the very pinnacle of piracy.

Governor Bennett of Bermuda, in a letter addressed to the Council of Trade and Plantations, dated May 31, 1718, reported hearing that among the pirates prowling the adjacent seas was "one Tatch with whom is Major Bonnett of Barbados in a ship of 36 guns and 300 men, also in company with them a sloop of 12 guns and 115 men, and two other ships, in all of which, it is computed there are 700 men or thereabout."[21] Governor Bennett was probably not correctly informed as to the total number of men on Blackbeard's ships. More reliable sources seem to indicate that there were about four hundred men on board Teach's flotilla when it approached the harbor of Charleston shortly thereafter.

This small squadron, to which was subsequently attached another sloop and one or more tenders, was the force with which Teach was to attempt his boldest and most daring sea exploit—the blockade of the port of Charleston, South Carolina.

Chapter 4

Blockade of Charleston

NEAR THE END of May, 1718, Blackbeard and his armed flotilla appeared outside the entrance to the harbor of Charleston, South Carolina. Determined to blockade the busiest and most important port of the southern colonies, Teach had assumed the title of Commodore, placing himself in charge of all administrative and judicial acts on board his ships. It was as if all persons on the pirate ships were inhabitants of a legally constituted commonwealth. The acknowledged sovereign of the seas—so far as the people of Charleston and those on ships wanting to ply in and out of the harbor were concerned—Edward Teach was at the high tide of his piratical career.

All vessels, whether inbound or outbound, were stopped. The pilot boat of Charleston was the first ship captured. Next was a large vessel, the *Crowley*, commanded by Captain Robert Clark and headed for London with many of Charleston's leading citizens aboard as passengers. During a period of five or six days, a total of eight or nine of these vessels were seized and plundered on the high seas off the bar of Charleston.

It did not take the citizens of Charleston long to discover what was happening at the entrance to their harbor. Shipping in the harbor was at a standstill. No ships came in from the ocean, and the eight vessels in the harbor, ready to go to sea, dared not venture outside the bar.

The *Queen Anne's Revenge*, with her forty guns, was the flagship of the pirate's fleet. Major Stede Bonnet was aboard as an unwilling guest of the Commodore. Lieutenant Richards was in command of Bonnet's former ship, the *Revenge*, with its ten or twelve guns. Israel Hands commanded the *Adventure*, which carried eight guns. In addition, there was another sloop of considerable size, with possibly one or more tenders used by the pirates to transport the overflow of captured cargoes.[1]

The passengers and crew on board the *Crowley*, bound for London, were made prisoners and brought aboard Blackbeard's flagship, where they were strictly examined concerning the number of vessels remaining in port, their cargoes, when they might be sailing, and their destination. As the inquiry was solemnly carried out, the pirates swore that death would be the portion of those who lied or evaded. The papers of the captured ship were scrutinized.

Blackbeard discovered that among the passengers was one Samuel Wragg, a man of considerable wealth[2] and a member of the Council of the Province of Carolina, and his son William, then four years old, who in later years became one of the most distinguished men in the American colonies.

He [William Wragg] was educated in England, and held many responsible public positions in South Carolina during the period just prior to the Revolution. In 1771 he was tendered the Chief Justiceship of the Province, which he declined. He was a devoted loyalist during the struggle for independence, but such was his character that he retained the highest esteem of his fellow-countrymen. Foreseeing the success of the American arms, he disposed of his Carolina estates and in 1777 sailed for England. His vessel was lost on the coast of Holland in September of that year, and he was drowned with the entire crew. Such was the regard in which he was held that George III had a memorial erected in Westminster Abbey in his honor.[3]

Upon the completion of the interrogation, the passengers and crew of the *Crowley* were returned to their ship and thrown below the lower deck, where the cargo was carried. Here they remained in darkness and silence, under locked hatches, for half a day. The prisoners' treatment had been so rough and hurried that a great terror seized the minds of all those innocent people. No one believed he would emerge from the ordeal alive. No distinction was made in the status of the prisoners. The captain of the ship, ordinary seamen, merchants, gentlemen of rank, and even the child of Mr. Wragg, were thrust alike, tumultuously, into the hold.

Blackbeard's image as a ruthless pirate was having an instantaneous effect upon his intended victims. At the same time, Captain Teach intended to capitalize on the fortuitous capture of some of Charleston's best citizens. Especially in Samuel Wragg, Teach recognized a valuable hostage. He was in a favorable position to bargain with the authorities of Charleston.

Finally a gleam of light shot in upon the prisoners huddled in the belly of the *Crowley*. The hatches were opened, and the trembling prisoners were hauled up on deck. The pirates ordered the more important of them to return to the *Queen Anne's Revenge* for a conference with Captain Teach in his cabin.

Blackbeard personally explained to them that it had become necessary to adopt the extraordinary procedure of placing them all in detention so that a general council of his crew could be held on board his flagship. His council had unanimously decided that the pirate ships needed a chest of medicine, and a list of the required drugs had been drawn up by his first surgeon. The drugs on this list, he informed them, were to be supplied by the colonial government of South Carolina. Lieutenant Richards and another of Blackbeard's officers had been selected to go into Charleston and submit their demands to Governor Johnson and the members of his Council.[4]

Blackbeard further announced that the Governor would be told that, to assure the safe return of his messengers, the pirates had voted to keep all prisoners as hostages; and that, if their demands were not complied with punctually, all prisoners would

be put to death, their heads sent to the Governor, and all captured ships at the entrance to the port set on fire.

On the heels of his broadside, Teach asked the prisoners
whether they had any suggestions. Samuel Wragg, their
spokesman,

answered that perhaps it might not be in their power to comply with
every part of it, and, he feared, that some certain drugs in the surgeon's list, were not to be had in the Province; and if it should prove
so, he hoped they would be contented to have that want made up by
substituting something else in the place. He likewise proposed that
one of them might go with the two gentlemen that were to be sent
on the embassy, who might truly represent the danger they were in,
and induce them more readily to submit, in order to save the lives
of so many of the King's subjects, and further, to prevent any insult
from the common people (for whose conduct on such an occasion,
they could not answer) on the person of his envoys.[5]

His Excellency thought well of Wragg's suggestion. He
called into session another meeting of the pirate crew, and
Wragg's amendments to their former resolution were approved,
all of which was in keeping with a kind of rough democracy
that prevailed on board the pirate ships.

The question arose as to which of the prisoners should be
sent into Charleston with the two representatives. Samuel
Wragg volunteered. As a member of the Governor's Council,
he pointed out, he would be in a favorable position to present
the demands of Blackbeard; and, to indicate his good faith, he
would leave his young son with the pirates as a hostage until
his return. Blackbeard instantly rejected this offer, averring
that a person of Wragg's importance would probably not be
permitted to return to the pirate fleet. Teach shrewdly calculated that his own bargaining power would be lessened if he
were to let go his most valuable hostage.

After some debate, a Mr. Marks, a citizen of Charleston, was
selected to accompany the two pirates and lay the situation be-

fore the Governor. Marks was given two days to accomplish his mission and was informed that, if any harm came to the pirates, Blackbeard would pass over the bar with his fleet, burn every vessel in the harbor, and "beat the town about their ears." The trio departed for Charleston in a small boat.[6]

In the meantime, Teach moved his pirate fleet, together with the captured ships, about five or six leagues from land and impatiently awaited the return of the embassy. The anxiety on the part of the prisoners was, understandably, great.

Two days passed with no sign of the embassy's return. Blackbeard, becoming furious, sent for Wragg. Putting on a terrible countenance, he roared that he was not a pirate to be trifled with, that some kind of foul treachery had been practiced upon him, and that Wragg and all his party might prepare for immediate death.[7]

Wragg, pleading for the lives of his fellow hostages, attempted to reason with the raging pirate. He was confident that South Carolina valued the lives of her captured citizens and would do everything possible to redeem them. He argued that some unforeseen difficulty had caused the delay. Possibly some misfortune had befallen the small boat in going or returning, or the two pirates themselves might have occasioned the delay. In either event it would be unfair to take the lives of innocent prisoners for something that neither they nor the people of Charleston could control. He begged for a postponement of at least one day more, stressing the fact that nothing was to be gained by haste.

This appeal from such an outstanding citizen of South Carolina as Wragg appeared to pacify Blackbeard for the time. He granted a reprieve of one day; but he vowed, cursing, that if the boat was not seen at the end of another day all prisoners would die within two hours.

Many believed themselves surely doomed, their minds already suffering the agonies of death. Before the end of the long day's reprieve, however, a lookout in the forecastle sang out that a small boat could be seen coming out of the harbor. Blackbeard examined the approaching boat with his spyglass and announced approvingly that he could see his own scarlet cloak, which he had lent Mr. Marks to symbolize, perhaps, that he was clothed, when he spoke to the Governor, with the authority of the commodore himself. But when the boat came alongside the *Queen Anne's Revenge*, it was obvious that it was not carrying the two pirates, nor Marks, nor a chest of medicine. The man who mounted the ladder in the midst of stunned silence was a messenger from Mr. Marks.

Reaching the deck, this man promptly informed Blackbeard that the envoys, on the way to Charleston, had been caught in a sudden squall that had capsized their small boat. Cast into the sea, they had been forced to swim to an uninhabited island, located several leagues from the mainland. Fully conscious of what might happen as a consequence of delay, according to Johnson, the two pirates

set Mr. Marks on a hatch and floated it upon the sea, after which they stripped and flung themselves in, and swimming after it, thrust the float forward, endeavoring by that means to get to town. This proved a tedious voiture and in all likelihood they would have perished, had not this fishing boat sailed by in the morning, and perceiving something in the water, made to it, and took them in, when they were near spent with their labour.[8]

Hiring a boat to carry him and his two companions to Charleston, Mr. Marks paid the fisherman to sail out and explain to Blackbeard what had occurred.

Teach grumpily accepted the explanation. He granted his prisoners the freedom of their ships and stayed their execution for two more days.

When the two additional days of grace had expired and the envoys had not returned, Blackbeard burst into another frenzied rampage. Strolling the deck and roaring forth that he had lost all patience, he swore that the Governor of South Carolina had imprisoned two of his men and that he would revenge them by killing not only his prisoners, but every other South Carolinian who might fall into his hands. He could not be persuaded to give them any longer to live than the following morning, if the envoys had not returned by that time. The prisoners had ample reason to believe him a man of his word.

Captain Johnson, in his contemporary history, states that a number of the prisoners, in a desperate attempt to save their own lives, offered to pilot the pirate ships into the harbor. They promised that if, after ranging up before the town, they did not see the envoys coming out shortly thereafter, "they would stand by [the pirates] to the last man" if Blackbeard decided to batter down the town. They professed themselves unable to understand why the demands of the pirates had not been complied with, unless the people of Charleston "put a greater value on the chest of medicines than on the lives of fourscore men now on the verge of destruction."[9]

There is no indication that Wragg himself was among those making this proposition to the pirates; considering his high character, it is difficult to believe that he would have done so. It is conceivable, however, that among the prisoners there could have been some who, to save their own lives, would have promised anything at the moment, even if they did not intend to carry out their promise.

Blackbeard, who welcomed the opportunity to square accounts for the supposed treachery, as he termed it, of the Governor, instantly agreed to this proposal of taking revenge against Charleston. He called a meeting of the pirates, and they approved the plan. Eight ships, the four fighting vessels of the buccaneer and the four captured ones held as prizes, weighed anchor and moved into the harbor.

The ships ranged in full view of the town, whose inhabitants now shared the fright which the prisoners were experiencing. The citizenry expected a general attack, and pandemonium broke out. They were terror-stricken. Both old and young men were hurriedly and haphazardly given arms and told to defend their town, while "women and children ran about the streets like mad things." Blackbeard, the most feared of all bloodthirsty pirates, was training his cannon on Charleston. "However, before matters came to extremities, the boat was seen coming out, which brought redemption to the poor captives and peace to all."[10]

In the boat which pulled alongside the *Queen Anne's Revenge* were the two pirates, Mr. Marks, and the medicine chest, the contents of which were satisfactory to Blackbeard.

Mr. Marks explained the long delay. Upon arriving in Charleston, he had presented the demands of Blackbeard to Governor Robert Johnson, who instantly recognized that the town was in great danger of demolishment and in no condition to defend itself. The Governor hurriedly convened his Council and sought the views of its members. Shirley Carter Hughson, in a scholarly treatise published in 1894, writes:

The members realized that but one course was open to them; the pirates had them at the greatest disadvantage, and the only thing feasible was to accede to their insolent demands, and, if possible, to seek to punish their audacity later. The colony was in no condition to repel the invasion at this time. The harbor was wholly unprotected, and there was not an armed vessel within hundreds of miles. The Indian wars had bankrupted the treasury, and it was impossible to arm any of the merchant vessels in the harbor for a movement against the blockading fleet.[11]

The decision to submit coincided with the wishes of the inhabitants, who had no wish to sacrifice the lives of valued citizens for a few dollars' worth of medicine.[12]

While Marks was pleading the case of the pirates before the Governor and his Council, Lieutenant Richards and his co-pirate openly and insolently walked the streets of Charleston within "the sight of all the people, who were fired with utmost indignation, looking upon them as robbers and murderers and particularly the authors of their wrongs and oppressions; but durst not so much as think of executing their revenge, for fear of bringing more calamities upon themselves, and so they were forced to let the villains pass with impunity."[13]

The Governor and his Council acted with dispatch. Only a few hours were required to assemble the items of drugs on Blackbeard's list. But when Mr. Marks began to look for the two pirates to accompany him on the return trip, they could not be found. They had run upon drinking friends and acquaintances, and were visiting from house to house with them. Mr. Marks became greatly concerned. He knew well that if he did not return with Blackbeard's men he would have a difficult problem in convincing Blackbeard that no foul play had befallen them. A general alarm was given, and a search was made for the missing pirates. They were finally discovered, smiling and gloriously drunk.

Upon the return of the two pirates and the receipt of the chest of medicines, Blackbeard released the captured ships and the prisoners, as he had promised. Both the ships and the prisoners were, however, plucked clean of all valuables. The best-dressed of the prisoners were stripped of their fine clothes and sent back to shore half-naked.

Contemporary accounts have placed the value of the contents of the medicine chest at £300–400 sterling.[14] Since Blackbeard had an armed fleet of more than 400 pirates and was holding an entire town to ransom, one wonders why he did not demand in money or jewels a much larger sum. It would seem that much more could just as easily have been obtained. Since the pirates had not recently engaged in any battles, it is difficult to understand why there was an urgent need for medical supplies. There could have been, of course, some epidemic of infectious disease existing on board the ships. But it would seem that such ordinary medical supplies as were demanded could have been procured from the eight or nine vessels plundered at the entrance to the port or from those encountered earlier in the cruise. One writer has suggested: "Probably the answer is that they wanted mercurial preparations for the treatment of syphilis. Brothel casualties were usually higher than battle casualties among the pirates."[15] Another writer has speculated that Blackbeard "wanted the mercurial preparations in the chest because his most recent girl friend had not only married him but also left him with a venereal disease to remember her by."[16]

It may be assumed that Blackbeard and his crew had other good reasons for demanding only a chest of medicines from the inhabitants of Charleston. The blockade of the harbor had not been without profit to them. A total of eight or nine ships had been plundered during the period of the blockade, and everything of value thereon was removed to the four sloops and two tenders of the pirate fleet. From the ship on which Wragg was a passenger, or some say, from Wragg himself, there were acquired gold and silver coins amounting to £1,500 sterling.[17]

Sailing from Charleston harbor in gay spirits, Blackbeard and his crew headed for North Carolina. The pirate king had committed his most brazen and highhanded act of piracy. In the hulls of his ships he carried the most valuable loot of his piratical career.

Commodore Teach, the boldest and most ruthless corsair of them all, had reduced to total submission the proud and militant people of South Carolina without the firing of a single gun. No physical injury was suffered by either the conquerors or the victims. The horrifying image of a savage and fearless pirate captain that Blackbeard had sought to establish had paid rich dividends.

The blockade of Charleston provided its citizens with the

stimulus and the rich challenge to undertake the difficult task of subduing piracy. The people of Charleston had been terrified and humiliated. They had been affronted. They were determined to have, in due time, their revenge on Blackbeard and his hellish company. Major Stede Bonnet, Blackbeard's "guest" during the whole period of the blockade, was destined to be the victim of this angry vengeance four months later.

Chapter 5

Treachery at Beaufort Inlet

*A*FTER THE DARING and bizarre blockade of Charleston, Captain Teach and his small fleet sailed northward up the Atlantic coast, the vessels heavily laden with seized loot.

While lying off the entrance to the harbor of Charleston for almost a week, Blackbeard had learned, from the crews of inbound and outbound ships, news both of the colonies and of England. He knew that Woodes Rogers, with several men-of-war, had left England on his way to Nassau with orders to clear the West Indies of pirates. Captain Hornigold and other pirate captains and their crews were already in Nassau awaiting the promised pardons for those who voluntarily surrendered by a specified date.

Intelligent as he was, and undoubtedly aware that the boom days of piracy were almost over, Teach decided to disband his company and find retirement in the less exciting surroundings of coastal North Carolina. For reasons known only to himself, he preferred to surrender to, and obtain his pardon from, Governor Charles Eden of North Carolina rather than Governor Woodes Rogers of the Bahama Islands.

Teach and Rogers were about the same age, and both had spent their boyhood in Bristol, England. It is not impossible that they may have been acquainted with each other, or even close friends, during their youth. Since Blackbeard used a number of assumed names, the chances are that Rogers, as the newly commissioned "Captain-General and Governor-in-Chief of the Bahama Islands" in 1718, did not know the true identity of the most notorious pirate of the times. Blackbeard could have had little desire to reveal himself to a fellow townsman and thereby bring dishonor to his true family name in Bristol.

Blackbeard devised a plan whereby he and his closest companions might acquire possession of the money and the most valuable portions of the plundered merchandise. Only those in on his scheme were aware that the best of the booty had been transferred to one of the small sloops.

On the pretense of careening his ships for the purpose of scraping their hulls, Blackbeard, in early June, 1718, ordered his entire fleet to sail into what was then known as Topsail Inlet on the coast of North Carolina. Today Topsail Inlet is commonly known as Beaufort Inlet and is the inlet used to reach the towns of Beaufort and Morehead City. It is not to be confused with the much smaller Topsail Inlet presently located about fifty or sixty miles to the south. In later years (1826–1834) Fort Macon was constructed at the point where Blackbeard's fleet entered Bogue Sound from the Atlantic Ocean. The fortifications, used in the War Between the States and captured by Federal forces on April 26, 1862, are in an excellent state of preservation and constitute the chief attraction of the Fort Macon State Park. On the other side of this inlet are Shackleford Banks.

Sailing through Topsail Inlet, Blackbeard deliberately ran the *Queen Anne's Revenge* aground on a sandbar. Her mainmast cracked and many of her timbers started to do so. And then, "as if it had been done undesignedly and by accident," Blackbeard, in his best style, hailed Israel Hands on the *Adventure*, roaring out orders to man one of the other sloops and to warp the *Queen Anne's Revenge* off the bar. Hands, fully aware of what his chief intended, threw the lines of the nearest sloops, as well as his own, across the *Queen Anne's Revenge* and struggled to extricate the big ship. In doing so, he ran his own sloop ashore, and it, too, stuck fast in the sand. Both vessels appeared to be damaged beyond further use.[1]

Blackbeard meanwhile calmly informed Major Bonnet, still an involuntary guest on board, of his own future plans. Having learned that King George had extended his offer of pardon to all pirates who would voluntarily seek clemency before September 5 and take the oath not to engage further in piracy, he confided his intention of going to Bath, North Carolina, to receive the pardon from the hands of Governor Eden. He suggested that Bonnet do the same. Furthermore, if Bonnet was so inclined, since war was threatening between the Quadruple Alliance and Spain, he might go to the West Indies and obtain a privateer's commission, flying the colors of King George against the Spaniards. Declaring himself a man of his word, Blackbeard coolly offered, as of that moment, to return Bonnet to his ship, the *Revenge*, and to its command.

Such generosity overwhelmed Bonnet. Waiting for no more, and taking a part of his original crew, he left immediately in a small boat for Bath, apparently using the inland waterways of Core and Pamlico Sounds. The remaining members of the crew had been instructed to prepare the *Revenge* for sailing to St. Thomas Island, where Bonnet intended to obtain a privateer's commission against the Spaniards.

Arriving in Bath, Bonnet surrendered to Governor Charles Eden and received a certificate of pardon, obtaining also the necessary clearance papers for a voyage to St. Thomas with the *Revenge*. Bonnet promptly turned back to pick up his ship and the remainder of his crew.[2]

After the departure of Stede Bonnet, Blackbeard proceeded with his private plans. A scattering of the crew, if effectively carried out, would mean a vastly larger share for the forty men chosen to remain with their captain. Some of the crew got wind of Blackbeard's treachery and protested violently. This was the group of twenty-five whom Blackbeard forced to give up their arms and money and who were marooned on "a small sandy island, about a league from the Main, where there was neither bird, beast or herb for their subsistence, and where they must have perished if Major Bonnet had not two days after taken them off."[3] This may have been the island on which is now located Atlantic Beach and the ruins of Fort Macon.

Before the rest knew what was happening, Blackbeard quietly slipped through the inlet aboard the *Adventure*, laden with her rich spoils, and headed northward up the Atlantic coast. A number of fishermen and small traders from the nearby hamlet of Beaufort had been peddling provisions to the fleet during its stay in Bogue Sound. Blackbeard had dropped a hint to them that he intended to go northward to Ocracoke Inlet. Some of the abandoned pirates made their way in the boats of the peddlers to the mainland and overland to northern points, some as far away as Philadelphia and New York.

Returning from Bath, Major Bonnet found his ship, the *Revenge*, awaiting him exactly as Blackbeard had promised. But otherwise Blackbeard had outwitted him. All valuables and provisions had been removed. Bonnet was furious, and so were the marooned men on the sandy island, whose signals he had seen and whom he had rescued. Together they set out to seek revenge. But Blackbeard was too crafty for them. He and Bonnet were never to meet again.[4]

Stede Bonnet, the pirate with scruples, was nearing the end of his race for fame and fortune. Thwarted in his attempt to avenge himself upon Blackbeard, he cruised aimlessly. Less than three months later, on September 27, 1718, Bonnet and the members of his crew were captured, in a running fight, by the citizens of Charleston in the mouth of the Cape Fear River.

During the course of the battle seven pirates were killed and five wounded, two of whom later died of their wounds. Aboard the two vessels of Colonel William Rhett, the captor of Bonnet and his crew, ten or twelve men were killed and eighteen wounded, several of whom afterwards died of their injuries.[5] Taken to Charleston and tried, all but four of the pirates were convicted and hanged. David Harriot, who had agreed to act as a King's witness against his fellow pirates, escaped from the residence of the Charleston marshal, where he was being held. Several days later, his whereabouts being discovered, he was killed in the process of recapture. Captain Bonnet and Ignatius Pell, another pirate being used as a witness for the King, were also kept in the residence of the marshal; but the other members of Bonnet's crew were imprisoned under heavy guard at the watch house, believed to have been located at the eastern end of Broad Street.[6]

On November 4, 1718, the Governor of South Carolina, placing himself in personal command of a fleet of four heavily armed vessels, including the one taken from Bonnet, sailed out onto the high seas to destroy the pirate ships then hovering around the entrance to Charleston harbor. In one of the fiercest battles ever fought in those waters, he captured the notorious Captain Richard Worley, who had terrorized the coasts in the vicinity of New York and Philadelphia only a few weeks before and had captured ships off the coast of Cape Henry, Virginia, and Cape Hatteras, North Carolina, as he moved southward.[7]

Not only were pirates slain aboard their ships, while others died from their wounds; the courts of Charleston tried, convicted, and caused to be hanged within the period of a month a total of forty-nine pirates. "This execution of forty-nine outlaws in a month stands unparalleled in America as an attack of an aroused community on crime."[8]

The pirates were strung up on gibbets erected at White Point. The exact location of the spot cannot be stated with historical accuracy. The bodies of the bold sea robbers were buried in the desolate mud flats then surrounding White Point, as was the custom in the burial of pirates, somewhere between the high and low tide marks. Their burial place has since been filled in and is presently the site of the beautiful White Point Gardens, which mark the southern boundary of a proud and historic city.

Chapter 6

Blackbeard Settles in Bath Town

*B*LACKBEARD passed through Ocracoke Inlet, North Carolina, entered Pamlico Sound, and headed for Bath Town, located in the county of Bath on the Pamlico River fifty-odd miles from the Atlantic Ocean. Captain Teach was in familiar waters, thoroughly acquainted with the shoals, channels, and shifting sands of shallow Pamlico Sound.

Arriving in Bath sometime in June, 1718, Blackbeard and at least twenty members of his crew sought out Governor Charles Eden and received, perhaps for the second time, the "gracious pardon" of the Royal Proclamation.[1] Major Bonnet had departed from Bath with his pardon just two days before Blackbeard arrived.

It was in and near Bath, North Carolina, that Blackbeard completed his rendezvous with history. He became the small town's most notorious inhabitant, and it was there that he played a part in the story of a great nation yet unborn.

The town of Bath, located on a small peninsula formed by the confluence of Bath Creek (formerly Old Town Creek) and Back Creek (formerly Adams Creek), faces out onto a beautiful little bay that opens into the Pamlico River. Founded on March 8, 1705/1706, it is the oldest incorporated town in North Carolina.[2] The planters of the area had taken the initiative to incorporate the town, hopeful that it would become the commercial and political center of the colony. The site selected was on the east bank of Bath Creek. John Lawson, Joel Martin, Sr., and Simon Anderson purchased from David Perkins sixty acres adjoining the plantation of William Barrow, and they proceeded to lay out the town and to sell or to give away options on the town lots, on which the wealthier plantation owners were expected to build town houses.

In 1709 Bath Town had about twelve houses within its corporate limits.[3] The town derived its name from one of the Lords Proprietors, John Granville, the Earl of Bath, who had bought the share owned originally by the Duke of Albemarle. The town survived the horrible Indian massacre of September, 1711, although three of its houses were burned. It was reported to have had over 300 refugees "in a pitiful condition" from the surrounding region.[4] Most of them were widows and orphans, whose husbands and fathers had died defending their homes.

Not until February 11, 1715, had the long and dreary Tuscarora War finally come to an end with the signing of a peace treaty. Bath Town launched upon a rebuilding program and experienced a minor boom. Governor Charles Eden, who became Governor on May 28, 1714,[5] honored Bath Town by purchasing several lots and a house in the town.[6]

A number of North Carolina governors, both before and after Blackbeard's arrival, lived in or near Bath Town.[7] In 1718 North Carolina did not have, in the true sense of the word, a capital. The governors lived in various regions of the colony, and the Assembly and Council met in private homes at several places. In fact, there were, except in the northeastern section, no settlements in the whole of what is now North Carolina; the poorly organized government of the colony might be described as migratory. During the latter part of 1718, however, a courthouse was completed on Queen Anne's Creek (now Edenton, in Chowan County).[8] The minutes of the Council Journal show that Governor Eden and four members of his council met "at the Court House in Chowan" on November 11, 1718.[9] During subsequent years this building was available for use and was actually used from time to time by the Council, the Assembly, the General Court, and the Chowan Precinct Court.[10] It is said to have been located on the south side of King Street, directly across from the present Chowan County Courthouse.[11] William Byrd II, of Westover, Virginia, wrote in 1729 that it had "much the Air of a Common Tobacco-House."[12] The present Chowan County Courthouse, built in 1767, is widely considered the finest Georgian courthouse in the South.

Nowhere in the town or county of Bath, or in the entire province, was there, during Blackbeard's stay in North Carolina, a courthouse, a jail, a schoolhouse, or a church building.[13] The church meetings were held in private homes. The population of the entire colony was thinly scattered. It has been estimated that the white population did not in 1718 exceed 7,500 or 8,000 persons.[14]

Except for a number of merchants, a few skilled artisans, and a handful of public officials, there were few permanent residents in Bath Town. Most persons "drifted into Bath and out again, as quickly and quietly as they had come, others paused long enough to purchase lots and sell them before going on their way, still others acquired a house and lived there for a short time before moving on to more distant fields."[15] Bath was in effect a seaboard frontier town. By virtue of an instrument dated August 1, 1716, Bath Town was designated by the Lords Proprietors as the official seaport for the Province of North Carolina.[16] As a consequence, the collection of customs and the clearance of vessels were conducted at Bath. It was one of the few places in North Carolina where money for patented land and the annual quitrents could be paid.[17]

Although Bath Town was a place of considerable political and commercial importance in the early eighteenth century, it grew very slowly and never became populous. The census of 1960 listed but 346 persons living in the town. In 1970 the number had dwindled to 231. Today there is not a single structure in Bath which was in existence when Blackbeard lived there.

George Whitefield, the famous English preacher and revivalist, visited Bath in 1739, 1747–1748, 1764, and 1765.[18] He wrote that he was "here, hunting in the woods, these ungospelized wilds for sinners" and, somewhat sardonically, that the conversion of "North Carolina sinners would be glad news in heaven."[19] According to legend, once when he was leaving, having been mistreated by some of the citizens of Bath, he "shook the dust of Bath from his feet," thereby invoking a curse of heaven upon the town, which "has doomed it forever to the life of a small village."[20]

Upon the recommendation of the Lords Proprietors of Carolina, Queen Anne, by an Order in Council on May 18, 1713, appointed Charles Eden Governor of North Carolina.[21] His royal instructions were the same as those issued for Governor Edward Hyde.[22] In addition to his annual salary of £300, Eden received statutory fees for services rendered incidental to the office, the latter apparently being a substantial part of his total income. He was required, aside from any salary, to give security of £1,000 for his due performance of the Trade and Navigation Acts.[23]

A little past forty years of age when he arrived in North Carolina, Charles Eden was a member of an ancient and distinguished English family seated in the County Palatine of Durham.[24] Sir Robert Eden, the last colonial governor of Maryland, also belonged to this family, as did many other outstanding men, including peers, bishops, and statesmen. Sir Robert Anthony Eden, Prime Minister of England from 1955 to 1957, born at Windlestone Hall, Durham County, of a family holding a baronetcy since 1672, was a descendant of the same family.

The British records of the Lords Proprietors, dated August 13, 1713, contain instructions to the Surveyor General of North Carolina to measure and set out 1,000 acres for the use of Governor Eden and his heirs, reserving an annual quitrent of ten shillings.[25] Governor Eden presented the commission appointing him Governor, Captain General, and Admiral, at a meeting of the members of the North Carolina Council held on May 28, 1714, in the home of Captain John Hecklefield on Little River at Durant's Neck in Perquimans Precinct. On that day he took and subscribed to the oaths required by law.[26]

The Lords Proprietors on February 19, 1717/1718, had made Governor Eden a landgrave.[27] Only two of North Carolina's governors, Eden and Robert Daniel, held the proprietary dignity of landgrave. The charter of June 30, 1665, granted by Charles II to the Lords Proprietors, authorized them to grant titles of honor provided they were not the same as those in use in England.[28] The Fundamental Constitutions of the Colony of Carolina, in the version approved on April 11, 1698, by the Lords Proprietors pursuant to their charter from Charles II, defined the term "landgrave" as a county nobleman invested with "great powers and privileges."[29] In Germany a landgrave was a count having territorial jurisdiction; later, it became the title of certain German princes.[30] The conferring of the title in Carolina was an attempt on the part of the Lords Proprietors to establish a kind of feudal nobility. Their efforts were never successful.

Governor Eden occupied a plantation of 400 acres on the west side of Bath Creek, across from the incorporated town of Bath.[31] Legend has it that a subterranean passage was cut from the cellar of "the Governor's Mansion" to the steep bank of the creek, so that Blackbeard could enter and depart without being seen.[32] This tale would have one believe that under cover of darkness Blackbeard's crew quietly carried Eden's share of the pirates' loot through the tunnel to Eden's cellar.

There exist today merely the foundation ruins of Eden's plantation home on the west side of Bath Creek.[33] Those who have studied colonial Bath's history are of the opinion that there never was a tunnel leading from Governor Eden's cellar to the water's edge. There was, however, a path made of ballast rocks leading from the cellar of his house to his pier. Rocks of that type are not common in this section of North Carolina. Brought to Bath in the bottom of unladen vessels from England, the rocks were dumped when cargoes were put on board for the return voyage.

Apparently during Blackbeard's stay in North Carolina, Governor Eden maintained two homes: the one on Bath Creek, and another on a larger plantation in Chowan Precinct (now Bertie County) on the west bank of the Chowan River, across from the present town of Edenton. In a letter addressed to the Society for the Propagation of the Gospel (the foreign missionary society of the Anglican Church), dated May 10, 1716, and written from "Chowan, North Carolina," he wrote, "I entend in the fall to settle at Pemptisough with my family."[34] The minutes of the Council Journal record that a meeting of the Council was held on Saturday, August 4, 1716, in the Precinct of Chowan "at the house of the honorable governor,"[35] a distance of almost fifty miles from Bath Town.

Tobias Knight, who figured prominently in later events relating to Blackbeard, became Governor Eden's neighbor on the west bank of Bath Creek by purchasing, on June 15, 1718, the adjoining plantation home and estate of the late Landgrave Robert Daniel, first governor to live in or near Bath Town.[36] The house was located on what is now Archbell Point.[37] Living at an earlier time in Pasquotank Precinct, Knight had married Catherine, the widow of William Glover, who as President of the Council had for a time been Acting Governor.[38] In 1718 Knight was the Secretary of the Colony, Collector of Customs, Chief Justice, and member of the Council. He was sworn in as Secretary of the Colony and Collector of Customs at a meeting of the Council held on May 9, 1712, the same meeting at which Edward Hyde was sworn in as Governor of North Carolina.[39] This was also the occasion on which North Carolina acquired both a governor and a government separate and distinct from those of South Carolina.[40] In consequence of Chief Justice Christopher Gale's departing for England in 1717, "Tobias Knight, Esq., was by the Governor with the consent of the Council constituted Chief Justice of this Province,"[41] according to the minutes of the Council Journal, dated August 1, 1717.

When Blackbeard settled in Bath, he established his home and base of operations at Plum Point on the east side of Bath Creek, across from Governor Eden's home.[42] Plum Point has a high elevation, commanding a beautiful view of the bay. It was an idyllic location. Still to be discerned today, a depression in the ground and sufficient ruins of a foundation indicate that many years ago a house stood on this spot. It is equally obvious that in the past many diggings were made nearby for buried treasure, possibly that which Blackbeard was believed to have hidden.

Persons now living remember that, located in a shallow field between Plum Point and Bath Town, there was "a round brick structure resembling a huge oven, called Teach's Kettle, in which the notorious pirate captain is said to have boiled the tar with which to calk his vessels."[43] So many tourists came to see it, thereby damaging the growing crops, that the farmer who owned the land covered the brick oven with earth and plowed it over.

One of the legends often repeated is that Captain Teach courted unsuccessfully Governor Eden's daughter. Already engaged to another young man, she is said to have rejected his suit. Angered and jealous of his rival, Blackbeard supposedly captured him one night, cut off his hands, and dumped his body into the sea. He then placed the severed hands in a jeweled casket, which he sent to Miss Eden. The heartbroken Miss Eden "languished and died," as was the fashion in the case of disrupted romance.[44]

There is, of course, no historical basis for this legend. Governor Eden did not have a daughter. He died childless.[45]

Eden himself married, shortly after his arrival in the colony, Mrs. Penelope Golland, the widow of a Mr. Golland of Mount Golland (now Mount Gould), on the west side of the Chowan River.[46] Eden built his own home, Eden House, some six or seven miles south on the same side of the river. Mrs. Eden, who died on January 4, 1716, at the age of thirty-nine,[47] had at least two children, John and Penelope Golland, by her earlier marriage.[48] Her daughter was married four times:[49] first, to Colonel William Maule;[50] second, to Captain John Lovick,[51] Secretary of the Province; third to George Phenney,[52] former Governor of the Bahama Islands; and fourth, to Governor Gabriel Johnston of North Carolina.[53]

John Lovick was the Secretary of the province and a member of the Council at the close of Eden's administration,[54] and apparently continued so until the end of the proprietary period, in 1729.[55] Under the terms of Governor Eden's will, Lovick was his sole executor and residuary beneficiary.[56] Penelope, the Governor's stepdaughter, was at the time married to Colonel Maule. Neither she nor her husband was left anything under the will of Governor Eden, and it was by virtue of the will of her second husband, Captain Lovick, that she acquired ownership of the plantation home of Governor Eden on the west side of the Chowan River, she being designated Lovick's sole executrix and residuary beneficiary.[57] It has been frequently supposed, and often stated in print, that Penelope was Governor Eden's own daughter, but she was in fact, of course, Governor Eden's stepdaughter.[58]

Penelope Golland became one of the wealthiest women of the province and was for a long time mistress of Eden House. Governor Johnston, her fourth and last husband, made his home at Eden House for a number of years, and his body is believed to be buried near there, though no marker has been found for his grave.[59] Colonel John Dawson, a lawyer from Virginia, married the daughter of Penelope Golland and Governor Johnston, also named Penelope, and moved into Eden House, which was noted for its "splendid hospitality" and the "refined society generally assembled there."[60]

It was not customary during colonial times for a person, after the death of his or her spouse, to remain long bereaved. For this there were good economic and social reasons. An attractive widow, especially an inheritrix of a sizable estate from her late husband, had a palpable advantage. There was a large surplus of males in the colony, so that the young and attractive widow was in great demand. The competition for her forced the men to seek her out and propose marriage before she became committed to another. So great was the haste that a friend of a widow would meet her and extend condolence upon the death of her former husband and congratulate her upon her choice of a second mate at the same time. It was not unusual for a woman's second husband to become the administrator of the estate of her first husband.

Eden sold his plantation on Bath Creek in 1718 to John Lillington and moved to Eden House in what was then Chowan Precinct, on the west bank of the Chowan River. There he died on March 26, 1722, from a lingering yellow fever. The members of the Council met in Eden House on March 30 and elected Eden's friend and neighbor, Thomas Pollock, President of the

Council, which automatically raised him to the position of Acting Governor. Pollock himself died on August 30, 1722.[61]

In 1889, the remains of Governor Eden and his wife were exhumed from their burial spot near Eden House, carried across the Chowan River to Edenton, and there placed in the burial ground of St. Paul's Church, of which Governor Eden at one time was a vestryman.[62] The original slate slab, set in brownstone, marks his grave. But the historic town of Edenton, named in his honor, is a nobler and more enduring memorial. The inscriptions on his tombstone are as follows:

Here lyes ye body of
CHARLES EDEN, E.S.Q.,

Who governed this Province Eight years, to ye greatest satisfaction of ye Lords Proprietors, and ye ease and happiness of ye people, he brought ye Country into a flourishing condition, and died much lamented March ye 26, 1722. Aetatis 49.

And near this place lyes also ye body of Penelope Eden, his virtuous consort, who died January 4 1716. Aetatis 39. Vivit post funera. Ille quem virtus marmor in aeternum sacrat.[63]

Chapter 7

Refuge in North Carolina

CAPTAIN EDWARD TEACH had, by the summer of 1718, attained an image buttressed with achievements. Bath undoubtedly was a lively place when he and his crew came into port. They traded their hard-earned booty at reasonable prices for wild sprees and replenished their ships for other forays, bringing an economic windfall to the area. People came great distances to buy merchandise from foreign lands in the shops of Bath. The ordinaries (the hotels of colonial times) and bars were crowded with customers. The village came to life.

The pirates proved to be lavish scoundrels who spent and gave with hands as open as when they took. Blackbeard's crew yarned with great pleasure of their acts of piracy, boasting of exploits on the high seas. It was a time of braggadocio, of pomposity and hard drinking and swearing. The pirates were admired for their primitive qualities of strength and arrogance.

The people of the colony were not fearful of the swaggering Blackbeard on land. He was strictly a sea robber, and there is no record of his ever committing a crime on land. Nearly everybody wanted to meet and talk with him, to learn of his maraudings and adventures in faraway places. He was a celebrity, pardoned by a royal proclamation and seeking retirement in their midst. The planters invited him into their houses, and Captain Teach in turn lavishly entertained in his Bath home.[1] He often boasted that there was not a home in North Carolina into which he could not be invited for dinner.[2] With his personality, wealth, and bonhomie, he was able to convince many, with many wishing to be convinced, that, after all, pirates on land were their good friends and not their foes.

Living in a location where, and an era when, unpardoned acts of piracy were condoned, if not sanctioned, by the law, it was not beneath persons of family and respectability to take part in such acts. Lawlessness has existed in every newly-opened country. A frontier morality was in full swing in North Carolina when Blackbeard arrived in 1718. Piracy was a fashionable vice. Blackbeard entered upon the scene of this piratical craze when it was at its height, and he easily became the star of the melodrama.

During the latter part of the seventeenth century nearly every colony in North America was, "in one way or another, offering encouragement to the pirates,"[3] these being the years that the fabulous cargoes of silks, gold, diamonds, and jewelry stolen in the area of the Red Sea were being disposed of in Boston, New York, and Philadelphia. Many of the great fortunes of colonial families in those places were founded upon pirate loot purchased as cheaply as possible. There was very little moral deterrence to piracy. No one asked where the gold or exotic merchandise came from, yet everyone knew. Politicians and churchmen had a knack for presenting pious faces and making condemnations of evil while working as fences for the sea robbers. Pirate gold was an irresistible lure for Puritans, Anglicans, and Quakers alike.

During this *laissez faire* period, pirate crews circulated freely along the wharves and in the stores and bars of Boston, Providence, Newport, New York, and Philadelphia. The merchants bought the pirates' pickings at a small fraction of their market value and sold to the pirates, at an enormous profit, rum, shot, gunpowder, and supplies for another voyage. Young men were enthralled with the stories told by pirates, stories of great adventure and boundless riches on the high seas and in faraway places. When Captain Thomas Tew sailed into Newport in 1693 aboard a ship laden with merchandise stolen from the

Moslems, young men of most respectable colonial families hastened to join him for additional maraudings. "Men told one another joyfully that in the Red Sea 'money was plenty as stones and sand—the people there were Infidels and it was no sin to kill them.' "[4]

The worst charges of corruption were made against Governor Benjamin Fletcher of New York and five members of his Council, all of whom were dismissed from public office.[5] They were accused of accepting gold and even ships in return for guaranteeing immunity from arrest. It was the Earl of Bellomont, Governor of New York, Massachusetts, and New Hampshire between 1698 and 1701, who stamped out piracy in New York.

Fletcher's hobnobbing with known pirates was an open scandal, not only in New York, but also in other colonies and in England. Having openly welcomed the notorious Captain Tew upon his return from the Red Sea, Fletcher rode with him in his own carriage and dined and drank with him far into the night at the Governor's Mansion. Questioned about such incidents in London, Governor Fletcher attempted to explain them away by saying that he was trying to reform Tew, and that he was personally interested in the pirate's remarkable stories of romance and adventure on the other side of the globe. Fletcher declared that Captain Tew was

not only a man of courage and activity, but of the greatest sense and remembrance of what he had seen, of any seaman I had met. He was also what they call a very pleasant man, soe that at some times when the labours of my day were over it was some divertisement as well as information to me, to heare him talke. I wish'd in my mind to make him a sober mind, and in particular to reclaime him from a vile habit of swearing. I gave him a booke for that purpose, and to gaine the more upon him, I gave him a gunn of some value. In return herefor he made me also a present which was a curiosity and in value not much.[6]

William Markham, Lieutenant Governor of Pennsylvania from 1694 until William Penn's arrival in December, 1699, was the official head of the proprietary colony of Pennsylvania at the time that populous colony is said to have given encouragement to piracy.[7] In 1699, Philadelphia, with 12,000 inhabitants, had twice the population of New York. The leadership of the colony was vested mainly in Quakers, "who, for religious or selfish reasons, advocated mild measures against smugglers and pirates, with some of their leaders setting themselves severely against the formation of a militia which could definitely have restrained these enemies of the province."[8] S. C. Hughson writes: "The minutes of the Province of Pennsylvania teem with notices of the freebooters on that coast and were all the references given, the array would weary the eye of the reader."[9]

Although Markham himself denied any kind of dealings with pirates, it has been said that he gave sanctuary to pirates at the rate of £100 per head.[10] "Practically everyone was aware of the fact that he had married his daughter to Captain James Brown, a notorious pirate, and that this couple associated with the best families in Philadelphia."[11] It has been stated by a Philadelphian, however, that Markham's son was refused a seat in the assembly because of his association with pirates.[12]

It was William Penn's great delight to prove that the Reverend Edward Portlock, rector of the famous Christ Church in Philadelphia, had been entrusted with 624 pieces of pirate gold, amounting to £414 in Philadelphia money, by Dr. Robert Bradenham, one of the craftiest of pirate politicians, and that the rector had given to the pirate a written receipt for the specie. Portlock had "been thundering from his pulpit Sunday after Sunday against Quakers and 'other instruments of the Devil' who trafficked with pirates."[13] Dr. Bradenham, who had sailed as the physician of Captain William Kidd's crew, was shipped to London for trial. But, because of the evidence he gave in London enabling the Crown to convict Captain Kidd, Bradenham was rewarded with his own freedom.

Part of the money used for the founding, in 1693, of the College of William and Mary came from pirate loot. The sum, according to the records of the college, was £300. It was only a small part of much money, plate, and goods piratically taken on an expedition that began on August 23, 1683, after four months of preparation in Accomac, Virginia, and ended on June 22, 1688, at the mouth of the James River. Only three pirates, Captain Edward Davis, Lionel Delawafer, and John Hinson, and a Negro servant belonging to Captain Davis, were found in a small boat stopped on suspicion by Captain Simon Rowe, commander of the *Dunbarton*, a frigate stationed in Virginia waters to protect shipping from pirate attack.[14]

Davis's large crew had been disbanded. The shares of the three captured pirates were inventoried, and they were lodged in the Jamestown gaol. An attorney, Micajah Perry, was retained to defend them. Contending that they had been coming into Virginia to surrender under the terms of King James's proclamation, the pirates won their freedom during the summer of 1689. After prolonged litigation, the King, on March 10, 1692, ordered a restitution of all their possessions, except that "three hundred pounds of the goods belonging unto them and now lying in their Majestys Warehouse, together with a fourth part of what shall be recovered belonging to the Petitioners from the said Capt Rowe or his executors shall be employed towards the Erecting a College or free Schoole in Virginia or some other Pious or Charitable uses as their Majesties shall direct."[15]

Lloyd Haynes Williams, in his *Pirates of Colonial Virginia*, states: "According to one account, the pirates themselves proposed the giving of this amount; another states that the Reverend James Blair offered to use his influence in having their goods returned provided they gave three hundred pounds toward the college the clergymen was so interested in founding."[16] James Blair, a shrewd Scotsman, was the first President of the College of William and Mary.

North Carolina's experience with piracy during the second decade of the eighteenth century was not unlike that of other English colonies of an earlier date. Because of its isolation and its thinly scattered population, the troubles incident to colonial piracy were delayed in reaching North Carolina. Since, however, North Carolina was the last of the colonies to stamp out piracy, it has been only natural for persons to associate the worst of piracy with this province. The extent to which it flourished has been greatly exaggerated. Most of the reports of the period came from Governor Alexander Spotswood of Virginia and crown officials, and their reports were a part of the propaganda waged for many years for the purpose of discrediting the proprietary colony in order to pave the way for its seizure by the Crown.

Hugh Talmadge Lefler and Arthur R. Newsome, in their history of North Carolina, said:

It should be borne in mind that the attitude toward these questionable and illegal practices was different then from that which developed later. English trade laws were extremely unpopular in the colonies, and it was smart, proper, and profitable to evade them. Hence, smuggling prevailed almost everywhere. Piracy was not considered an unmitigated evil and many of the pirates were regarded as respectable men and were sheltered and protected by the people. After all, they brought in many desirable articles which they usually sold at reasonable prices; they also helped to keep out French and Spanish vessels, and thus enabled England to expand its trade with the colonies.[17]

In any case, North Carolina was in no position to inflict either ostracism or judicial punishment upon these wayfaring corsairs. The times were not ripe. The habit of easy dealing with pirates had grown too strong to be broken by Governor Eden's limited resources. Far from investing their funds in a section of the province that was not yielding a profit, the Lords Proprietors were directing their attention and resources to the Charleston area, which had begun to pay them dividends.[18] Since Carolina was not a Crown Colony, the British government was little inclined to send out its men-of-war to police the waterways of a private investment of eight Lords Proprietors who were operating "a real estate office offering to supply the ever-present land hunger of the peoples of Europe."[19]

When the profits from their business venture were no longer forthcoming and the inhabitants had become increasingly difficult to govern, in 1729 the Lords Proprietors, not surprisingly, sold their interests to the Crown.[20] South Carolina had become a Crown Colony in 1719, the year after Blackbeard's death, while Virginia had done so as early as 1624. The administration of a Crown Colony theoretically implied a direct relationship between the colony and the Crown. North Carolina's government prior to 1729 was virtually independent of the Crown, having its own administration, assembly, and court system.[21]

The powers of the proprietary governor were restricted. All public matters had to be determined by the concurrence of at least four of the seven members of his Council, who were scattered throughout the province, and it was difficult to get them to attend the called sessions.[22]

Caught in the undertow of piracy and undeterred by government, North Carolina's colonists, in 1718, "could hardly have been expected to resign a profitable connection with the pirates, merely at the command of a board of gentlemen three thousand miles across the sea, who only looked upon the colony as an enterprise for the betterment of their private fortunes."[23]

The people of North Carolina tended, furthermore, to be mutinous, so used to disposing of their governors that they assumed they had the right to do so. The governor and his Council meanwhile had much difficulty defending the colony from Indian attacks and establishing law and order.[24] The Indian fighting, of course, had to be done by the colonists themselves.

In 1715, the Assembly of North Carolina, under the leadership of Edward Moseley, flung the following challenge into the teeth of Governor Eden and his Council: *"Resolved,* that the impressing of the inhabitants, or their property, under the pretense of its being for the public service, without authority from the Assembly, was unwarrantable, a great infringement of the liberty of the subject, and very much weakened the government by causing many to leave it."[25]

There is no indication that, when Blackbeard surrendered and accepted his pardon, he intended at the time to return ultimately to piracy. He had wealth and could easily yield to the inevitable and settle down to a quieter life.

For a time Captain Teach lived the life of a gentleman of leisure. His fast-sailing sloop became a yacht, as it were, and her owner amused himself by sailing the quiet inland waters of North Carolina, occasionally taking excursions on the high seas to break the tedium.

Johnson states:

He often diverted himself with going on shore among the planters, where he revelled night and day. By these he was well received, but whether out of love or fear, I cannot say. Sometimes he used them courteously enough, and made them presents of rum and sugar, in recompense of what he took from them; but as for liberties which, 'tis said, he and his companions often took with the wives and daughters of the planters, I cannot take upon me to say whether he paid them *ad valorem* or no.[26]

To the people of North Carolina, Blackbeard was the king of his profession. He liked them, and most of them, it appears, liked him. He possessed the ability to adapt to different situations, and whatever he undertook he did well and with great aplomb. He knew the homes into which it would not be proper for him to be accompanied by pirate companions. When he visited them, his crew remained aboard ship.

Having settled in Bath, Blackbeard took little time in selecting his fourteenth bride. Visiting the plantations on the sounds and rivers, he chose a girl who was about sixteen years old and the daughter of a Bath County planter. Governor Charles Eden performed the marriage ceremony.[27]

Writers have seized upon this marriage performed by Governor Eden as sufficient proof that Blackbeard and the governor were bosom friends allied in the commission of piratical acts. Such a conclusion reveals ignorance both of the laws and of the conditions existing in North Carolina in 1718 with respect to marriages. There was no minister or missionary in the whole of Bath County at the time Blackbeard's ceremony was performed. Furthermore, the marriage was in strict accordance with the statute of North Carolina, codified in 1715,[28] which expressly authorized the governor or any member of his Council to conduct marriage ceremonies.

Diligent research has not produced any historical proof that a child was born to the bride Blackbeard married in Bath.[29] The pirate was slain only a few months after his marriage. If a child fathered by Blackbeard was born to Mrs. Teach after the death of her husband, this child may have been reared under some surname other than Teach or Thatch. There has not been found any authenticated record or any statement of the identity of the girl whom Blackbeard married. Tradition has it that the girl's name was Mary Ormond, and there exists a letter written by a relative of a Mary Ormond so stating.[30]

According to Colonel C. Wingate Reed's *History of Beaufort County*, a family named Ormond played a prominent role in the history of Bath Town and what later became Beaufort County. William Ormond in 1738 was appointed the first sheriff of Beaufort County. Wyriott Ormond represented Bath Town in the 1746, 1749, 1762, 1764, and 1773 sessions of the General Assembly, and in the 1749 session he represented Beaufort

County. Roger Ormond, brother of Wyriott, represented Beaufort County in the 1773, 1774, and 1775 sessions.[31] It was Roger Ormond and William Brown, members of the Committee of Safety for Bath, who on May 6, 1775, heard the pounding hoofs of a "foam-flecked horse" galloping down the post road from Edenton to enter the town gate, bearing an express rider who informed them of the battles of Lexington and Concord in Massachusetts.[32]

Blackbeard's settling in Bath, his surrender and marriage, seemed to indicate that he planned to live out the rest of his days as a wealthy "gentleman." Blackbeard was, however, not the kind of man to live in virtuous inactivity. He possessed an unquieted passion for adventure. He wanted to be where things were happening, which to him was on the high seas. He had been bred to the sea, and the old lure was something his adventurous soul could not resist. If in good faith he had accepted the King's gracious pardon, it was inevitable that he would backslide, for he was constitutionally beyond redemption. He was soon on the high seas bringing back to Bath Town his spoils.

It bears out the story of a band of buccaneers who crashed the pearly gates of heaven. St. Peter, particularly anxious to get rid of his uninvited guests, solved the problem by a stratagem capable of dispersing only the Brethren of the Coast. Pointing to a place outside of heaven, he yelled, "A sail!" "Where?" demanded the pirates. "To the leeward on the port side," replied St. Peter. "*Chasse dessous!*" they cried, instinctively rushing out the gates, which were shut tightly behind them.[33]

North Carolina was a pirate's utopia. It was close to the traffic lanes of the seas. Cape Hatteras, often called the Graveyard of the Atlantic, made coastal navigation treacherous. The inlets between the sandbars allowed the pirates' shallow-draft ships to escape into the safety of shallow sounds and rivers, where the heavy, pursuing men-of-war dared not follow. The circuitous channels had to be known, but these inland waters were convenient hideouts, places for cleaning, caulking, and refitting ships for another cruise. It was very difficult to police such a large expanse of water. The pirates were able to move about without causing any particular stir.

Violent and frequent storms have for centuries been constantly at work changing the coastline of North Carolina. Nature did not place any rocks or stones to anchor the Outer Banks, the long and narrow strips of land separating the sounds from the ocean. Storms have closed old inlets and opened new ones at random. In 1718 no commercially usable inlet existed north of Ocracoke Inlet, because the earlier ones had been closed. The present Hatteras and Oregon inlets were cut through the sandbars by storms occurring in 1846. Oregon Inlet derived its name from that of a steamboat named the *Oregon*, the first vessel to pass through it.[34]

Blackbeard claimed undisputed sway over the rivers and sounds of North Carolina that could be reached by ocean travel. Respecting his authority, the natives looked to him to protect them from other pirates. Blackbeard knew well that in this "land of Eden" piracy would flourish like an indigenous and fertile seed dropped into rich soil.

Even Teach's pirate cronies who remained in North Carolina had developed a hankering for their old trade. They were unable to adjust to the restraints of society, and their behavior would have been much worse had it not been for the stabilizing influence of Captain Teach in their midst. So many pirates in the province at this particular time could easily have brought chaos and a complete breakdown of organized society, had Blackbeard not been there to restrain them. He could, and did, do far more to curb the pirates than any other person in the province.

The increasing restlessness of his men may have been one of the factors that caused Blackbeard to return to the high seas. He could handle his villains better on board ship than was possible on land. A man both respected and feared, he never had any trouble with so-called "sea lawyers," who knew their rights under the law and protested too much. If one manifested himself, his mates soon singled him out for special treatment. Such a man was sent aloft under perilous conditions, or knocked down from behind and kicked in the ribs or face until he staggered forward to his bunk. With such treatment, most sea lawyers learned to exercise discretion.

Governor Eden was probably most happy to see the Vice-Admiralty Court in Bath Town clear the title to the *Adventure*, officially placing the vessel in the name of Captain Teach for use in trading expeditions on the high seas.[35] Since the petition by Teach was not contested, this was undoubtedly a routine adjudication, making possible the issuance of clearance papers for a trip to the island of St. Thomas, and thereby removing Teach's crew for a time from Bath Town, where Governor Eden reported to his Council that there had been "some disorders committed by them."[36] It would relieve some of the tension in the colony; the pirates could blow off their steam at sea.

A proper certificate of registration was among the most important of the ship's papers when the *Adventure* sailed. Teach had no intention of being caught on the high seas or entering a port without such a paper. This, along with documentation of his "gracious pardon" of prior piratical offenses, would thereafter always be aboard his ship.

Chapter 8

Seafaring Activities
of a Pardoned Pirate

*W*ITH NOT THE slightest intention of going to St. Thomas for the purpose of engaging in honest trade, Teach's freebooters headed north for Philadelphia, the largest city in America. Blackbeard had on numerous prior occasions visited Philadelphia; he had friends in the area and was well known to frequenters of the taverns on the waterfront. But on this occasion the captain had scarcely more than appeared in the taverns when, to his astonishment, he was informed that Governor William Keith had, on August 11, 1718, reported to his Council the issuance of a warrant for Teach's apprehension.[1] It was impossible for a character as colorful as Blackbeard to go unnoticed in Philadelphia. Too shrewd to be caught in a trap, he and his crew retreated to their ship and departed. On October 17, 1718, Governor Keith submitted a bill of £90 to cover the expenses of an expedition of two sloops, commanded by Captains Raymond and Taylor, sent out to the nearby capes in pursuit of Blackbeard.[2]

John F. Watson, in his *Annals of Philadelphia and Pennsylvania*, has collected antiquarian materials indicating that Blackbeard was as well known to the citizens of Philadelphia as to the people of Bath, Nassau, and the West Indies:

Mrs. Bulah Coates, (once Jacquet—this was the name of the Dutch governor in Delaware, in 1658,) the grandmother of Samuel Coates, Esq., late an aged citizen, told him [Coates] that she had seen and sold goods to the celebrated Blackbeard, she then keeping a store in

High street, No. 77, where Beninghove owned and dwelt—a little west of Second street. He bought freely and paid well. She then knew it was he, and so did some others. But they were afraid to arrest him, lest his crew, when they should hear of it, should avenge his cause by some midnight assault. He was too politic to bring his vessel or crew within immediate reach; and at the same time was careful to give no direct offense to any of the settlements where they wished to be regarded as visitors and purchasers, &c. . .

Blackbeard was also seen at sea by the mother of the late Dr. Hugh Williamson, of New York; she was then, in her youth, coming to this country, and their vessel was captured by him. The very aged John Hutton, who died in Philadelphia in 1792, well remembered to have seen Blackbeard, at Barbadoes, after he had come in under the Act of Oblivion. This was but shortly before he made his last cruise, and was killed, in 1718. The late aged Benjamin Kite has told me, that he had seen in his youth an old black man, nearly a hundred years of age, who had been one of Blackbeard's pirates, by impressment. He lived many years with George Grey's family, the brewer in Chestnut street, near to Third street. The same Mr. Kite's grandfather told him he well knew one Crane, a Swede, at the Upper ferry, on Schuylkill, who used to go regularly in his boat to supply Blackbeard's vessel at State island. He also said it was known that that freebooter used to visit an inn in High street, near to Second street, with his sword by his side. There is a traditionary story, that Blackbeard and his crew used to visit and revel at Marcus Hook, at the house of a Swedish woman, whom he was accustomed to call Marcus, as an abbreviation of Margaret.[3]

It was probably after leaving Philadelphia that Blackbeard set sail for Bermuda. On the way he encountered several English vessels, but robbed them only of the provisions necessary for the expedition.[4] Toward the end of August, his sloop *Adventure*, equipped with eight cannons, fell in with two French merchant ships, one sailing light but the other laden with sugar and cocoa, both bound for home from Martinique. For the experienced Blackbeard, it was a simple matter to take the Frenchmen. After putting the crew of the laden vessel aboard the other, he permitted them to proceed on their way. The captured ship, with her cargo, was taken to North Carolina.[5] Because of her size, this ship was probably kept in a cove at Ocracoke Inlet.

On or about September 24, 1718, Teach reported to Governor Eden that he had "found the French ship at sea without a soul on board her."[6] He and four members of his crew made affidavits to this effect. Governor Eden immediately convened a Vice-Admiralty Court in Bath Town. Tobias Knight, the Chief Justice and Secretary of the Colony, as well as the Collector of Customs, presided.[7] The Vice-Admiralty Court adjudged that the ship was a derelict found at sea. Twenty hogsheads of sugar were awarded to Knight and sixty hogsheads of sugar to Eden. The rest of the cargo was assigned to Captain Teach and his crew.

It is chiefly in connection with the court's decision "that the names of Eden and Knight have been handed down in history besmirched with infamy."[8] The decision of the Vice-Admiralty Court was legally sound under principles recognized, not only in 1718, but also in admiralty courts in the United States today.[9] Historians who have heretofore dealt with the incident have been unfamiliar with certain rules of admiralty law. As a consequence, they have done less than justice to Governor Eden and others.

The case involved the doctrine of "salvage," altogether different from the rules governing the saving of another's property on land. Salvage is the compensation allowed by a court of admiralty as a reward, or bounty, offered, from motives of public policy, to encourage the saving of a ship and the cargo thereof in peril at sea, bringing back into circulation property that might otherwise have been lost. The saving of a derelict on the high seas or the carrying of shipwrecked property to shore by human agency is a matter within the jurisdiction of an admiralty court and to which the doctrine of salvage applies. But, on the other hand, property shipwrecked at sea and by the sea cast up onto the shore is within the jurisdiction of the common law, and the doctrine of salvage has no application.[10]

The United States Supreme Court has said:

Compensation as salvage is not viewed by the admiralty courts merely as pay, on the principle of a *quantum meruit* or as remuneration *pro opere et labore*, but as a reward given for perilous services, voluntarily rendered, and as an inducement to seamen and others to embark in such undertakings to save life and property. Public policy encourages the hardy and adventurous mariner to engage in these laborious and sometimes dangerous enterprises, and with a view to withdraw from him every temptation to embezzlement and dishonesty, the law allows him, in case he is successful, a liberal compensation.[11]

The owner of the vessel engaged in a salvage operation is entitled to a reward corresponding with the value of his own property risked in rendering the service; the remainder of the award goes to the members of his crew.

There is no fixed rule as to the amount of the salvage award. "So many elements enter into the determination of the award that a considerable latitude of discretion must be allowed the trial court and, were it otherwise, every salvage suit would result in an appeal."[12] As a consequence, in the absence of a clear abuse of discretion, appeals involving only the amount of the award are not encouraged. In the past, the usual amount awarded to the salvor was one-half of the property saved, but the tendency in recent years has been toward a lesser percentage. In a federal case decided in the United States in 1909, the salvors were paid one-half of the proceeds of derelict property. When, after the lapse of years, no claimant appeared for the other half, that also was given to the salvors.[13]

In the United States, admiralty jurisdiction is vested exclusively in the federal courts. But under the early English law, that portion of the saved property which was not awarded to the salvor, if not claimed by the true owner, "belonged to the crown, and later to the admiral, as admiralty droits, unless the privilege of taking them had been granted as a franchise to an individual or a corporation."[14]

William S. Holdsworth, in his monumental treatise, *History of English Law*, says that wrecks or abandoned ships found at sea belonged to the office of Admiral, who might or might not reward the finder. "If a claimant appeared, he was entitled to a restoration on proof of his claim, and the payment of a reasonable salvage. Such salvage was often allowed to the Vice-Admirals of the court as a reward for taking possession of, and looking after, the property."[15]

It must be remembered that Eden had been commissioned not only as Governor, but also as Captain General and Admiral of North Carolina. The sixty hogsheads of sugar he was awarded by the Vice-Admiralty Court in Bath Town were in consequence of his admiralship. The twenty hogsheads awarded to Knight could have been awarded to him either as court costs or by virtue of his office of Collector of Customs.

The rules of the vice-admiralty courts in those early days were so tangled that no historian has succeeded in unraveling them completely. There is no doubt that the jurisdiction and practices in vice-admiralty courts in the colonies were quite different from those of the corresponding courts in England, the colonists having no direct knowledge of the general rules of practice being followed in England and there being no printed reports of England's High Court of Admiralty prior to 1799.[16]

Only after Blackbeard had been slain, and solely on the testimony of Israel Hands, a member of Blackbeard's crew, given at a trial in Williamsburg, Virginia, the following year, was there any evidence that the sugar and cocoa had been piratically taken from the French ship. The Vice-Admiralty Court in Bath Town rendered its decision on the basis of sworn testimony therein given. There was no claimant other than Blackbeard, and no conflicting testimony given in that proceeding.

Writers have ridiculed as preposterous the affidavits, presented in the Vice-Admiralty Court at Bath Town, as to how the French ship came to be found wrecked at sea. Accordingly, they have proceeded to cite the decision there as positive evidence that Eden and Knight had leagued themselves with Blackbeard for the conduct of piracy. Such writers must be thoroughly unacquainted with the fact that many foundered ships lie in the treacherous waters off the coast of North Carolina as the result of storms, ancient and modern. C. C. Crittenden has illustrated contemporary accounts of wrecks as follows:

> Peleg Greene, the master of a vessel plying between North Carolina and the West Indies, wrote ungrammatically of a storm at Ocracoke in April, 1774, so terrific that "there was fourteen sails of vessels drove on shore, and five of which will be entirely lost, and one drove over the South breakers and gone to [sea] and every soul perished." In February, 1784, after a vessel had got aground at the mouth of the Cape Fear, her crew left her, and at high tide she went off "God knows where."[17]

David Stick, a native of the Outer Banks, who wrote a history of shipwrecks on the North Carolina coast, *Graveyard of the Atlantic*, tells of more than six hundred wrecked vessels, all totally lost.[18]

The *Patriot*, a former New York pilot boat and privateer, drifted ashore at Nags Head, North Carolina, in January, 1813, with no one on board. What happened to the passengers and crew of the schooner has never been determined. She had departed from Georgetown, South Carolina, on December 30, 1812, bound for New York. Among the passengers on board was Theodosia Burr Alston, the twenty-nine-year-old wife of Governor John Alston of South Carolina and the daughter of Aaron Burr, former Vice-President of the United States.[19]

On the early morning of January 31, 1921, the man on lookout duty at the Cape Hatteras Coast Guard Station sighted a five-masted schooner, with all sails set, on Diamond Shoals. It turned out to be the *Carroll A. Deering*, which had been built at Bath, Maine, during 1919. An exceptionally large sailing ship, measuring 225 feet in length and 44 feet across the beam, and registered at 1,879 tons, she had made a voyage to South America and was en route home to Norfolk, Virginia. There was no one on board. Prepared food was on the table of the dining room and on the stove. All the ship's lifeboats had disappeared, and there was a ladder hanging over the side. Indications were that the passengers and crew had hurriedly departed. Their fate has never been learned. Because this particular vessel had beached without anyone on board, and the whereabouts of her crew and passengers has never been determined, she has been labeled the "ghost ship."[20]

Captain Johnson, more conversant with maritime law and customs than are most writers, states:

And as to condemning the French Martiniqueman that Blackbeard brought into North Carolina afterwards, the Governor proceeded judicially upon her. He called a court of Vice Admiralty, by virtue of his commission, at which four of the crew swore they found the ship at sea with no person on board her; so the Court condemned her, as any other court must have done, and the cargo was disposed of according to law.[21]

Subsequently Teach considered the possibility that some seaman or other person coming into Ocracoke Inlet might have knowledge of the French ship and report that the facts were different from what he and his crew had testified to in the Vice-Admiralty Court. "But Teach thought of a contrivance to prevent this, for, upon a pretense that she was leaky, and that she might sink and so stop up the mouth of the inlet or cove where she lay, he obtained an order from the Governor to bring her out into the river, and set her on fire, which was accordingly executed."[22] When the ship was burned to the water line and the hull sunk, Teach's anxiety must have been greatly relieved.

Except for the capture of the French vessel with the sugar and cocoa, there are no records of Blackbeard's having taken over a vessel on the high seas after he received his pardon from Governor Eden in June, 1718. He apparently was in semiretirement and was trying to live as circumspectly as his restless nature would permit. If not visiting in the homes of planters located on the sounds and rivers, he could usually be found either at Bath Town or at Ocracoke Inlet.

There were occasional rumors that he had molested some of the small trading vessels in the inland waters of the province. Occasionally he stopped the trading sloops, to swap the plunder he had taken as a pirate for articles which they had on board and which he needed. If he was in a good humor, he could be generous. At other times, he boldly took what he needed without a great deal of negotiation as to what, if anything, he would give in exchange.[23] He must have known it would be difficult to prove that he had actually robbed the trader. Very likely there were traders who yielded through fear.

Ocracoke Inlet was Blackbeard's favorite anchorage. All ocean-going vessels bound for or leaving the settlements in northeastern North Carolina passed through this inlet, which was located about thirty miles southwest of Cape Hatteras and fifty miles northeast of Cape Lookout. Blackbeard's base of operations was near the southern tip of Ocracoke Island, which is eighteen miles long and from one-half to two miles wide, and is one of the sand islands of the Outer Banks. He customarily anchored in a narrow channel on the sound side, to the extreme right after passing through the inlet from the Atlantic. The particular spot, located south of Springer's Point, near Ocracoke Inlet, has been known since the 1700's as Teach's Hole.[24] A keen-eyed sentinel posted on one of the sand dunes could, with a spyglass, descry with ease the name of a ship and the number of her crew, and, depending upon whether she was heavily laden, he could estimate the value of her cargo.

The word "Ocracoke," undoubtedly of Indian origin, passed

through a dozen or so spellings before assuming its present form. There is a fine old legend that Blackbeard's lookout sentinel spotted the two ships that had been sent from Virginia to capture him anchored outside the bar, awaiting the early dawn in order to come through the inlet. Blackbeard, during the long night, stalked the deck of his ship, impatient for the arrival of the fateful dawn of November 22, 1718, and cried out, "O Crow Cock! O Crow Cock!" He knew that the first cock's crow would signal the beginning of the Battle of Ocracoke Inlet. This, the legend states, is how the name "Occocock," "Occacock," "Ocracock," and finally "Ocracoke" came about. Actually, however, old maps of North Carolina, dating back to the map drawn by John White in 1585, had designated the inlet as "Wokokin," or sometimes as "Wocon" or "Woccocock." About 1715, some writer, either scorning or misinterpreting Indian pronunciation, dropped the "W" and introduced spellings more closely approaching the present form. Governor Spotswood of Virginia apparently never learned to spell the word. In letters written to England during 1718 and 1719, he used the following spellings: "Ocracock," "Oecceh," and "Oeccent."[25]

Probably in 1719, shortly after Blackbeard's death, the whole of "Ocacock" Island, then consisting of 2,110 acres, was granted to John Lovick.[26] Lovick was Secretary of State for the province, member of the Council, and the second of the four husbands of Penelope Golland, Governor Eden's stepdaughter. The island was subsequently acquired by Richard Sanderson, who upon his death in 1733 devised to his son, Richard Sanderson, "ye Island of Ocreecock w'th all the Stock of Horses, Cattle, Sheep and hoggs, thereunto belonging."[27] The elder Sanderson, for whom the existing Cupola House in Edenton was built in 1725, was a prominent member of the Council.[28] Neither of the first two private owners of the island ever lived on it.

There were probably no settlers in 1718 in what is now the

village of Ocracoke. There is no historical basis for statements that Blackbeard built for himself a large, comfortable house near the present village, that the house was two stories high and had many large rooms and a turret from which he viewed all passing ships. It would have been impossible for him to build such a house during the less than five months between his surrender and pardon, and his death. Nor were there available at that time either the materials or the facilities for the construction of such an elaborate structure. It was not until around 1730 that sawmills made their appearance in North Carolina.

There was a structure of the general type described once standing near the present village of Ocracoke, but this was constructed at a date much later than 1718. Persons now living remember seeing this old, abandoned wooden house before it was torn down. Years ago someone called it "Blackbeard's Castle," perhaps to amuse a tourist; the story was repeated and became a part of the folklore of the area.

The lives of the people of Ocracoke have been closely interwoven with shipwrecks. During a storm of August, 1750, a five-hundred-ton Spanish frigate, *Nuestra Señora de Guadalupe*, without masts or rudder, drifted through Ocracoke Inlet with a merchandise cargo valued in Spain at one million pieces of eight and an additional four hundred thousand pieces of eight in specie. Other notable shipwrecks include that of the steam packet *Home* in 1837, in which ninety people were killed, that of the steamer *Ariosto* in 1899, in which twenty-one people were killed, and that of the six-masted schooner *George W. Wells* in 1913.[29] Many of the present inhabitants are descended from survivors of wrecked ships. To live on an island which is little more than a narrow strip of land separating the ocean from the sound is to them the next closest thing to treading the deck of a sailing vessel. Some have built and furnished their homes from the materials of wrecked ships. According to David Stick: "As for wrecked property that drifted ashore, it has been said of the people of Ocracoke Island, for example, that they would drop a corpse on the way to a burial if they heard the cry of 'Ship Ashore!' "[30]

Near the end of September, 1718, while Blackbeard was anchored in his favorite channel at Ocracoke Island, his lookout sentinel signaled that a large brigantine and several smaller vessels were approaching the inlet from the south. Captain Teach alerted his men and, employing the spyglass, his experienced eye, and his mind, appraised the situation. As the ships drew closer, he recognized the visitors as other Brethren of the Coast. Hauling up the anchor, he sailed out into the inlet, his gunners standing by their positions, ready to welcome friends or to do battle.

The commander of the approaching vessels was Captain Charles Vane, the most sought-after unpardoned pirate then roving the waters of the Atlantic. Vane had no difficulty in recognizing the unmistakable Blackbeard; without a moment's hesitation, he ordered a salute to the greatest living pirate. His great guns boomed and thudded across the quiet waters. As was the custom of the Brethren of the Coast, Captain Teach answered the salute in like manner.[31]

Captain Vane and ninety members of his crew had been in Nassau when Captain Woodes Rogers arrived at nightfall on July 26, 1718, from London, bringing with him his commission as Governor of the Bahama Islands and authority to grant pardons to all pirates. Rogers did not land until the following day. Vane was the only pirate captain in the harbor who did not accept a pardon, sending instead a letter to Rogers stating the terms under which he would surrender. Not receiving the reply as speedily as he expected, Vane, on the evening of July 26, 1718, launched a French prize ship then in the harbor directly towards the grouped vessels of Rogers. All of its guns, double-shotted, were aimed pointblank at the men-of-war. Setting the French ship afire, Vane abandoned it, escaping in a waiting sloop. The burning vessel's guns exploded, scattering the English men-of-war before the French ship blew up. Under this spectacular diversion, Vane and his crew had no difficulty in reaching the high seas.[32]

Shortly thereafter, Vane sent back word to Governor Rogers that he intended to return to New Providence and burn his guardship because he had attempted pursuit instead of answering his letter. Benjamin Hornigold, Blackbeard's pardoned former tutor, was sent out by Rogers to capture the elusive Vane but was able only to bring in the sloop *Woolfe*, Nicholas Woodall, master, which had traded with Vane.[33]

During August, 1718, Vane and his crew, lying off the coast of South Carolina, took and plundered a number of vessels.[34] Governor Robert Johnson dispatched Colonel William Rhett in two well-armed sloops to capture Vane. Rhett was of the opinion, on September 27, 1718, that he had Vane cornered in the Cape Fear River; but the pirate there turned out to be Captain Stede Bonnet, who was captured, tried, and hanged.[35]

It is unlikely that Vane knew of Bonnet's capture and impending trial when, on his way northward from the South Carolina coast, he met Blackbeard and his crew at Ocracoke. The "mutual civilities,"[36] as Captain Johnson described Vane's visit with Blackbeard, actually constituted the largest pirate festival ever held on the mainland of North America. Among the celebrities who attended the festivities near what is now the village of Ocracoke were Edward Teach, Israel Hands, Charles Vane, Robert Deal, and John Rackham, all of whom at some time during their lives had commanded a pirate ship.

The unspoiled and primitive southern tip of Ocracoke Island became a pirate playground. Johnson says the rendezvous lasted for "some days,"[37] with Blackbeard as the host. A number of hogs and cows were barbecued, and many of the fishermen and traders passing the inlet, upon seeing such a throng of people, stopped to trade with them and furnish them with fresh provisions. They were well aware that they had nothing to fear so long as Blackbeard's *Adventure* was anchored among the visiting vessels.

The visiting pirates had an ample supply of rum, and the punch bowls were never empty. Some of the pirates hunted and fished, but most of them simply relaxed. During the evening the musicians furnished music, and there were always among a group of pirates of this size some who were capable of entertaining the others.

At this summit meeting of the elite of coastal piracy, Teach and Vane exchanged such news as they had. Teach had recently made his trips to Philadelphia and Bermuda, and Vane was thoroughly acquainted with events in the West Indies and along the southern coast.

This chance meeting of so many notorious pirates was undoubtedly a factor in causing Governor Spotswood of Virginia to organize only a few weeks later an expedition to set forth to Ocracoke Inlet to capture Blackbeard. The well-known "grapevine" of eastern North Carolina had carried the information to him, the twisted version that he received being to the effect that the pirates were planning to build a fortress at Ocracoke Inlet and turn the island into "another Madagascar."[38]

Leaving Ocracoke Inlet after the meeting with Blackbeard, Captain Vane headed northward. On October 23, 1718, off the coast of Long Island, Vane robbed a sloop and a small brigantine bound from Jamaica to Salem, Massachusetts, with John Shattock as master.[39]

On November 23, 1718, Vane came upon a ship which he expected to surrender as soon as he hoisted his pirate's black colors. Much to his surprise, the ship discharged a broadside and raised her own colors, which revealed her to be a French man-of-war. Vane judged it too rash and desperate an enterprise to attempt to board her. Robert Deal, who was his mate, and about fifteen others shared his opinion; but the majority, championed by John Rackham, the quartermaster, held a contrary view. Since the captain of the ship was in absolute command during the course of a battle, Vane chose to withdraw in the faster brigantine. In all other matters the captain was governed by a majority vote of the pirates.[40]

The next day, November 24, 1718, Jack Rackham branded Vane a coward and demanded that he submit to a test vote of confidence. The Brethren of the Coast passed a resolution ousting Vane and installing Rackham as their captain. Vane and the handful of supporters who had not favored the boarding of the French man-of-war were given a small sloop, taken some time before, along with a sufficient quantity of provisions and ammunition, and were told to depart. The following spring Vane was captured in the Caribbean by Captain Holford, an old acquaintance, who carried him and his companion, Robert Deal, to Jamaica, where they were tried, convicted, and hanged.[41]

Captain Rackham, known as "Calico Jack" (because, says Johnson, "his jacket and drawers were always made of calico"[42]), was fairly successful as a pirate captain scouring the harbors and inlets of the West Indies. About the middle of May, 1719, at a time during which England was again at war with Spain, he put into the harbor at Nassau and sued for a pardon from Governor Rogers. Shortly thereafter he became acquainted with Anne Bonny and fell in love with her. Rackham lavishly spent his money upon the young and reputedly attractive Anne, then married to James Bonny, a pardoned pirate living a sober and unexceptionable life.[43]

Born in a town near Cork, Ireland, Anne was the illegitimate daughter of a lawyer, in whose home her mother was a maid-servant. The scandal caused him to lose his law practice, and, converting his assets to ready money, he and "his maid and daughter embarked for Carolina. At first he followed the practice of law in that Province, but afterwards fell into merchandise, which proved more successful to him, for he gained by it sufficient to purchase a considerable plantation." His maid passed in Carolina as his wife.[44]

Rackham, by his free spending in Nassau, soon ran through his money, and, like so many other pardoned pirates, returned to piracy. Anne went to sea with him dressed in the clothing of a man, proving herself a brave and reckless pirate. Few persons on board, it is said, knew that she was a woman. In fact, on Rackham's ship at the time of its capture by Captain Jonathan Barret in November, 1720, there was another female pirate, Mary Read, also dressed in the clothes of a man.[45] The crew were taken to the town of St. Jago de la Vega in Jamaica and there tried before a court of admiralty, without a jury, under the Act of 11 and 12 William III. Twelve male pirates, including Rackham, were convicted; and, according to the official records, "were hung on Gibbits in Chains, for a publick Example, and to terrify others from such-like evil Practices."[46] Rackham was executed on November 18, 1720. The pirates' bodies were strung up at various points on the island.

Anne Bonny and Mary Read were tried in the same Court of Admiralty on November 28, 1720, Sir Nicholas Lawes, Governor of Jamaica, presiding. Neither of the defendants elected to testify or to interrogate the witnesses who gave testimony against them. The commissioners of the court unanimously found them guilty of "piracies, robberies, and felonies," as charged in the third and fourth items of the articles of piracy. Governor Lawes sentenced them to be hanged by the neck until dead. After the judgment was pronounced, the prisoners informed the court that both were "quick with child and prayed that the execution of the sentence might be stayed. Whereupon the court ordered that execution of the said sentence should be respited, and that an inspection should be made."[47] A physical examination revealed that they had spoken the truth. Mary, seized by a violent fever soon after the trial, died in prison.[48] Anne was detained in prison to the time of her lying-in and afterwards was reprieved from time to time. She was never executed.[49]

Chapter 9

Virginia Trial of Blackbeard's Quartermaster

GOVERNOR ALEXANDER SPOTSWOOD of Virginia was greatly concerned that Blackbeard and some of his crew had surrendered in North Carolina and were living there. He had just cause to fear that they might return to piracy and interrupt the profitable coastwise commerce being carried on by Virginians. Spotswood had very little confidence in the integrity of the government of North Carolina or its power to control the pirates, some of whom had already migrated to Virginia and had been seen in several of its seaport towns. He feared that they would associate themselves with others, seize some vessel, and return to their old pursuits as soon as their money was spent.[1] On July 10, 1718, Spotswood issued a proclamation requiring all former pirates, immediately upon their arrival in Virginia, to make themselves known to some justice of the peace or officer of the militia, to deliver up their arms, and not to travel or associate in a greater number than a company of three.[2]

Spotswood had been bred to the Army. Born in 1676 at Tangier, then an English colony in Africa, where his father was resident surgeon to the English garrison,[3] he had already attained the rank of colonel at the time of his appointment as Lieutenant Governor of Virginia in 1710. General George Hamilton, Earl of Orkney, was the Governor and Commander-in-Chief of the colony. It was the policy of the British crown to give station and emolument to those of the aristocracy whom it desired to favor. For twenty-seven years (1710–1737) Orkney enjoyed immense revenue as the ranking official of Virginia without ever visiting the colony or performing personally a single act of government. As Lieutenant Governor, Spotswood was a royal appointee and not simply a deputy of the Governor.[4]

A master at military strategy, Spotswood had at his disposal in Virginia a sizable and well-disciplined militia. He was a leader and a forceful personality, egotistical and autocratic. As a consequence of his egotism and his autocratic ways, he became, as a colonial official, controversial, ever anxious to be cast as hero and patriot. Historians have found, for information about him, their richest lode in the many lengthy letters he wrote, two volumes of which have been published. But few historians have checked the letters against the facts and against the opinions of others during the period in which they were written. All of the letters contain the most fulsome praise, both indirectly and directly, of the author. Herbert L. Osgood, an analytical and careful historian, concludes that Spotswood expressed with vigor his own views "and assailed those of his opponents." Leonidas Dodson, Spotswood's biographer, states that "Spotswood's correspondence is far from depicting its author at his worst."[5]

As an official of a Crown Colony, Spotswood was possessed of a deep prejudice against the proprietary colony to the south. "He held up North Carolina as a fearful example of the anarchy into which failure to provide for defense would plunge a colony."[6] In the words of his biographer, "This uncouth neighbor was regarded by Virginia with a patronizing air which at times approached the supercilious."[7] William Best Hesseltine and David L. Smiley, in *The South in American History*, state: "Virginians never learned to regard North Carolinians with anything but contempt."[8] Giving an unfriendly coloring to everything connected with the Province of North Carolina, Spotswood discouraged adventurers from settling there, seeking instead to sell or lease portions of the large tract of wilderness he had personally acquired on Virginia's western frontier. He hopefully looked forward to the day when the Crown would be forced to buy the rights of the Carolina Lords Proprietors and annex the territory to Virginia.[9] The days of the tracts, written by John Lawson and others, idealizing North Carolina as a good place into which to immigrate, were, in Spotswood's view, near an end. Furthermore, a boundary dispute, still unsettled in 1718, had long disturbed relations between Virginia and North Carolina.

But it was the long series of Virginia statutes prohibiting North Carolina tobacco from being carried into Virginia that impaired most the relationship between the two colonies.[10] Tobacco was then, as it is now, North Carolinians' chief money crop. Richard Fitz-Williams, Surveyor General of Customs in the Southern Provinces in America and also a member of the Virginia Council, protested against the renewal of the embargo in 1726 because, among other reasons,

the restraining of the people of North Carolina from selling or shipping off their tobacco to Virginia, when they have neither shipping of their own, nor ports to receive them, must of consequence force them upon manufactures of clothes for themselves, since they are thus prevented of all supplies by the produce of their labor, and thus by a partial restraint of trade from one part of his Majesty's dominions to another his Majesty's customs are lessened, the consumption of British manufactures diminished, and instead thereof a country which begins to grow numerous laid under the necessity of falling into manufactures of their own, for it is impossible to imagine that a number of people should continue long under the want of necessary cloathing without exerting their industry, expecially when the country they inhabit is capable of furnishing them with the materials.[11]

The editor of *The Colonial Records of North Carolina*, in his prefatory notes to volume two, states:

The happy time was long in coming. Indeed, it may well be doubted whether the history of any other American colony shows a struggle for existence as prolonged as that through which North Carolina passed in the days of her Proprietors, or as hard. But those days of adversity were not without their good results, constituting, as they doubtlessly did, the formative period in the character of the people. Shut in on every side and left to struggle with her enemies as best she might, unaided and alone she worked out her own salvation.[12]

Although Spotswood divided equally with the Earl of Orkney the £2,000 sterling annual salary he received, he was able to accumulate a pretty fortune during the twelve years (1710–1722) he was Lieutenant Governor. The perquisites of the office apparently were Spotswood's alone.[13] He began early, like a typical Virginian of that time, to acquire large tracts of land. By the end of his administration he had in Spotsylvania County alone more than 85,000 acres, some of which carried a special tax exemption for seven years.[14] Acting in the sovereign's stead, and having thereby the power and authority to convey crown lands, Spotswood originally conveyed much of this land to one or more friends, who shortly thereafter quietly reconveyed it to Spotswood. Later, Spotswood sought to justify his practice of granting land to others, in secret trust for himself, on the somewhat ingenuous premise that he did so in good faith and on the assumption that he could not be both grantor and grantee.[15] Many Virginians of his time, as well as historians of a later date, suspected Spotswood of having acquired these lands, in large part, by means not always irreproachable.

Spotswood lived well in Williamsburg. The first occupant of the Governor's Palace, he had devoted his personal attention to its construction. The colonists, resenting the additional levies required to complete it, gave it the derisive sobriquet "Palace." Undeterred, Spotswood prided himself on his elaborate entertainments there. In a letter to the Lords Commissioners of Trade and Plantations, he wrote:

I appeal to all the Gentlemen of these parts, and Strangers resorting hither, whether ever they knew any Governor of Virginia to keep up, by his constant way of Living, the Honour and Dignity of his

Majesty's Government so greatly as I have done, and whether ever they saw before in this Colony their Sovereign's Birth day celebrated with so much magnificence as in my time and at my Expense.[16]

In 1718, both the House of Burgesses and the Council were bitterly opposed to Spotswood and were seeking his removal. Surprisingly, eight of the twelve members of his own Council were against him, these being of the so-called Ludwell-Blair faction.[17] Philip Ludwell II "was the son of Philip Ludwell, who had been secretary of state of Virginia and councillor, and sometime governor of North Carolina. . . . Like his father, he was prominent in Virginia affairs, serving as burgess and speaker of the House . . . trustee and rector of the College of William and Mary, councillor, auditor general, and one of the directors in the laying out of Williamsburg."[18] Ludwell's associate, the Reverend James Blair, was the first president of William and Mary. William Byrd II, of Westover, then in England, was also aligned with the Ludwell-Blair faction.

Attempting a reconciliation with his restive councilors, but disappointed in that object, Spotswood wrote, on June 24, 1718, to the Board of Trade:

An invitation to my House after this Reconciliation was slighted by them, and an Entertainment with all the freedom and Civility I could give, has not prevailed with one of the Eight to make me ye common compliment of a Visit, Nay, when in Order to the Solemnizing his Majesty's Birthday [May 28, 1718], I gave a publick Entertainment at my House, all Gentlemen that would come were Admitted; These Eight Counselors would neither come to my House nor go to the Play which was Acted on that occasion, but got together all the Turbulent and disaffected Burgesses, had an Entertainment of their own in the Burgesses' House and invited all ye Mobb to a Bonfire, where they were plentifully Supplyed with Liquors to Drink the same healths without, as their M'rs did within, which were chiefly those of the Council and their associated Burgesses, without taking any notice of the Governor, than if there had been none upon the place.[19]

Facing as he did a crisis in his government, Spotswood needed to capture Blackbeard at this particular time. Success would restore, even if only temporarily, his prestige and harmony in his government. Bruce, in his *History of Virginia*, says that Spotswood was "always wrapped about with the atmosphere of romantic adventure."[20] Very probably he resented Blackbeard's taking the limelight; he must have wanted the second decade of the eighteenth century reserved for himself.

Thus, it was for the governor a stroke of very good fortune that William Howard, who at one time had been quartermaster of Blackbeard's ship, the *Queen Anne's Revenge*, was among those seen in the taverns and around the docks of Virginia's seaport towns. He had formerly lived in Virginia. According to Spotswood, Howard had brought with him into Virginia two Negro slaves, piratically taken, one from a French ship and the other from an English brigantine.[21] Spotswood saw in him a man within his jurisdiction from whom he might be successful in wringing all he knew about Blackbeard, including the location of his loot.

Governor Spotswood caused a justice of the peace to seize Howard and his two Negroes. The £50 Howard had in his possession was confiscated. On the ground that he was insolent and unable to prove that he had any lawful business, he was hustled on board one of the King's ships as a vagrant seaman.[22]

Apparently it was not until the receipt of a letter dated December 24, 1718, with its enclosures, that any of the colonial governors had a commission to establish courts and appoint persons to conduct trials of pirates during the reign of George I, which began in 1714.[23] It has been said that commissions for the trying of pirates other than in England were terminated upon the death of the sovereign who issued them, and that acts of Parliament dealing with piracy were to be distinguished from colonial commissions for the trial of pirates. A number of the governors had written to the Council of Trade and Plantations requesting such commissions. The Council in turn had urged crown officials to issue them, but to no avail. As a consequence, a number of colonial governors found themselves with captured pirates on their hands. It is possible, of course, that some governors had special commissions authorizing them to establish courts for the trial of pirates. But most governors, reflecting the pioneer spirit of the times, improvised by appointing a commission of judges to try pirates without a Royal Commission. The ends of justice, as viewed by them, were thereby met.[24]

Probably through the assistance of influential friends ashore who had become incensed by Howard's treatment, John Holloway, in Spotswood's words "one of the chief lawyers" of the colony, was retained to espouse his cause. Holloway, an attorney of the Marshalsea Court of London before emigrating to Virginia, was indeed one of the most eminent lawyers of Virginia.[25] For fourteen years the Speaker of the Virginia House of Burgesses and for eleven years the Treasurer of the Colony, he became the first Mayor of Williamsburg. His wife was the former Elizabeth Catesby, sister of the famous naturalist, Mark Catesby, who wrote, among other things, *The Natural History of Carolina, Florida, and the Bahama Island.* Governor Eden of North Carolina in his will referred to John Holloway as "my very dear friend" and bequeathed to him his gold watch and a Negro slave.[26] Holloway died at sixty-nine years of age on December 14, 1739.

Accepting from Howard an attorney's fee of three ounces of gold dust, Holloway promptly caused the arrest of not only the justice of peace who had signed Howard's warrant, but also Captain George Gordon and Lieutenant Robert Maynard of the man-of-war *Pearl*, on which Howard was detained. Alleging that Howard was being held under false imprisonment, he instituted a civil action against the two naval officers in the common-law court of Virginia, asking damages of £500.[27]

Spotswood then instituted criminal proceedings against Howard. In a letter to the Council of Trade and Plantations, he wrote as follows:

This extraordinary behaviour of a pirate well known to have been very active in plundering divers vessells on this coast but the year before, occasioned a more strict inquiry into his course of life after his departure from hence, and at last it came to be discovered that, tho he and the rest of Tache's crew, pretended to surrender and to claim the benefits of H.M. Proclamation, they had nevertheless been guilty of divers piracys after the fifth of January for which they were not entitled to H.M. pardon. I therefore thought fitt to have him brought to a tryal, but found a strong opposition from some of the Council agt. trying him by vertue of the Commission under the great Seal pursuant to the Act of the 11th and 12th of King Wm. tho I produced the King's Instruction directing that manner of tryal; but having at length overcome their scruples, I had this person tryed. . . .[28]

At a meeting of the Governor's Council, October 29, 1718, eight of the twelve members were in attendance, and nearly all were of the opinion that Howard should be given a jury trial pursuant to the Statute of Henry VIII, c. 15. Spotswood pulled down the law books and convinced them that Howard should be tried without a jury under the Statute 11 and 12 William III, c. 7.[29] The law was probably on the side of Spotswood,[30] although in a trial of pirates previously held in Virginia, on May 13, 1700, both grand and petit juries were used,[31] and in the trials of Stede Bonnet and other pirates conducted in Charleston, South Carolina (October 28, 1718, through Nov. 12, 1718) grand and petit juries were likewise used.[32]

The indictment under which Howard was tried read as follows:

Articles exhibited before the Honble his Majtsy Commr appointed under the great Seal in Pursuance of an Act of Parliament made in the Eleventh and twelfth years of the Reign of King William the third Entituled an Act for the more Effectual Suppression of Pyracy

Against

William Howard For Pyracy and Robbery committed by him on the High Seas

First

That the Said Wm Howard not having the Fear of God before his Eyes nor Regarding the Allegiancy due to his Majesty nor the Just Obedience he Ow'd to the Laws of the Land did some time in the Year of our Lord 1717 Join and Associate him self with one Edward Tach and other Wicked and desolute Persons & with them did combine to fit out in Hostile manner a Certain Sloop or Vessel Call'd the Revenge to commit Pyracys and depridations upon the High Seas on the Subjects of our Lord the King and of other Princes & States in Amity with his Majesty trading in America

And   2.

That in pursuance of the Said Felonious and Pyratical Combination the said Willm Howard did together with his Associates and Confederates on or about the 29th day of Septr in the Year Afforsaid in an Hostile manner with force and Arms on the high Seas near Cape Charles in this Colony within the Jurisdiction of the Admiralty of this Court attack & force a Sloop Calld the Betty of Virginia belonging to the Subjects of our said Lord the King, and the said Sloop did then and there Rob and plunder of Certain Pipes of Medera Wine and other Goods and Merchandizes and thereafter the said Wm Howard did Sink and destroy the said Sloop with the remaining Part of the Cargo.

3.

That the Said Wm Howard and his Associates and Confederates did on or about the 22d of Octo^r in the year aforesaid in the Bay of Delaware in America w^thin the Jurisdiction of the Admiralty of Great Brittain & of this Court Pyratically take Seize and Rob the Sloop Robert of Philadelphia and the Ship Good Intent of Dublin both bound for Philadelphia aforesaid and divers goods and Merchandize then on board the s^d Ship & Sloop belonging to the Subjects of our Lord the King did feloneously and piratically take seize and carry away.

4.

That on or about the —— day of December the said Wm Howard
and other of his Associates did Pyratically take and Seize the ship
Concord of Saint Malo commanded by Capt D'Ocier belonging to
the Subjects of the French King one of the Allyes of our Sovereign
Lord the King near the Island of Saint Vincent in the West Indias
within the Jurisdiction aforesaid and having Rob'd and feloniously
spoiled the said Subjects of the French King of their Merchandize
and Effects consisting of Negroes Gold dust money Plate, and Jewels, did Carry away the said Ship and Convert the Same towards
the Carrying on and Prosecuting his the said Howards Pyratical
designs.

5.

That whereas his Sacred Maj^{ty} by his Royal Proclamation bearing
date at Hampton Court the 5th day of Septr and in the fourth year
of his Reign was graciously pleased to promise and declare that all
Pyrates surrendering themselves to Any of his Maj^{tys} Principal
Sec^{ys} of State in Great Brittain or Ireland or to any Governor or
Deputy Govr of his Maj^{tys} Plantations Beyond the Seas should have
Maj^{tys} most Gracious Pardon for such Pyracys by them Committed
before the fifth of January then next ensuing nevertheless the said
Wm Howard not being Ignorant of his Maj^{tys} Gracious Intentions
declar'd in the said Proclamation but Dispising his Maj^{tys} Royal
offers of Mercy did after the said fifth of Jany continue to Perpetrate
his wicked and Pyratical designs at sundry times and places more
particularly he the said Wm Howard in Company with the afforesaid
Edwd Tach and other their Confederates and associates in the afforesaid ship called the Concord of St Malo and afterwards denominated
by the said Pyrates by the name of Queen Anns Revenge on or about
the —— month of April 1718 a sloop belonging to ye subjects of
the King of Spain upon the high seas near the Isl^d of Cuba did
piratically take & seize ye same did detain and upon the —— day
of May in year of our Lord 1718 the Brginteen ——————— of
London bound on a Voyage from Guinea to South Carolina in and
upon the high seas near the Post of the said province and within y^e
Jurisdiction aforesd did pyraticaly take and [seize] divers Negro
Slaves & other goods and Merchandise belonging to the Subjects
of our said Lord the King did then and there feloniously take seize
& carry away all which acts of Pyracy and Premises are notoriously

known to be true and for which the said Wm Howard ought by the Judgm^t and Sentence of this Court to suffer such pains Penalties and Forfeitures as by the Laws of Great Britain are inflicted upon Pyrats and Robbers on the high seas.[33]

Howard was transferred to the public gaol in Williamsburg to await trial before a Court of Vice-Admiralty on the charge of piracy.[34] Captains Ellis Brand and George Gordon, in command of British men-of-war stationed in the Chesapeake Bay to give protection against pirates, were, along with John Holloway, among the commissioners notified to sit as judges. The two captains stiffly informed the Governor that they would not serve with Holloway because he had accepted in a different case an attorney's fee from the man on trial in this case. In explaining his actions the following year to the Secretary of the Council of Trade and Plantations, Spotswood wrote: "To prevent any disturbance on the Bench, which I apprehended would ensue upon their publickly excepting against Mr. Holloway, I sent him a civil Message to desire him not to expose himself by appearing on that Tryal."[35]

This infuriated Holloway, who refused to sit in any further vice-admiralty cases. As a lawyer, he could see nothing ethically wrong in accepting a professional fee from a client in a civil action in a common-law court and later sitting as one of several judges in a criminal case in a vice-admiralty court involving the same individual. The members of the Governor's Council in Virginia, in their judicial capacity as the General Court, did not hesitate to sit "in judgment upon cases in which they themselves were interested."[36]

Spotswood appointed in Holloway's place the Attorney General of Virginia, John Clayton, whom Spotswood described as "an honester man" in contrast with Holloway, whom he termed "a constant patron and advocate of pirates."[37] Thus, Spotswood unjustifiably imputed the character and reputation of the client to his attorney, a frequent mistake of laymen.

With the Attorney General and two naval dignitaries sitting as judges, there was no doubt as to the outcome of the trial. William Howard was found guilty of piracy and sentenced to be hanged. Fortunately for him, his life was saved by the timely arrival, on the night before he was to be executed,[38] of a commission from London directing the Governor to pardon surrendering pirates for all acts of piracy committed before July 23, 1718.[39]

But Howard's arrest and trial had served Spotswood's purposes. Virginia's law-enforcement officials had obtained from William Howard valuable information about Blackbeard. Spotswood accordingly knew the locations of Teach's various hideouts in North Carolina and the number of men on his ship. The Governor was now ready to invade the neighboring colony and capture both the pirate and his treasure.

Chapter 10

Preparations in Virginia for the Capture of Blackbeard

*R*UMORS WERE COMMON that Blackbeard sallied forth at his pleasure to commit robberies on the Virginia coast, that he and other pirate captains had met at Ocracoke Inlet and were planning to fortify Ocracoke Island, and that an invasion of Virginia was being plotted to avenge the arrest of Howard. Every act of piracy along the coast, including especially those recently committed by Captain Richard Worley,[1] was credited to Blackbeard. These were rumors; the facts were unknown.

But the image Teach had created had made him a marked man. Governor Spotswood was determined that the pirates should not be permitted, through either the weakness or the connivance of the government of North Carolina, to gather strength and establish at a remote Carolina inlet a rendezvous very dangerous to Virginia shipping.[2] If the Governor had his way, Teach would not be allowed to live out, as he hoped to be able to do, even a moderately larcenous life on the inland waterways of the neighboring colony. Spotswood planned a two-pronged invasion by land and by sea for the purpose of capturing Blackbeard.

Spotswood employed the greatest secrecy in his design to invade North Carolina, withholding all information from his Council and revealing his plans only to those indispensable in carrying them out. There were few in Virginia whom, apparently, he judged trustworthy, and fewer who would have approved his methods. He could little afford a breach of intelligence that would permit his prey to escape; Blackbeard had friends not only in North Carolina but also in Virginia. Addressing the Council of Trade and Plantations in a letter after the Battle of Ocracoke Inlet, Spotswood confided: "I did not communicate to the Assembly nor Council, the project then forming against Tach's crew for fear of his having intelligence, there being in this country and more especially among the present faction, an unaccountable inclination to favour pyrates."[3]

Spotswood shrewdly wanted the leaders and makers of opinion in Virginia and England to believe there were repeated applications from the trading people of North Carolina for him to invade that province. In a letter dated December 22, 1718, Spotswood wrote his superiors in London on the Council of Trade and Plantations:

. . . and having at the same time received complaints from divers of the trading people of that Province of the insolence of that gang of pyrates, and the weakness of that Government to restrain them, I judged it high time to destroy that crew of villains, and not to suffer them to gather strength in the neighborhood of so valuable a trade as that of this Colony. Having gained sufficient intelligence of the strength of Tache's crew, and sent for pylots from Carolina, I communicated to the Captains of H.M. ships of war on this station the project I had formed to extirpate this nest of pyrates. It was found impracticable for the men of war to go into shallow and difficult channells of that country, and the Captains were unwilling to be at the charge of hyring sloops which they had no order to do, and must therefore have paid out of their own pocketts, but as they readily consented to furnish men, I undertook the other part of supplying at my own charge sloops and pilots. Accordingly, I hyred two sloops and put pilotes on board, and the Captains of H.M. ships having put 55 men on board under the command of the first Lieutenant of the *Pearle* and an officer from the *Lyme*, they came up with Tach at Ocracock Inlett on the 22nd of last month, he was on board a sloop which carryed 8 guns and very well fitted for fight.[4]

There were undoubtedly some requests for help from North Carolina, but there could not have been many. Colonel Thomas Pollock, who was twice Acting Governor of North Carolina and for thirty years a member of her Council, who lived close to the Virginia border and had many friends in both colonies, wrote to Governor Eden on December 8, 1718: "I declare that I never heard any thing of any applications to Virginia concerning Captain Thach, nor nothing of any intended expedition out of Virginia, until I heard that Captain Brand was come in, and that he and Colonel Moore and Captain Veall [Vail] were gone to Pamplico."[5] Pollock's veracity has never been questioned.

The knowledgeable Spotswood realized that there were bound to be persons in North Carolina who were in opposition to those in power and who would welcome an opportunity to discredit Eden's administration, just as there were many in Virginia who were at the time seeking to bring embarrassment to his administration and thereby cause his removal. Spotswood sought Eden's enemies out, and they were not hard to find.

He gained the support of two men, Edward Moseley and Colonel Maurice Moore, men of considerable political influence, who were the chief antagonists of Governor Eden and others in power. Both Moseley and Moore would find their place in the colonial history of North Carolina. Each was an adventurer of great courage, mettle, and intellect. Anxious to discredit Eden's administration and thereby gain control of the colony, both found it expedient to assist Governor Spotswood.

Spotswood further wanted it to appear that the Crown might benefit by the expedition against Blackbeard. In a letter to the Lords of Trade, dated May 26, 1719, Spotswood suggested:

If the owners make out their property, the produce must be paid to them according to his Majesty's Treatys, allowing a usual Salvage to those who rescued them from the Pyrats. If no Claimer appears and that the same comes to the King, no doubt his Majesty will think fit to reward the Officers of his Ships and other Concerned in so considerable a Service as the destroying of that crew of Pirats.[6]

Thus, by his own words, the Governor was seeing to it that his personal financial investment in what amounted to a business adventure was to be no economic loss to himself. There were never any claimants to the alleged stolen goods captured in North Carolina and taken to Virginia.

As it turned out, however, only ordinary merchandise amounting to £2,238 sterling was brought back to Virginia, and the government of North Carolina vigorously challenged Spotswood's legal right to invade the jurisdiction of a province owned and controlled by the Carolina Lords Proprietors. Spotswood consequently asserted only the right to deduct "the Charges of recovering ye s'd Effects out of the hands of the Pyrats, the Transportation from Carolina, the Storage and Expense of the Sale."[7]

Having found adequate political support in North Carolina, Spotswood began to develop his military strategy. He looked, for military strength, to Captains George Gordon and Ellis Brand, who commanded two men-of-war of the Royal Navy, the *Pearl* and the *Lyme*. Both ships, in November, 1718, were lying at anchor in the James River, the *Pearl* commanded by Captain Gordon and the *Lyme* by Captain Brand. Furnished by the Crown to give Virginia some protection against pirates, these vessels had been in Virginia waters for about ten months.[8] If they had as yet made no punitive voyages, their presence was alike a source of comfort to the Virginians and a partial deterrent to the pirates. Although the Governor had only tenuous authority over these officers, in spite of the fact that he had been appointed Admiral of Virginia, the direct orders of the Governor and his Council were generally obeyed. When they were not, however, his only recourse was to complain to the Admiralty Office in London.[9]

Spotswood gave Brand overall command of the expedition. He was to travel overland with a force to Bath Town.[10] Lieutenant Robert Maynard, of the *Pearl*, was put in command of the two leased sloops that were to approach Bath Town by water.[11] This was the double-pronged strategy of the invasion.

Gordon was to remain in charge of the more powerfully armed battleships then in the James River.

The trained fighting crews of the *Pearl* and the *Lyme* were selected to man the two sloops, which were equipped with sufficient ammunition and small arms but not with mounted cannons. The sloops, fast anyhow, were kept light for maximum speed and for maneuvering in the shallow waters of the sounds and inlets. North Carolina pilots familiar with the channels and shoals of these waters were employed.[12]

Spotswood had leased the two sloops at his own expense. He surely believed, as did most persons, that Blackbeard had cached fabulous treasures in North Carolina, and this may have been a factor in causing him personally to finance the expedition. Should valuable unclaimed loot be recovered from the pirates, he would be in a position to claim much of it for himself.

Knowing that seamen on British warships were reluctant to risk their lives unless there was some prospect of gain, Spotswood had to find an incentive for the seamen to fight Blackbeard instead of simply deserting to him, as others had done in the past. So Spotswood promised a liberal bonus from the Assembly of Virginia for the capture of Blackbeard and his crew, over and above any reward the seamen might receive under the proclamation of the Crown.[13]

Captain Johnson states, "What seems a little odd is that some of these men who behaved so bravely against Blackbeard went afterwards apirating themselves." One was captured with the notorious Captain Bartholomew Roberts and later hanged.[14]

On Thursday, November 13, 1718, the Governor and his Council dispatched an official message to the House of Burgesses urging rewards for the capture of the pirates. The message referred to information elicited at the recent trial of Howard, and emphasized "certain Advice that they [the pirates] threaten to revenge on the Shipping of this Country the taking up of the above mentioned Quarter Master. For these reasons the Governor and Council think it absolutely necessary that some speedy and Effectual Measures be taken for breaking that Knott of Robbers." The proposed "Act to Encourage the Apprehending and Destroying of Pirates" was hurried back and forth from chamber to chamber, with several amendments; on Monday, November 24, 1718, it was signed by the Governor and duly enrolled.[15] That the entire matter could be pushed through both houses in just eleven days, considering the strained relations then existing between Assembly and Governor, indicates the alarm that had seized the Virginians with respect to Blackbeard.

Four days previously, on November 20, the House of Burgesses had engrossed a recital of its grievances against Spotswood and had instructed William Byrd II, then in England, to present them to the King.[16] This now open opposition lingered and festered until April 3, 1722, when Spotswood was finally removed, "doubtlessly the result of an accumulation of grievances against him."[17]

Spotswood used a proclamation as the means of publicly announcing the statute concerning piracy. The proclamation, issued on the day the statute was enacted, offered a reward of one hundred pounds for the capture or killing of Blackbeard, and lesser amounts for the pirate crew, in the order of their designated importance.[18] It is significant that this proclamation was dated two days after the Battle of Ocracoke Inlet.

Spotswood did not wait for the conclusion of the legislation then pending in the Assembly. His two armed sloops quietly raised anchor and slipped out of Kecoughtan (now Hampton), Virginia, at about three o'clock on the afternoon of November 17, 1718. Heading for Blackbeard's North Carolina hideout, they proceeded slowly southward. Time had to be allowed for Brand's land forces to reach Bath Town. Information as to the exact whereabouts of Blackbeard was obtained from vessels sailing northward.[19]

Captain Brand, meanwhile, set forth for North Carolina on the night of November 17. According to a letter to the Lords of Admiralty, his force came within fifty miles of Bath Town on November 21. On the following day, Colonel Edward Moseley and Colonel Maurice Moore, the two North Carolinians who were political foes of Governor Eden and his Council, assisted Brand in getting his men and horses across Albemarle Sound; and at about ten o'clock on the night of November 23, they came within three miles of Bath Town.[20]

Colonel Moore, Captain Jeremiah Vail, and a number of other North Carolinians were with Brand when he approached Bath.[21] Their presence among the invaders tended to restrain the inhabitants, who were disinclined to resist the armed forces of the King when officers of their own militia were associated with them. Brand requested Moore to proceed to the town of Bath and determine whether Teach was there. Returning shortly afterwards, Moore reported that Teach was not there but was expected at "every minute."[22] Brand proceeded to the home of Governor Eden and informed him coldly that he was in North Carolina in quest of Blackbeard.[23] Presumably Eden was staying at his house on the west side of Bath Creek, across from the incorporated town. Undoubtedly Brand handed him on this occasion a letter from Spotswood, addressed to Eden and dated November 7, 1718.[24]

Having obtained no information as to the whereabouts of either Blackbeard or Lieutenant Maynard, Brand, on November 24, sent men in two canoes down the Pamlico River towards Ocracoke Inlet in search of Maynard and the sloops under his command. They returned two days later with an account of the battle fought between Blackbeard and Maynard on November 22.[25]

Chapter *II*

Battle of Ocracoke Inlet

*L*IEUTENANT MAYNARD, having ascertained from vessels he stopped the exact point at which Blackbeard was lurking, arrived with two armed sloops at Ocracoke Inlet at sundown on Thursday, November 21. Unfamiliar with the channels and shoals, he decided to wait for the tide at early dawn of the following day to make the attack. Lieutenant Maynard had no difficulty in locating the pirate ship of Captain Teach. It was anchored in his favorite spot at the sound side of the southern tip of Ocracoke Island. Maynard permitted no boat or vessel to enter the inlet, thus preventing any warning from reaching Blackbeard.[1] Also, he posted a lookout aboard both sloops throughout the night to prevent any attempted escape to the open seas. The mast of Blackbeard's sloop could be seen across the sand dunes at the tip of the island. It is not known for certain whether Captain Teach understood on the evening of November 21 that armed sloops lay outside the bar of Ocracoke Inlet waiting to capture him. For six months he had frequented these waters unmolested. There seemed every reason to believe that all seagoing vessels considered him a pardoned and retired pirate. The chances are good that on this particular evening he had posted no sentinel to keep a lookout on the top of a cold sand dune.

Captain Teach had a greatly reduced crew; his experienced officers and fighting men of former days were no longer with him. There was no profit in associating with him if he was not actively engaged in looting vessels. A number of his former crew, including Israel Hands, were in Bath Town at the time of the fighting at Ocracoke Inlet on November 22, 1718.[2] Johnson says that Teach had "no more than twenty-five on board" his vessel, the *Adventure*, although Teach gave out to all passing boats that he had forty.[3] Governor Spotswood, reporting the battle to the Council of Trade and Plantations in a letter dated December 22, stated that Teach had a crew of eighteen.[4]

A number of Teach's crew were probably retainers performing menial services on board, and at least a third of them were Negroes.[5] The existence of Negro pirates in a time of slavery may come as surprise; but the Brethren of the Coast made no distinctions in race, color, or country of origin. No one asked or cared, a man's status being determined by his achievements alone.

Tobias Knight, the Secretary of the Colony, had written from Bath Town, on November 17, a letter addressed to Teach and found by Maynard aboard the *Adventure*; but, in the opinion of this writer, the letter gives no intimation of the intended attack or warning to Teach to be on guard.[6]

Blackbeard had in the past received warnings of possible capture, which had turned out to be little more than wild rumors. He probably took no greater precaution than to alert his men, which ordinarily meant the stacking of powder, cannon balls, and scrap shot near the eight mounted guns; soaking blankets to hang around the powder magazine and to smother any fires breaking out on deck; and piling pistols and cutlasses near the battle stations.

Each pirate was expected to furnish his own cutlass and pistols, the latter thrust in a sling of leather or ribbon across the chest. The cutlass, swung from a belt at the hip, had its origin in "the medieval curtal axe, a short, wide-bladed weapon more like a cleaver than either axe or sword. It had gradually evolved from this into a yard-long, wide-bladed sword, slightly curved like a saber, but a good deal heavier. A rounded brass guard ... protected the hand and wrist."[7]

A strong advocate of the use of the cutlass on the high seas, Blackbeard had taught his pirates how to manipulate this weapon, lethal when used with skill and brutal strength. Wildly swinging pirate cutlasses were a fearful thing to behold; few sailors on merchant ships failed to surrender within minutes of exposure to the sight. "Blackbeard knew that half the advantage of this attack was psychological, which was one reason why he cultivated it, just as he used every other trick he could devise for terrifying his victims and making his name hated everywhere."[8] Unfortunately for Blackbeard, there were now few members of his crew capable of effectively using the cutlass.

Far from preparing his crew for battle, Blackbeard spent the greater part of Thursday night in his cabin drinking with the master of a trading sloop and three members of his crew who were visiting on board the *Adventure*.[9]

Lieutenant Maynard, during the early gray light before sunrise on Friday, November 22, ordered the anchors weighed and headed for what in later years became known as "Teach's Hole."[10] Off the tip of Ocracoke Island, and before passing into the sound waters, men in a rowboat were lowered with instructions to proceed ahead of the sloops and take soundings. Maynard did not care to run the risk of being grounded on a shoal, so the men in the rowboat signaled the course to be followed. Upon coming into firing range of the *Adventure*, the men in the rowboat were greeted with a round of shot and immediately "scurried back to the protection of the sloops."[11]

The smaller of the two sloops was the *Ranger*. The other, never identified by name, was commanded by Lieutenant Maynard, then an officer of His Majesty's man-of-war *Pearl*, stationed in Virginia. The *Ranger* was commanded by a Mr. Hyde, an officer of His Majesty's man-of-war *Lyme*, also stationed in Virginia.[12]

According to a letter written on December 17, 1718, by Lieutenant Maynard, who was in overall command of the trained fighting crew from the Royal Navy, there were under his command twenty-two men on board the sloop of Mr. Hyde and thirty-two men on board his own sloop.[13] Counting himself, Mr. Hyde, and at least two pilots, there were no less than fifty-eight in the attacking force, according to the Maynard version. Maynard undoubtedly was not including as being under his "command" any non-naval personnel aboard the two sloops. In a letter dated September 14, 1721, addressed to the British Admiralty, Captain George Gordon stated that there were the two masters of the two sloops hired by Governor Spotswood "at his own charge for the expedition, and their crews they making a twelfth part of the whole number of men that went with them."[14] Captain Ellis Brand, in his report to the British Admiralty, dated February 6, 1718/1719, stated that he furnished a midshipman and twenty-five men from the *Lyme* and that Captain George Gordon furnished his lieutenant and thirty-five men from the *Pearl*. The seamen from the *Lyme* were placed in the *Ranger* with Hyde; those from the *Pearl* were under Maynard in the other sloop.[15]

In the old days vessels at sea did not fly their national flags, which were reserved for special events or for battle. "When two strange ships met at sea and after examining one another and deciding at last to fight, the flags went up as the first broadside boomed, not before. It would have been considered the height of rashness for a master to show a stranger at sea who he was before they were within speaking-trumpet distance."[16] It was the custom to carry on board ship the flags or colors of several nations. For example, any master sailing in waters controlled by the Spanish, and thinking an approaching vessel Spanish, would run up the Spanish flag. If the ship was hailed in Spanish, someone on board who spoke that tongue would answer. If, on the other hand, the vessel was French, the tricolor was run up and anyone on board who spoke French handled the trumpet. If further probing was indicated, the challenger ordered the unknown captain aboard in a rowboat to prove his identity.[17]

The rowboat, with the men sent in advance of Maynard's sloops, was hauled up. Blackbeard's crew had fired the first shot and the battle was on. At this point the pirate could easily have evaded his attackers and fled northward through channels thoroughly familiar to him. But Teach was no coward. It was not his nature to run away from a fight because the odds were against him. He cut his cable and elected to engage in a running fight, keeping up a continual fire at his enemies.

Maynard ordered the Union Jack hoisted to the masthead of his two vessels. They tacked directly towards the oncoming *Adventure*. Hyde maneuvered his *Ranger* to the left of Maynard's sloop as the two vessels moved forward for the conflict. Many of the latter's men maintained a constant fire with small arms, while the rest of the crew labored at the oars. Neither side thus far was doing any effective damage to the other.

Blackbeard, a master navigator, in home waters, grabbed the wheel and began easing the *Adventure* over toward the beach of Ocracoke Island.

His men looked up from their guns, glanced at the approaching shore, at the helm, and then at each other in surprise. Thomas Miller, the quartermaster, ran to the helm, grabbed Blackbeard by the shoulder, and pointed to the approaching land. Blackbeard knocked him to the deck. He did not try to explain, but as the quartermaster got to his feet again and noted the slowly changing course of the pirate sloop, he divined Blackbeard's plan.[18]

He was entering a narrow channel that would separate the *Adventure* from her attackers by a sand bar, hidden by the shallow waters. Shortly thereafter both of Maynard's vessels would be grounded temporarily on it.

Blackbeard roared rudely across the water: "Damn you for villains, who are you? And from whence come you?"

"You may see by our colors we are no pirates," answered Maynard.

"Send your boat on board so that I might see who you are," demanded Blackbeard.

"I cannot spare my boat, but I will come aboard you as soon as I can with my sloop," replied Maynard.

Seeing that they intended to board by storm, Blackbeard took up a bowl of liquor; and calling out to the officers of the other sloops, drank to them with these words: "Damnation seize my soul if I give you quarter or take any from you."

In reply to this, Maynard yelled back, "I expect no quarter from you, nor shall I give any."[19]

For the moment, the fortunes of war were in Blackbeard's favor. The two royal sloops had crunched the sands of the submerged bar and their crews set to working feverishly to dislodge them. The rising tide would shortly set them afloat again. Blackbeard acted with dispatch, ordering Philip Morton, his gunner, to train the eight[20] cannons of the *Adventure* towards the attackers in a general broadside. Four were to concentrate their fire upon the *Ranger*, and the other four, upon the larger sloop. At a signal from Blackbeard, the eight cannons were touched off. The thunder echoed and re-echoed around the sand dunes of the island. The mighty thrust of power caused the *Adventure* herself to be grounded in the sands of the shoreline.

This single broadside of eight cannons was devastating. Johnson states that twenty on Maynard's sloop were wounded or killed and nine on the other.[21] Hyde was killed and his second and third officers either killed or seriously wounded.[22] The *Ranger* was so badly disabled that she made no further attempt to participate in the battle until near its end. With a single broadside from his eight cannons, Blackbeard had reduced the attacking force to half its original size.

While Blackbeard was getting the *Adventure* refloated, Maynard frantically hastened to get his sloop back into action, well knowing that another broadside could doom him. Striving to get close enough for a boarding before Blackbeard could fire again, Maynard ordered all his water barrels staved, and the ballast jettisoned. Finally, with the aid of a breeze, his craft was able to push free of the sand bar and move toward the *Adventure*.

At this juncture Maynard came up with a typical trick of sea warfare. He ordered all his men below deck, their pistols and swords ready for close fighting, to remain in the hold until he gave the signal. Two ladders were placed in the hatchway to insure their expeditious appearance when ordered. Maynard's strategy was to ensnare the pirates into doing the fighting aboard his own ship. Maynard himself went into the cabin, ordering the midshipman at the helm and William Butler, the pilot, to inform him of anything that happened.[23]

Blackbeard, seeing Maynard's sloop approaching, alerted his men to prepare to board, with grappling irons and weapons ready for instant use. In addition, he had a lethal surprise which he intended to introduce to His Majesty's Royal Navy—hand grenades: in this case, bottles filled with powder, small shot, and pieces of iron and lead and ignited by fuses worked into the center of the bottle. Captain Teach's own invention, it had served him well during numerous pirate attacks, the resulting explosion invariably creating pandemonium on deck.

Most of the light grenades landed on the deck of Maynard's sloop, exploding resoundingly and rendering the sloop almost invisible in the enveloping smoke. Since most of the men were below deck, the grenades this time failed to achieve their effect. The royal sloop continued to drift forward. Seeing through the smoke only a few or no hands aboard, Blackbeard jubilantly shouted to his crew: "They were all knocked on the head but three or four. Blast you—board her and cut them to pieces!"

Maynard's sloop bumped against the side of Blackbeard's

sloop. The grappling irons clanked across the bulwarks of Maynard's vessel. Carrying in his hand a rope to lash and make fast the two sloops, Teach was the first aboard. Butler, the pilot, gave this intelligence to Maynard. According to Maynard's version, ten pirates followed their leader and scrambled aboard, howling and firing at anything that moved. Maynard's men in the hold burst out, shouting and shooting.[24]

The effect of the men pouring out of the hold was as shocking as Maynard had calculated. Everything was in confusion. The pirates were taken aback. Blackbeard instantly saw what was happening. Like the leader he was, he paused to rally and inspire his men.

The blood of the twenty British seamen wounded or killed by the terrific broadside had slickened the deck. The bodies of the dead were still there. Additional blood was to flow from the butchery and the savage melee that was to follow—the bloodiest battle ever fought on the deck of a small craft. Johnson says that "the sea was tinctured with blood around the vessel."[25]

Every man engaged in the hand-to-hand fight that ensued knew that his own life was at stake. It was kill or be killed, a deadly struggle for survival. On both sides the men fought furiously. There could be no stopping because of a wound. Many skidded or fell on the blood-slicked deck, but regained their stride and relentlessly sought to close with their foes amidst the bang and smoke of pistols, the clashing of swords, the shrieks of the wounded, and the groans of the dying.

Blackbeard waded into the melee, swinging his great cutlass. It was a wild windmill attack that no one in front of him could repel with a blade. He had to be stopped by a pistol shot or by someone from the rear. Both methods were tried. Blackbeard from time to time supplemented his blade swinging with a pistol snatched from the bandolier of pistols across his chest. These were single-shot pistols, thrown aside after being used.

An heroic touch was given to the battle by the ferocious confrontation of Maynard and Blackbeard—the champion of law and order and the champion of piracy—face to face. In this epic struggle, one or the other had to be annihilated. When they met, each pulled a pistol and fired. Blackbeard was being rushed at the time from all sides, and his shot missed its target. But the shot discharged by Maynard plowed through the great body of Blackbeard. It failed to halt him, however; he fought on with fury.

In the heat of combat they engaged each other with swords. A powerful blow of Blackbeard's cutlass snapped off Maynard's sword blade near its hilt. A blow of such terrific force would ordinarily have knocked the sword flying, but apparently Maynard was holding it with a frenzied grasp. Hurling the hilt at his adversary, Maynard stepped back to cock his pistol, and at the same instant Blackbeard moved in for the finishing blow with his cutlass. But at the moment in which he swung his cutlass aloft, a British seaman approached Blackbeard from the rear and "gave him a terrific wound in the neck and throat."[26] The cutlass, raised for the finishing blow, swerved as it came down, merely grazing the knuckles of Maynard, cutting them slightly.

The blood spurted from Blackbeard's gashed neck. He staggered, but fought on. Shouting defiance, he continued to swing the heavy cutlass about him. The bullet and sword wounds which he had sustained were, however, weakening him. Others saw that he was approaching his end. The British seamen, who had kept clear of him until now, closed in for the kill. They ducked in behind him to stab him with their swords. "At length, as he was cocking another pistol, having fired several before, he fell down dead."[27] Edward Teach died a violent death, but it was in the heat of battle, as he would have wished, still fighting as he fell with the insensate rage of a mortally wounded lion.

Lieutenant Maynard afterwards conducted an informal autopsy, to discover that his opponent had fallen with five pistol shots in him and no less than twenty severe cuts in various parts of his body.[28] Maynard unquestionably recognized Blackbeard as a man superior to others in talent, in courage, and, moreover, in physical strength. Johnson says: "Here was the end of that courageous brute, who might have passed in the world for a hero had he been employed in a good cause."[29]

Seeing their brave leader slaughtered and many pirate companions already dead, Johnson continues, "all of the rest, much wounded, jumped overboard and called out for quarter, which was granted; though it was only prolonging their lives for a few days."[30] Captain George Gordon, in a letter to the British Admiralty, stated that "in less than ten minutes tyme Tatch and five or six of his men were killed; the rest of these rogues jumped in the water where they were demolished, one of them being discovered some days after in the reeds by the fowls hovering over him."[31]

The *Ranger* had advanced, towards the end of the action, to attack the few members of Blackbeard's crew remaining aboard the *Adventure*.[32] While on board Blackbeard's sloop, one of the *Ranger*'s crew was shot by another member of the Royal Navy, "taking him by mistake for one of the pirates."[33]

Maynard and his men were fortunate indeed that the fighting took place on the British sloop and not on board Blackbeard's *Adventure*. Teach had posted in the hold a huge Negro, Caesar, "whom he had bred up," and whom he had instructed to set fire to the powder room and blow up the *Adventure* if the pirates lost the fight. When Caesar learned how his master had fared, he sought to carry out these orders. Two crew members of a trading sloop who had been visiting and drinking with Blackbeard the night before and who had lain in the hold throughout the battle, rushed forward and prevented him from taking this rash action.[34]

Rummaging through the *Adventure*'s papers, Maynard discovered correspondence between Blackbeard and prominent New York traders, as well as the letter of November 17, 1718, which he had received from Tobias Knight, Secretary of the Colony of North Carolina.[35] Maynard, on instructions from Governor Spotswood, hoped to find among the pirate's papers some indication of the whereabouts of his loot.

There is a variance in the casualty statistics of the battle as reported by four fairly reliable contemporary writers. Johnson, in his book published in 1724, stated that twenty-nine of Maynard's men were killed and wounded as a result of the broadside fired from Blackbeard's sloop; he does not list the number of Maynard's casualties resulting from the hand-to-hand fighting, but states that Blackbeard and eight members of his crew were killed in the engagement.[36] Governor Spotswood, on December 22, 1718, wrote that Blackbeard and nine of his crew were killed, and that nine others taken alive were "all much wounded"; that ten of the King's men were killed in action, and twenty-four wounded, "of whom one is since dead of his wounds."[37] Lieutenant Maynard, in his letter dated December 17, 1718, later published in a British newspaper, stated that eight of his own men were killed and eighteen wounded; that Blackbeard and twelve of his men were killed and that all nine of his prisoners were wounded.[38] Captain Ellis Brand, on February 6, 1718/ 1719, reported that ten pirates were killed and that all of the remainder were badly wounded; that "the *Pearl* sloop had killed and died of their wounds nine, my sloop [the *Ranger*, with men removed from the *Lyme*] had two killed, in both sloops there were upwards of twenty wounded."[39]

If Maynard's statement is interpreted as referring only to those killed or wounded from the crew of his own sloop, the *Pearl*, and not to the two mentioned by Brand as being killed from the crew of the *Lyme*, then, with respect to the casualties of the King's men, the only discrepancy among the four writers is that Spotswood and Brand listed as killed one more than did Maynard. Since Spotswood's and Brand's letters were written after Maynard's, one of the King's men may well have died of his wounds during the interval. In fact, in a later letter dated February 14, 1718/1719, Spotswood stated that of the King's men there were "no less than 12 killed and 22 wounded."[40] Hence the chief variance lies in the number of Blackbeard's crew said either to have been killed or to have died from their wounds. This is to be expected. There was little reason for the Royal Navy to keep an accurate record of these, especially since, as reported by Captain George Gordon, there were rogues who, after the battle, "jumped into the water where they were demolished."[41]

In addition to Blackbeard, Johnson names the following pirates killed in battle: Philip Morton, gunner; Garrat Gibbens, boatswain; Owen Roberts, carpenter; Thomas Miller, quartermaster; John Husk; Joseph Curtice; Joseph Brooks, Sr.; and Nathaniel Jackson.[42]

Maynard ordered Blackbeard's head severed from his body and suspended from the bowsprit of Maynard's sloop. The rest of Blackbeard's corpse was thrown overboard. According to legend, when the headless body hit the cold water it defiantly swam around the sloop several times before it sank.[43]

The head of Blackbeard would be proof irrefutable that Maynard and his crew had slain the pirate chieftain, enabling them to collect the reward of £100 sterling offered by the Colony of Virginia. Therefore, the hideous trophy was hanging from the bowsprit of Maynard's sloop when he arrived in Bath Town, as well as weeks later when he returned in triumph to the waters of Virginia's James River.[44]

According to the legends of Virginia and the statements of a number of writers, Blackbeard's skull dangled from a high pole on the west side of the mouth of the Hampton River for many years as a warning to seafarers.[45] The place is still known as "Blackbeard's Point." In time, someone took down the grim souvenir and fashioned it into the base of a large punch bowl. Watson states that the bowl "was long used as a drinking vessel at the Raleigh Tavern in Williamsburg. It was enlarged with silver, or silver plate; and I have seen those whose forefathers have spoken of their drinking punch from it; with a silver ladle appurtenant to that bowl."[46] If these statements are true, one suspects that the original shoulderer of this skull would heartily approve. Next to roaming the trackless seas, Blackbeard enjoyed most the companionship that attended a well-filled punch bowl.

After administering first aid to the injured and policing the scene of carnage at Ocracoke, Maynard sailed with his forbidding cargo to Bath Town, where he sought further relief for his wounded men.[47] According to the plans for the expedition, as drafted by Governor Spotswood, Maynard was to join Captain Brand's forces, which had moved into North Carolina overland from Virginia. Perhaps most important, in terms of the financial arrangements of the invasion, he was to carry back to Virginia as much of Blackbeard's loot as could be found.

Maynard had remained on Ocracoke Island for two or three weeks. Captain Brand had dispatched several letters to him, telling him to proceed to Bath Town as soon as possible.[48] Brand was waiting in Bath Town when Maynard arrived with his vessels. According to Johnson, there were discovered in "pirate sloops and ashore in a tent where the sloops lay, 25 hogshead of sugar, 11 tierces [casks containing about 304–330 pounds] and 145 bags of cocoa, a barrel of indigo, and a bale of cotton," in addition probably to twenty barrels of sugar and two bags of cotton found under hay in Tobias Knight's barn.[49] This merchandise was taken to Virginia and sold at auction for £2,238 sterling.[50]

Israel Hands, Blackbeard's former first mate, whom Blackbeard, executing one of his devilish pranks, had shot through the knee only a short time before, and five other former members of Blackbeard's crew were rounded up in Bath Town; these and the survivors of the battle at Ocracoke comprised a group of fifteen tried in Williamsburg on the charge of piracy.[51]

Brand and Maynard, with their invasion forces, did not depart from North Carolina earlier than the latter part of December,[52] the extended time being required for the healing of wounds and the repair of the vessels for the return voyage to Virginia. They used some of the time, no doubt, in tracing rumors of hidden treasure, never found, and in collecting evidence to be used in the forthcoming trial of their prisoners.

Governor Spotswood learned of the success of the invasion of North Carolina before the return of Lieutenant Maynard and his vessels to Virginia waters.[53] In one of his customarily lengthy letters to the Council of Trade and Plantations, dated December 22, he explained in great detail how he personally had planned and executed the expedition in the utmost secrecy, concluding: "I do myself the honour of giving yor. Lordps. the particulars of this action because, it has, I hope, prevented a design of the most pernicious consequences to the trade of these Plantations, wch. was that of the pyrats fortifying an Island at Ocracock Inlett and making that a general rendevouze of such robbers."[54]

Chapter 12

Dispute over Jurisdiction

GOVERNOR EDEN and many of his subjects resented, to be sure, not only Governor Spotswood's invasion of North Carolina but also the secret and highhanded manner in which he had conducted it. They felt that he had acted without authority; and, further, Spotswood's imputation of their being evil neighbors engendered in them an indignant displeasure. The episode served only to enkindle such ill feelings as already existed between the two colonies.

Governor Eden was doubtless in Bath Town during the period in which Captain Brand's land forces and Lieutenant Maynard's marines were in occupation of that town and the surrounding area.[1] Humiliated and helpless, he turned to Colonel Thomas Pollock, a trusted friend in Chowan Precinct, for counsel. Having arrived in the colony in 1683, Pollock had sat almost continuously since that time in the Council as a deputy of one of the Lords Proprietors.[2] Serving as Acting Governor when Eden came into North Carolina in 1714, he was to be reelected in the same capacity upon Eden's death in 1722.

Governor Eden dispatched a letter to Colonel Pollock, the contents of which, together with other papers delivered by the messenger, are unknown. There is preserved, however, Colonel Pollock's reply. Written only sixteen days after the Battle of Ocracoke Inlet,[3] it reveals much of what Governor Eden's communication must have contained.

Needless to say, over and above the lively resentment of Spotswood's invasion of North Carolina's jurisdiction, there were many knotty legal questions involved in this wholly unorthodox situation. Governor Eden's methodical mind warned him that if Spotswood went coolly to such lengths to suppress Blackbeard, in all probability he was prepared to go even further in support of his arrogant schemes.

Colonel Pollock's response to the Governor's letter was concerned wholly with the legal aspects of the matter. Like the Governor, he was fully aware of Virginia's superior military and naval strength and of the fact that physical resistance would be not only disastrous, but impossible. Legal redress was the only effective course available.

Eden understood that Tobias Knight was the weak link in his essentially impregnable legal position. It is plain that Eden asked Pollock how best to deal with this matter. The Colonel replied rather warily, pleading the excuse of haste, and neglecting to refer directly to Knight. Much of his letter is concerned with details of the royal statutes expressly forbidding the line of action already pursued by the Governor of Virginia.

Pollock specifically condemned ɪ ot only the invasion, but also the carrying of seized goods and valuables of the pirates into another colony for disposal to the advantage of Governor Spotswood. He also discussed critically the trials of the surviving pirate prisoners under another jurisdiction than that of North Carolina.

It is interesting now to note the extent to which all colonials in authority referred without question to basic law at home in England. Infringement of the statutes controlling the individual colonies could be detected, proven, and effectively punished by the Sovereign; but Governor Eden justifiably suspected treachery.

Each new reigning monarch in England issued his or her own commissions or instructions to the colonial governors in America, the commissions of a deceased sovereign being superseded thereby. Queen Anne died on August 1, 1714. Because time was required to determine the colonial policies of a new sovereign and to draft the necessary documents, King George I issued a proclamation stating in substance that all matters should proceed in the colonies exactly as before for at least six months after the death of the late queen, so that the government of the colonies should not suffer by the lapse. James Stanhope, the Principal Secretary of State, enclosed this proclamation with a letter addressed to Governor Spotswood, dated November 30, 1714.[4] Spotswood was asked to notify the other governors.

There were 136 numbered paragraphs in the set of instructions, dated April 15, 1715, received by Spotswood from the King. The form and contents of the instructions sent to the other colonial governors were substantially the same.[5] Governor Spotswood's actual commission from George I is dated April 28, 1715.

A colonial governor invariably read to the members of his council the commission appointing him governor, but he customarily did not reveal to them his instructions. Spotswood's 1715 instructions, paragraph 5, expressly provided: "You are forthwith to Communicate unto our Said Council such and so many of these our Instructions wherein their advice and Consent are mentioned to be requisite, as likewise all such others from time to time as you shall find Convenient for our Service to be Imported to them." Most governors wanted the subjects to believe they had greater powers than they actually had, and, at the same time, did not want others to know when they were derelict in carrying out their instructions.

There is nothing in the instructions received from King George I which might conceivably confer upon Governor Spotswood authority to invade the jurisdiction of North Carolina. In fact, there are paragraphs which seem expressly to negate such authority. Instruction number 108 provides: "You are not to

Grant Commissions of Mark or Reprisals against any Prince or State, or their Subjects in Amity with us, to any person whatsoever without our Especial Command." Instruction number 120 states: "In case of Distress of any other of our Plantations, you shall upon the Application of the respective Governors thereof to you, Assist them with what Aid, the Condition of our Colony under your Government, can Spare."

The only instruction directly pertaining to piracy is found in paragraph 56:

In case any goods, money, or other Estate of pirates or Piratically taken, shall be brought in or found within said Colony of Virginia, or taken on board any Ships or Vessels, you are to cause the same to be seized or secured, until our Pleasure Concerning the disposal of the same, but in Case such Goods or any part of them, are perishable the same shall be publicly sold and disposed of, and the produce thereof in like manner secured, until our Further order.

If Governor Spotswood had any specific authority to justify his campaign into North Carolina, it was never revealed. He was a skillful and prolific letter writer, yet nowhere in his accounts of the affair to persons in England does he mention the source of his legal authority. Apparently he felt that the desired results justified the means adopted.

In a printed pamphlet, evidently prepared by the Virginia House of Burgesses during its quarrel with Governor Spotswood in 1719, there appears this statement:

As to the destroying of Thache and his Crew that Story had better be kept in silence than told for if all the Circumstances of it were known they would make little for his [Spotswood's] Reputation. For after Thache had surrendered himself upon the King's Pardon to the Governor of North Carolina, Colonel Spotswood being informed of some rude Actions he and his Crew were guilty of in that Government, instead of Acquainting the Governor of that Country therewith, or Offering to assist him to reduce Thache and his Crew;

Understanding that there was a good deale of money and a great many Negroes in the case, he persuades the King's Men of War to Surprise and Kill the men within the Country of Carolina, and to Seize the goods and to bring them away to Virginia, where he had them condemned as Pyrats goods, tho' taken within the time limitted in the King's Pardon, and the Money not put into the hands of the King's officers as it ought to be but, immediately into his own hands, in hopes grants will be more easily obtained of it, than if it were to come thro' the Treasury.[6]

Spotswood was fully cognizant of the fact that his actions had given rise to a jurisdictional dispute. In reporting to his superiors in London touching the Vice-Admiralty Court in Virginia that condemned the merchandise brought from North Carolina, he stated that an attorney representing the government of North Carolina had appeared and entered a plea questioning the jurisdiction of the Virginia court and insisting that the goods be returned to North Carolina and adjudged there. He further stated that, when the plea was overruled, Captain Brand was threatened with a lawsuit in England for trespassing on the lands of the Carolina Lords Proprietors and was made accountable for all property taken out of that province. In the words of Spotswood:

And tho' I am Credibly informed that Affidavits are taken in No. Carolina to contradict what has been plainly proved here upon the Tryal of the pirats, and to prove that Capt. Brand took away these piratical Effects by force, I hope the Lords proprietors themselves will give little Credit to such Clandestine Testimonials when they shall know how dark a part some of their Officers have acted, particularly one who enjoyed the post of Secretary, Chief Justice, one of the Lordships' Deputys and Collector of the Customs held a private Correspondence with Thach, concealed a Robbery he committed in that province, and received and concealed a considerable part of the Cargo of this very ffrench Ship which he knew Thack had no right to give or he to receive, admitting the same had been Wrecked Goods as was pretended.[7]

Governor Spotswood left no front uncovered, communicating further to Lord Carteret (whose name he spelled "Cartwright"), one of the Carolina Lords Proprietors, and stating in detail how he had eliminated pirates from a defenseless colony. Being an adroit reasoner, Spotswood strongly argued his case for reasons of expediency, playing on Lord Carteret's supposed apprehensions for his proprietorship, which Spotswood himself sought coolly to awaken. He took care to point out, not only that Lord Carteret might almost certainly stand to be a gainer through the transportation and sale of the pirates' confiscated loot in Virginia, "where there are many more purchasers for such Commoditys than in Carolina, and I may say . . . much better Payment," but added the reminder that "15 killed and 22 Wounded," among the Virginians, had been the price of this benevolence to His Lordship. Precisely who among the inhabitants of North Carolina had tendered their "Earnest Solicitations" for this service to them was left unmentioned.[8]

Spotswood further defended the secrecy of his operation on the ground that Governor Eden "could contribute nothing to the Success of the Design"; but that, in the event of his plan's miscarriage, Eden "must have been more exposed to [the pirates'] Revenge for being lett into that Secret." His shrewdest argument, aside from deliberately minimizing the legal technicalities of his position, was perhaps the assumption that Governor Eden, depending solely on his own resources, would have necessarily failed in any attempt to capture Blackbeard, if, indeed, he made the attempt at all.[9]

Spotswood had already finessed the jurisdictional question in three letters to Governor Eden, dated November 7, 1718, December 21, 1718, and January 28, 1718/1719. The first was apparently handed to Captain Ellis Brand for delivery to Eden. The bearer of the second was a Mr. Bray. The third was in reply to letters of December 30 and January 6, wherein, from the tenor of Spotswood's reply, Eden had apparently asked him to spell out in detail the source of his authority.[10]

In the last letter, Spotswood wrote:

In answer to the first of which I herewith send you a copy of that part of my Commission under the great Seal whereby I am impowered [faded word] Pyrats in or out this Dominion which I hope will satisfy you that I have not exceeded the power given me by sending a Force to suppress Tatch and his crew. As President of the Court appointed for Tryall of Piracies in Virginia and Carolina, I have Authority to issue Warrants for apprehending Pyrats in any of those Provinces. That power was so fully recited in the Warrant I gave Capt. Brand at his going into your province, and whereof I presume he gave you a Copy, that there needs little to be added for your further Information. . . . I perceive no pirate case can be tried in your Province, but must be sent hither for that purpose. And by Special Commission the Governor of Virginia is Impowered to Constitute the Judges and other officers of the vice admiralty courts in Carolina whenever the said offices are Vacant, a copy of this last Commission has (I understand) been long since sent to your Government, and if it should be now mislaid upon Notice I shall furnish another.[11]

Spotswood did not give the date of his commission, apparently referring to the commission issued to Governor Andros of Virginia in 1697, which, as pointed out earlier, had expired with the death of King William III.[12]

Although, in a letter to the Lords Commissioners of Trade in 1716, Spotswood had expressed doubts whether he had any authority under the commission of the former Governor, it was not to his interest to express such doubts in his letter to Eden. He went so far as to inform Eden in his last letter that pirates could not surrender themselves for a pardon in North Carolina and "that if there be in your Province any persons under that Circumstance you may be pleased to notify them to repair hither for their pardons."[13] This was, of course, contrary both to the language and to the intent of the Royal Proclamation, which expressly provided that a pirate might surrender himself "to any Governor or Deputy Governor of any of our Plantations beyond the Seas."[14]

Spotswood went to great length in his letter of January 28 to point out to Eden, as he later did to Carteret, why he did not seek the participation of Eden. He stated that he recognized the weakness of Eden's government in the neighborhood of Bath Town and that, had the expedition failed, Teach would have taken his resentment out against Eden "for being privy to the design formed against him . . . therefore I am confident when you reflect on this point of my Conduct, you will rather attribute it for a friendly concern for your safety."[15]

In the perspective of history, it was to Spotswood's interest that he should stress the considerations of practical reality, as it was to Governor Eden's to cling to the letter of the law. It remains a tribute to the Virginian governor's sense of his own importance that he was able to present so strong a case for himself.

Except for Colonel Pollock's letter to Eden,[16] there are no extant letters or other documents presenting the North Carolinians' view of the jurisdictional dispute. Apparently, few historians have read Pollock's letter or have been concerned with the legality of Spotswood's actions. In the opinion of this writer, Spotswood had no legal authority to enter the territorial limits of North Carolina and seize property therein, to transport the property to Virginia, to sell the same at public auction, and finally to divide the proceeds among persons in Virginia. Ownership rights to the merchandise from the French ship had already been determined according to the law of salvage in a properly convened Court of Vice-Admiralty held in Bath. The doctrine of *res adjudicata*, apart from the issue of jurisdiction, should have precluded the condemnation proceedings in Virginia.

A brief treatment of the jurisdiction of colonial courts of vice-admiralty and the commission for the trial of piracy cases therein may be found in Appendix C of this book.

Chapter 13

Virginia Trial
of the Captured Pirates

*T*HE FIFTEEN PRISONERS brought to Virginia by Lieutenant Maynard were lodged in the public gaol in Williamsburg and charged with piracy. As was then customary, they probably wore leg irons and handcuffs attached to chains, and spent the long, bitterly cold nights of the winter months in unheated cells on floor matting of fusty straw. Most likely, they fed on a diet of "salt beef damaged, and Indian meal." Sanitary arrangements, though crude, were superior to those of most other gaols; in case of illness, a "physick" was provided.[1]

According to the minutes of the meeting, Governor Spotswood informed his Council on March 11, 1718/1719, that five of the prisoners captured on Blackbeard's sloop were Negroes, and "he desired the opinion of this Board whether there be anything in the Circumstances of these Negroes to exempt them from undergoing the same Tryal as other pirates." The Council was of the opinion that the Negroes ought to be tried in the same manner as the others "and if any diversity appears in their circumstances the same may be considered on their tryal."[2]

The trial was held on March 12, in a Court of Vice-Admiralty constituted by a commission under the Great Seal of England.[3] It was undoubtedly held in the General Courtroom on the first floor of the Capitol, which today stands reconstructed as it was in 1719. There are in Virginia no existing records of the court proceedings of the trial. These were either destroyed by fire or lost. A diligent search has failed to discover any sign of them.[4]

Spotswood, feeling it his duty to advise Eden and his Council of a state of affairs in their government which was brought to light in a Virginia court, sent to Governor Eden copies of several depositions used in the Williamsburg proceeding which accused Tobias Knight of being an accessory to acts of piracy.[5] These depositions were entered in the North Carolina Journal for May 27, 1719.

From the Journal we know that Israel Hands and four of the Negro prisoners, along with Captain Ellis Brand and William Bell, owner of a trading vessel from Currituck Precinct, were among those testifying to acts of piracy. Hands and the four Negroes undoubtedly gave incriminating evidence in hope of mercy.

No jurors were used in the trial of the pirates, as this was not required under admiralty law. Since the commissioners for this special occasion had been appointed by Spotswood, who was probably the presiding officer,[6] the results were as expected. Fourteen of the fifteen prisoners, including the five Negroes, were convicted and sentenced to be hanged.[7]

Samuel Odell was the only prisoner acquitted. He was able to prove conclusively that he was not a pirate, explaining that he had come aboard Blackbeard's *Adventure* for a drinking party the night before. Having participated in the Battle of Ocracoke Inlet out of circumstantial necessity, he had received thereby some seventy wounds.[8] It seemed punishment enough.

Israel Hands, Blackbeard's first mate who was in command of one of his sloops at the time of the Charleston blockade and who was in Bath Town at the time of the Battle of Ocracoke Inlet, was convicted on these grounds and sentenced to die; "but just as he was about to be executed, a ship arrived at Virginia with a Proclamation for prolonging the time of His Majesty's pardon to such of the Pirates as should surrender by a limited time therein expressed." Upon regaining his freedom, Hands returned to England, where he was later seen begging his bread on the streets of London.[9]

The remaining thirteen pirates were hanged on gibbets or trees outside Williamsburg on the Capitol Landing Road, a thoroughfare known for many years afterwards as "Gallows Road."[10] Many persons in Virginia believed the pirates were unjustly condemned.

It was customary in Virginia, as elsewhere during colonial times, to transport the condemned man to the scene of his hanging in a cart.[11] The cart was stopped beneath the gallows. There was usually an attending minister. The doomed man was told to stand. He was allowed to speak his last words to the throng of spectators who had come to witness the macabre spectacle. Upon the completion of this formality, the executioner placed the noose snugly around his neck, and the cart was withdrawn.

During the seventeenth and eighteenth centuries, both in England and in America, pirates were often hanged in chains at some point near the entrance of a harbor. Their bodies were permitted to hang for years, drying in the sun until skeletons, as an example to passing seamen. Since chains were costly, this custom was not always followed by the colonial governments. In 1720, Governor Spotswood did, however, require it to be done to four "profligate wretches" who he said had behaved outrageously while being tried. He ordered two to be hanged in chains at Tindall's Point, on the York River, and the other two at Urbanna, on the Rappahannock.[12]

The expenses of trying and executing the members of Blackbeard's crew were paid out of the King's revenue of two shillings per hogshead of tobacco.[13]

Spotswood reported to his superiors in London that the "sundry effects piratically taken by one Thack" had been sold for a total sum of £2,238, "out of which is to be deducted the Charges of recovering the said Effects out of the hands of the Pyrates, the transportation from Carolina, the Storage and Expense of the Sale."[14] There is no record of the amount, if any, remaining, or of who received the remainder.

The promised rewards for the apprehending and killing of pirates under Spotswood's proclamation, which stated that "the said rewards shall be punctually and justly paid," were not actually paid until four years later.[15] Apparently an angry quarrel arose over how the rewards and prize money should be distributed. Captains Brand and Gordon insisted that the money should be divided among the companies of the two ships, *Lyme* and *Pearl*, from which Lieutenant Maynard's force had been recruited; while Maynard claimed that the money should go entirely to him and to those who had taken part in the expedition with him.[16] Maynard lost the argument. The brave survivors of the bloody battle received no more than those who had remained safely aboard ship in the James River.[17]

On August 24, 1721, the King's Privy Council considered a petition signed by Lieutenant Robert Maynard and Thomas Tucker, master's mate formerly on board the *Pearl*, complaining about the unjust distribution of the reward money by the Assembly of Virginia, and, on behalf of themselves and sundry others, "praying in regard to their services that His Majesty will be pleased to grant them the benefit and advantage of such bounty as has been granted to other Captains on like occasions at home." The Council ordered "that the said petition (a copy of which is hereby annexed) be, and it is hereby, referred to the Lords Commissioners of the Admiralty to consider the same, and report to His Majesty at this Board, what they conceive fitt to be done therein."[18]

Captain Gordon, then in London, prepared at the request of the Lords of Admiralty what he termed a true and real account of the whole affair,[19] stating that Governor Spotswood distributed one-twelfth of the bounty money among "the two masters of the sloops he had hired at his own charge for that expedition, and their crews, they making a twelfth part of the whole number of the men that went with them." He further stated that Captain Brand and he had received £334/13/4 for the companies of the two ships, and that the same was distributed in what they considered the usual way in time of war—except that, in his own case, every farthing he received as captain was given to Maynard and those who went with him.

Gordon reluctantly informed the Lords of Admiralty that Maynard had shown Captain Brand some gold dust, silver plate, and other "small things of plunder," as Maynard called them, taken on board Blackbeard's sloop at Ocracoke Inlet.[20] Brand had charged him not to dispose of anything until they returned to Virginia. Violating these orders and also the prior orders of Gordon, Maynard nevertheless took the liberty of distributing valuable loot among himself and some of his friends. Gordon declared he had been reliably informed that Maynard's own share from this illegal appropriation of the pirates' effects amounted to about £90.

The Governor of Virginia had been making a successful effort to obtain privately from the members of his Council and others a collection of money for Maynard, but he brought this to a sudden halt.[21] Apparently Spotswood discovered that Maynard was not quite the hero he had at first been led to believe. No praise of Maynard is to be found in any of Spotswood's numerous letters.

There is no certainty as to Maynard's subsequent fate. One account says that a few years later he "suffered a sudden death at the hand of two Negro slaves in Prince George County," Virginia.[22] Captain Brand, who was placed in overall command of the expedition and headed the land forces that entered North Carolina, continued to serve in the Royal Navy. In 1747 he was officially classified as a "superannuated rear-admiral."[23]

It is unfortunate that a record of the proceedings in the trial of Blackbeard's crew in Williamsburg has not been preserved. Historians have generally relied upon contemporary accounts found in the letters of Spotswood and in the *History of Pirates*, by Captain Charles Johnson. It was only natural that Spotswood's letters should lionize Spotswood. In building himself up as a colonial patriot and vanquisher of pirates, he did not hesitate by his innuendoes and derogatory implications to tarnish the name of Eden. Later writers were led to believe that Eden and Blackbeard were bosom friends, whereas, neither in Spotswood's letters nor elsewhere is there any evidence that Eden ever had improper dealings with Edward Teach.

Spotswood's letters presumably misled Captain Johnson, in the early editions of his widely circulated work. Johnson corrected his errors, however, in a fourth edition, published in 1726. But the damage had already been done. Apparently few later writers read the retraction, which runs as follows:

What follows, contains reflections on a gentleman now deceased, who was Governor of North Carolina, namely Charles Eden, Esq., which we apprehend, by accounts since received, to be without just grounds; therefore, it will be necessary to say something in this place, to take off the calumny thrown on his character by persons who have misjudged of his conduct by the light things appeared in at that time.

Upon a review of this part of Black-beard's story, it does not seem, by any matters of fact candidly considered, that the said Governor held any private or criminal correspondence with this Pirate; and I have been informed since, by very good hands, that Mr. Eden always behaved, as far as he had power, in a manner suitable to his post, and bore the character of a good governor and an honest man. . . .

As to the secret expedition from Virginia, undertaken by the Governor and the two captains of men-of-war, they had their secret views in it. The men-of-war had lain up these ten months while the Pirates infested the coast and did great mischief, for which 'tis likely, they might have been called to an account. But the success of the enterprise against Teach, *alias* Black-beard, perhaps prevented such enquiry, though I am at a loss to know what acts of Piracy he had committed after this surrender to the Proclamation. The French ship was lawfully condemned, as has been said before, and if he had committed any depredations amongst the planters, as they seemed to complain of, they were not upon the high sea, but either in the river, or on shore, and could not come within the jurisdiction of the Admiralty, nor under any laws of Piracy.

The Governor of Virginia found his interest in the affair, for he sent, at the same time, a force by land, and seized considerable effects of Black-beard's in Eden's Province; which was certainly a new thing for the Governor of one Province, whose commission was limited to that jurisdiction, to exercise authority in another government, and the Governor himself upon the spot. Thus was poor Mr. Eden insulted and abused on all sides, without having the power of doing himself justice, and asserting his lawful rights.

In fine, to do justice to Governor Eden's character, who is since dead, there did not appear from any writings or letters found in Black-beard's sloop or from any other evidence whatsoever, that the said Governor was concerned at all in any malpractice; but on the contrary that during his continuance in that post, he was honoured and beloved by his colony, for his uprightness, probity and prudent conduct in his administration. What affairs were carried on privately by his then Secretary I know not. He died a few days after Black-beard's destruction, and no enquiry was made; perhaps there might be no occasion for it.[24]

Chapter 14

Trial of Tobias Knight

*W*HEN GOVERNOR SPOTSWOOD transmitted to Governor Eden the depositions that were taken at the trial of Blackbeard's crew and that implicated Tobias Knight as an accessory to their acts of piracy, Eden laid them before the members of his Council at a meeting held on April 4, 1719, in the home of William Duckenfield.[1]

Since Knight was a member of the Council, Secretary of the Colony, Collector of Customs, and had only recently been Chief Justice, this was a serious charge which had to be duly considered. Knight was not present at the meeting. According to the minutes of the Council Journal, a thorough investigation was ordered. Copies of all documents received from Virginia were sent to Knight, and he was ordered to attend the next session of the Council "and bring with him all papers, Orders, Depositions, or anything else he may have by him relating to Theache and the Transactions of Captain Ellis Brand, Lieutenant Maynard, and all others concerned in that business."[2]

Knight was tried at a meeting held in the home of Frederick Jones on May 27, 1719. The members recorded as present were Governor Charles Eden, Thomas Pollock, William Reed, Francis Foster, Frederick Jones, and Richard Sanderson. Since Knight was the defendant, he was not on this occasion sitting as a member of the Council. The only historical facts we have relating to this trial are those appearing in the Council Journal.[3] Since the validity of Virginia's involvement hinged on its outcome, the entire proceeding merits close attention.

The depositions and other records of evidence produced before the Virginia Court of Admiralty on March 12, 1718/1719 were read to the members of Governor Eden's Council.

As Teach's first mate, Israel Hands gave evidence at the Virginia trial that he was on board Blackbeard's sloop *Adventure*, in August of the previous year, when the pirates captured two French ships, putting the crews of both on one of them, and bringing the other craft to North Carolina as a prize. On arrival at Ocracoke Inlet, Hands deposed, Teach traveled by small river boat up the Pamlico with four members of his crew to visit Tobias Knight. Teach carried with him as a present for Knight several casks of chocolate (cocoa), loaf sugar, and sweetmeats taken from the French ships. At Blackbeard's return to the *Adventure*, on this occasion, Hands declared that he saw loaded aboard various other goods "which Thache said he bought in the Country." Hearing later that one William Bell had been robbed on the river, and learning "as well by common report as by discourse with said Bell" what goods had been stolen, Hands well understood them to be the same that Teach had brought on board, though he dared not identify the thief to Bell.

On being questioned by Spotswood's Court of Vice-Admiralty, the four pirates who had accompanied Teach acknowledged both the visit to the home of Knight and the present of chocolate, sugar, and "some Boxes, the Contents of which they did not know." They added that they had reached Knight's home "about Twelve or one a Clock in the Night," that Knight was then at home, and that Captain Teach remained with him "till about an hour before the break of day," when Teach departed in the small boat. They testified to seeing a boat lying near the shore "at a place called Chesters landing," about three miles below Knight's on the river. Teach ordered them to row toward her, saying he would go ashore at Chester's; but on approaching the other boat, which contained a man, a boy, and an Indian, Teach called out asking for a dram. Leaping into the boat, after some dispute, he plundered her, carrying away "some money, one cask of pipes, a Cask of rum or Brandy, Some Linen and other things."

William Bell testified at the Virginia trial that while on board his periauger at the landing of John Chester, on the night of September 14, a somewhat larger boat passed by, heading up the river. Before daybreak the same boat returned, and turned toward him, and one of the men aboard asked if he had anything to drink. When Bell made the excuse of darkness, the man called for his sword, which was handed to him from his own boat, and he commanded Bell to "put his hands behind him to be tyed." Bell declared that, after rough words had passed, he immediately attacked the man who had approached the landing. In the process of beating Bell, the man's sword was broken about a foot from the point. The broken piece was found later in Bell's periauger and was put in evidence at the trial. Following a sharp struggle, Bell and his companions were made captive, and his pistols were demanded. He answered that they were in his chest, which he unlocked rather than having it broken open.

This done, Bell's boat was moved farther out into the river and there rifled, some "66 pounds and 10 shillings in cash, one peice of Crape Containing 58 yards, a box of pipes, half of barrel of Brandy and other goods" being taken. Bell also declared himself robbed of a "silver cup of remarkable fashion, being made to Screw in the midle, the upper part resembling a Chalice, the Lower a Tumbler." This cup, Bell later had been informed, was found on board Teach's sloop at its capture. Only in this manner, Bell averred, had he finally learned the identity of the robber.

Having plundered him, Bell's deposition continued, the thieves tossed his sail and oars overboard and proceeded down the river. Bell said he went to Governor Eden two hours later to complain, and was referred to Mr. Knight, then Chief Justice. Knight had given Bell the requested "Hue & Cry" (a warrant), which he produced in court. He described the boat and the men to Knight, repeating as well as he could the language used by the white man, and adding that the other four were Negroes, or white men disguised as such. If the periauger which first passed up the river, before returning to plunder him, had been bound for Knight's home, the Chief Justice had made no admission of the fact, nor did he indicate that he so much as knew of Teach's being in the country.

Following Bell's evidence, a letter purportedly from Tobias Knight addressed to Captain Edward Thache, on board his sloop *Adventure*, and found among Blackbeard's papers after his death, was put in the record:

> November 17, 1718
>
> My ffriend
>
> If this finds you yet in harbour I would have you make the best of your way up as soon as possible your affairs will let you. I have something more to say to you than at present I can write; the bearer will tell you the end of our Indian Warr, and Ganet can tell you in part what I have to say to you, so referr you in some measure to him.
>
> I really think these three men are heartily sorry at their difference with you and will be very willing to ask your pardon; if I may advise, be ffriends again, its better than falling out among your selves.
>
> I expect the Governor this night or tomorrow, who I believe would be likewise glad to see you before you goe, I have not time to add save my hearty respects to you, and am your real ffriend.
>
> And Servant
>
> T. Knight

The apparently guarded terms in which this letter was couched had persuaded Governor Spotswood, who knew nothing of existing conditions in North Carolina, that it was sufficiently damning in itself. To clinch the matter, he included among the papers in the case forwarded to Eden a sworn copy of Captain

Ellis Brand's deposition before the Vice-Admiralty Court. It was read into the record as a part of the charges in the examination of Knight's conduct.

Brand, commander of the *Lyme*, asserted in his statement that, having received information of twenty barrels of sugar and two bags of cotton delivered by Captain Teach at the house of Tobias Knight, he forthwith demanded the goods of Knight as a part of the cargo piratically taken from the French ships. Brand declared that Knight positively denied that the goods were anywhere about his plantation. But on the following day, when Captain Brand urged the matter home, citing the proofs he could bring and the inevitable consequences, Knight "owned the whole matter, and the piratical Goods aforesaid were found in his Barn covered over with fodder."

The final document Spotswood submitted to Governor Eden was ominous and, as he must have believed, justification in full of his highhanded course of action:

At a Court of Admiralty Continued and held at the Capital the 13th day of March 1718 [1719], Wherease it has appeared to this Court Mr. Tobias Knight, Secretary of North Carolina, hath given Just Cause to suspect his being privy to the Piracys committed by Edward Thache and his Crew, and hath recieved and concealed the Effects by them piratically taken, whereby he is become an accessary:

Its therefore the opinion of this Court that a coppy of the Evidence given to this Court, so farr as they relate to the said Tobias Knight's Behavior, be Transmitted to the Governor of North Carolina to the end he may cause the said Tobias Knight to be apprehended and proceeded against, pursuant to the directions of the Act of Parliament for the more effectual suppression of Piracy.

Knight's masterly rebuttal, offered before Governor Eden and the members of the Council, is of sufficient importance to merit quoting at length. It, along with other records of the proceeding, appears in the Council Journal, as follows:

The Humble remonstrance of Tobias Knight, Esquire, Secretary of this province and a member of this Board, in answer to the several Depossitions and other pretended Evidences taken against him at a Court of admiralty holden at the Capital of Verginia the 12th day of March 1718 [1719]: First, the said Tobias Knight doth averr, and doubt not to make it Evidently appeare, that he is not in any wise howsoever guilty of the least of those Crimes which are so Slyly, malitiously and falsely suggested and insinuated against him by the said pretended Evidence, the which to make more apparent to your Honours, the said Tobias Knight doth pray your Honours first to Consider as to the Evidence themselves, they being such as Contradict themselves, or as ought not to be taken in any Court of Record or else where against the said Tobias Knight or any other white man, for first Hesikia hands, master of Captain Thaches Sloop Adventure, seems to sweare possitively in his Depossition that the said Thache went from Ocacoch Inlet at his returne into this Country from his last voyage, with a present to the said Tobias Knights house, when by the same depossition he acknowledgth that to be out of the reach of his knoledge, he being all the time at the said Inlet, which lyes at above thirty leagues distance from his house; and further the said Tobias Knight doth pray your Honours to observe that the aforesaid Hesikias hands was (as he has been well informed) for some time before the giveing of the said Evidence kept in prison under the Terrors of Death, a most severe prosecution; and that there doth apparently appeare thro' out the whole Evidence more of Art, mallice and designe against the said Tobias Knight then truth; secondly, as to the four next Evidence pretended to be given against the said Tobias Knight, under the name and pretext of foure of Captain Thaches men, is utterly false and such as the said Tobias Knight humbly conceives ought not to be taken against him, for that they are (tho cuningly couched under the names of Christians) no other [than] the four Negro Slaves which, by the Laws and customs of all America, Aught not to be Examined as Evidence; neither is their Evidence of any Validity against any White person whatsoever, and further, that the said Negroes at the time of their giveing the pretended Evidence aforesaid (as the said Tobias Knight is informed), was upon Tryal for their own lives for the supposed piracy by them Committed on Board the said Thache; and that what they did then say was in hopes of Obtaining mercy, tho' they were then

Condemned and since Executed; so that, had they been never so Lawfull Evidences, the said Tobias Knights debarred from his right and benifit of an Examination of them.

Thirdly, as to the Depossition of William Bell I shall only observe to your Honours that there is nothing in it can Effect the said Tobias Knight, save that it is therein cunningly Suggested that Edward Thache was at the said Tobias Knight house that night in which he was robbed, which the said Tobias Knight has good reason to believe was rather an Artfull and malitious designe of those that drew the said Depossitions, for that had it been true, it was Impossible to have been within the reach of his knowledge; and besides, the said Bell upon his Examination the day after he was robbed had in Suspicsion one Smith Undey, Fiteing Dick and others, and hath since the date of that Depossition, Viz^t; on or about ye 25 of April last past, declared that he doth verily believe that the said Thache never was at that time at the said Tobias Knights house, for the truth of which the said Tobias Knight doth humbly refer to the Examination and Depossitions of Mr. Edmund Chamberlain.

Fourthly, as to the pretended Evidence of Captain Ellis Brand, the said Tobias Knight doth humbly conceive the same ought not to Effect him, for had it been true, it had and ought to have been upon Oath, which is not, tho' the said Tobias Knight doth in the most Solemn manner declare that the said pretended Evidence is every word false, and that the said Brand never did at any time speak one word or mention to the said Knight in any manner whatsoever touching or concerning the sugar mentioned in the said Evidence before the said Knight first mentioned them to him; neither was the said sugar ever denyed by the said Tobias Knight to be in his Custody, for the truth of which he humbly referrs to the Honble the Governor, but further Saith that when the said Tobias Knight was apprised that the said Brand had been informed that the said Sugars had been coniveingly put on shore for the said Knights use, and that there might be found in his Custody Several other things of value belonging to the said Thache, and that the said Brand did intend to send his people to search his, the said Knight house, he did then speak himself to the said Brand and did acquaint him truly how and for what reason the said sugars was there Lodged, Viz^t: at the request of the said Thache, only till a more Convenient store could be procured by the Governor for the whole, with assurance that the said Tobias Knight never did pretend any Claim or right to any part thereof, and did also at the same time desire the said Brand, if he had any other informations against him he would be so civel as either to come himself or send his Lieutenant to his house, and every lock in his house should be opened to him; which he only replied that tho' he had some spightfull things insinuated to him by Evil minded persons whose names he need not mention, intimating Mr. Maurice Moore, Jerimiah Veal and others of that family, yet he had more Honour than to do any such thing; for that ever Since his comeing into this Goverment he had found nothing in the said Tobias Knights but a great deal of readyness to assist him in the service of the Crowne, very much becomeing a Gent and one in his poast, which Character he should give of him in Verginia in opposition to all the false and malitious storys there suggested against him, or words to the same Effect; ffifthly, as to the Letter that was said to be found of the said Tobias Knights writeing on Board the said Thache Sloop, the said Knight doth beleive to be true, for that he did write such a Letter by the Governors orders, he having advised him by Letters that he had some earnest business with the said Thache; but he doth uterly deny that there was any evil intent in the writeing the said Letter, but that he did verily believe at the Same time that the said Thach was as ffree a Subject of our Lord the King as any person in this Goverment; and the said Tobias Knight doth further say in his owne Justification that when the said Thache and his Crew first came into this Goverment and Surrendered themselves, pursuant to his Majestys Proclamation of indemnity, the said Tobias Knight then was, and for a long time had been, confined to his bed by sickness; and that dureing his whole stay in this Government, he never was able to goe off from his owne plantation, nor did either the said Thache or any of his crew frequent the said Knights house, unless when they had business at his Office as Secretary or Collector of the Kings Customs; neither did the said Tobias Knight or any of his family contract any acquaintance with the said Thache or any of his crew, nor did deal, buy or Sell with or of any of them dureing their whole stay, Save only Two Negroe men which the said Knight purchased from Two men who had left the said Thache, and had rece'd their pardons, and since are gone Lawfully out of this Goverment and Stil Continue in their good Alegiance; and the said Tobias Knight doth aver for Truth, that from the time the said Thache tooke his departure from this Goverment, bound to St. Thomas's, he did never See the said Thache or any of his people until on or about the 24th of September last past, when he came and reported to the Governor that he had brought a wreck into this Goverment; and perticularly that the said Thache was not to the said Knight knowledge, nor to the knowledge of any of his family, at or near his house on or about the 14th day of September last past, as is most falsely suggested in the aforesaid Evidence given against him in Verginia; for the Truth whereof he refers himself to the Examination and Depossition of Mr. Edmund Chamberlaine aforesaid, all which is most humbly Submited by

Your Honours Most Dutifull and
Most obediant Servant
T. KNIGHT.

Knight's broadside was fully supported by the evidence of a witness, Edmund Chamberlaine, who was doubtless known to Governor Eden and every member of the Council, but whom Spotswood and Captain Brand could hardly have anticipated.

Couching his statement in terms of considerable exactness, Chamberlaine declared himself a resident continuously in Tobias Knight's home since August of the previous year. During the period including and following September 14, he was never absent either by day or night. At no time, he averred, did he have knowledge of a visit by Captain Edward Teach or any of his crew; nor did he believe it possible that such occurrence could have been kept secret or unknown to him, his own room being so near Knight's as to make concealment of such an event impossible. Chamberlaine was the more certain of this, he said, because a rumor, abroad at the time, that Indians were contemplating an uprising in Bath County had made him extremely watchful of everything that occurred about the house and plantation grounds. He added that Knight was then in so uncertain a state of health that he could not possibly have left home, for the purpose of the suggested communication with Teach, without hazard to his life.

Chamberlaine stated further that he neither saw nor heard anything of a present from Teach to Tobias Knight or anyone in his family, save one gun of some forty shillings value.

Chamberlaine was present, he said, when William Bell came on September 14 to complain of being robbed, asking Knight for a warrant. He heard Knight examine the man, who was unable to describe the robbers because of darkness, but strongly suspected "one Thomas Undey, and one Richard Snelling, commonly called Fitery Dick," adding that the others appeared to be Negroes. Later Bell came again to see Knight, and this time he had under suspicion William Smith and others. Captain Teach was not mentioned or thought of until on or about September 24, some ten days after this robbery, when Chamberlaine was informed that Teach reported to Governor Eden that he had "brought a wreck into this Government."

Chamberlaine concluded with an account of a conversation with William Bell, on April 25, 1719, concerning Teach's alleged robbery of his periauger. Asked whether Bell now thought Tobias Knight had any knowledge of that affair, Chamberlaine stated that Bell replied that in his estimation Knight was "a very Civil Gent and his wife a very Civil Gentlewoman," and that he "did not think or believe that Knight knew anything of the matter, or words to that Effect."

Chamberlaine's statement closed the examination. It was now up to Governor Eden's Council to pass judgment on the grave charges, true or false. The decision of the examining Council, as recorded in the minutes of the Council Journal, was terse and final:

And this Board, haveing taken the whole into their Serious Consideration, and it appearing to them that the foure Evidences called by the names of James Blake, Richard Stiles, James White and Thomas Gates were actually no other than foure negroe Slaves and since Executed, as in the remonstrances is set forth; and that the other Evidences, so far as it relate to the said Tobias Knight, are false and malitious; and that he hath behaved himself, in that and all other affairs wherein he hath been intrusted, as becomes a good and faithful Officer; and thereupon, it is the opinion of this Board that he is not guilty and ought to be acquited of the said Crimes, and every of them laid to his charge, as aforesaid.

The defense of Tobias Knight was a surprising feat for a gravely ill man, and one of the final major acts of his closing career. His broadside, in terms of style and content, leaves no doubt that he was an attorney of not inconsiderable ability. His argument, devoid of any emotionalism, was designed to influence six highly respected government officials sitting as a court of law. He succinctly stated the principles of law involved and sought to contradict, point by point, each of the terms of evidence contained in the charges.

Hesikeah Hands (more commonly referred to as Israel Hands) and four of the Negro pirates (Richard Stiles, James Blake, James White, and Thomas Gates), undoubtedly as the result of pressures brought upon them during the almost four months they were held prisoners before their trial, elected to become King's witnesses against their fellow pirates. Knight pointed out that their statements were "in hopes of obtaining mercy." It is interesting to note that the fifth Negro prisoner, known only as Caesar, who had long been a member of Black-beard's crew and was a favorite of all the pirates, could not be persuaded to turn against his Brethren of the Coast.

Knight reminded the Council that some of the testimony given by Hands in the Virginia trial was admitted in violation of the well-known "hearsay evidence rule." Hearsay evidence is a form of testimony not proceeding from the personal knowledge of the witness, but from the mere repetition of what he has heard others say, and it is generally inadmissible in court.

Knight probably considered it unnecessary to remind the

learned members hearing the charges that he had been denied the right to face his accusers and that they themselves had no opportunity of observing the demeanor of the witnesses giving their testimony.

Knight further correctly stated that under the laws and customs of the American colonies at that time, a Negro slave could not be a witness against a white person in the courts. Under a statute enacted in Virginia as early as 1705, Negroes, whether slave or free, "were forbidden to be witnesses in any case whatsoever." Upon later finding that this restriction provided protection for dishonest free Negroes when the only evidence available was that of other free Negroes, in 1744 the Virginia law was amended so that "any free negro, mulato or Indian being a Christian" should be admitted as a witness in both civil and criminal suits against any Negro, mulatto, or Indian, slave or free.[4]

In North Carolina in 1719 it appears to have been an unwritten law, or custom, which prohibited the testimony of Negroes against white persons, rather than an enactment of the provincial legislature. Not until 1746 do we find a positive statute on the subject: "All Negroes, Mullatoes, bound or free, to the Third Generation, and Indian Servants or Slaves, shall be deemed and taken to be Persons incapable in Law to be Witnesses in any Cause whatsoever, except against each other."[5] This statutory rule of evidence was renewed from time to time, and continued until the end of the War Between the States.[6]

All of the Southern states had similar rules of evidence until the abolition of slavery.[7] Seemingly, a white man could, with impunity if no other white person was present, assault, injure, or even murder a slave in the midst of any number of Negroes and mulattoes.

Professor John Spencer Bassett, writing in 1896, states:

. . . it is well to remember that in the days when slavery was introduced into America there were two good reasons, as the whites thought, why the negroes should not give evidence against a white man. 1. They were in the lowest moral condition. Those who have not examined contemporary testimony on the subject will not easily imagine how the negroes lived. They were naturally ignorant, superstitious, and filled with intense hatred for those who made them slaves and held them as such . . . . They were unchaste and mostly unreliable. 2. The Africans were pagans. Those few who professed conversion to Christianity could not have had any clearly defined idea of Christian principles. The mass who were unconverted could have very little regard for the Christian oath. How could such persons, argued the colonists, be allowed to imperil the lives of Christian whites? That such testimony should not be received was quite in keeping with the spirit of the times.[8]

Most historians have wholly ignored the defense of Knight. The letter found in the possession of Blackbeard has been either misstated or given an interpretation not strictly valid.

The verdict reached by the six members of the Council is not surprising, obliged as they were to accept either an abstract of evidence given in a Virginia trial, at which Knight was not a defendant and therefore had no opportunity to cross-examine his accusers, or the evidence of one of their own group whom they had known for many years. There is no doubt that the credibility of the evidence produced by Knight was superior to that of five convicted felons whom probably they had never seen. Knight had been a very sick man for almost a year, and died from his illness within a few weeks of the trial.[9]

Because of illness, Knight's last recorded attendance at a meeting of the Council prior to his trial had been on August 1, 1717, when, as a consequence of the departure of Chief Justice Christopher Gale for England, Knight was appointed to serve in his place by the Governor, with the advice and consent of his Council. Previous to this time he had been a regular attendant at the sessions of the Council.[10]

Captain Brand, upon his return to England, wrote a letter to the Lords Commissioners of the Admiralty, dated July 4, 1719, complaining about the conduct of Knight, Collector of Customs for North Carolina, and Richard Fitzwilliams, Collector of Customs for the Lower District of James River in Virginia. He accused both of constantly assisting pirates and maintaining activities that discouraged the rendition of His Majesty's Naval Service in those parts, and he suggested that their behavior be investigated. On November 26, 1719, J. Burchett, Secretary, forwarded extracts of Brand's letter to the Secretaries of the Lords of the Treasury.[11] The Admiralty Commissioners were of the opinion that the inquiry was a matter for consideration by the British customs officials. But before these officials could get around to investigating the matter, Tobias Knight had already died.

If the Treasury ever investigated Captain Brand's charges against Fitzwilliams, there is no indication that they were found to be true. The Lords may have considered Brand to have had selfish motives, since he was constantly feuding with the Customs Collector over jurisdictional matters.[12] Subsequently Fitzwilliams was appointed "Surveyor General of the southern district on the continent of America, in which is contained South and North Carolina, Maryland, Virginia, Pennsylvania, the Bahama Islands and Jamaica"; and at a still later date he was appointed Governor of the Bahama Islands.[13] Fitzwilliams was later named one of Virginia's commissioners to survey the Virginia–North Carolina boundary line, in which capacity he "was more in sympathy with North Carolina than [were] his fellow commissioners of Virginia," fraternizing with the North Carolina commissioners and backing them on significant issues.[14]

Chapter 15

Aftermath in North Carolina

*W*HEN CAPTAIN ELLIS BRAND and his armed men invaded North Carolina overland from Virginia under instructions from Governor Spotswood, Colonel Maurice Moore and Colonel Edward Moseley met and accompanied him on his journey to Bath. They undoubtedly assisted Brand in looking for the fabled treasure said to be secreted in North Carolina but never found. Moseley, Moore, and some of the other leaders of the opposition in North Carolina were not only willing to cooperate with Governor Spotswood, but also, apparently, to prove to the people of North Carolina and the authorities in England that the government officials in the colony were corrupt and that they were deriving a profit from the piratical acts of the notorious Blackbeard. This would please Spotswood and at the same time enable them to gain control over the colony.

There was nearly always going on in North Carolina during colonial times a struggle between two factions for the control of power: those who were in power and those who were out but maneuvering to get in. Each side used every available means either to keep or to gain position. All the political figures of the colony were in one or the other of the two camps.

During Governor Eden's administration, Edward Moseley was probably the colony's ablest lawyer. He had for a long time been intriguing for the governorship. As early as 1708 he was speaker of the Lower House of the General Assembly, and as such he was "the chief contriver and carryer-on" of Cary's Rebellion, and had succeeded in placing Thomas Cary at the head of the government for more than two years.[1] During this period actually "[t]here were two governments, each claiming to be regular and lawful, each with its adherents, who loudly proclaimed their opponents to be rebels and traitors."[2] Colonel Thomas Pollock supported the claims of William Glover to the governorship. Moseley disliked both Pollock and those who shared his thoughts and actions. Pollock held a similar dislike for Moseley and his followers.

Moseley was a member of the Council and Surveyor General during Cary's administration.[3] Both positions were lost, however, with the ouster of Cary. He had to wait until the death of Pollock before regaining power and prestige as an official within the government of the province. "For forty years Moseley's biography is practically the history of North Carolina, so varied were his activities and so deeply did he impress his personality on his times. He was that sort of character toward which men cannot be neutral. Those who did not hate him adored him."[4]

Like Pollock, Edward Moseley acquired considerable wealth. He listed more than thirty thousand acres and eighty-eight slaves in his will. In his library there were more than two hundred law books, plus 150 volumes on other subjects.[5] Moseley came into the province about 1704.[6] On August 4, 1705, he married Ann Lillington Walker, the widow of Henderson Walker, who had been president of the Council and the Acting Governor of the province from 1699 to the time of his death on April 14, 1704.[7] Ann was the daughter of Major Alexander Lillington, of Perquimans Precinct (now County), who had taken a prominent part in the affairs of the colony. Jeremiah Vail and Colonel Maurice Moore married sisters of Ann Lillington.

When Ann Lillington died in 1712,[8] her body was buried beside the remains of her first husband, at a place then called Moseley Point. Sometime in the late 1800's, the bodies of Ann and Governor Walker were exhumed and reinterred in the churchyard of St. Paul's Church in Edenton, to save them from "the encroachment of the water of Albemarle Sound."[9]

Moseley remarried, as is evidenced by the fact that he was survived in 1749 by a widow named Ann, who was designated the executrix of his estate under a will dated in 1745.[10]

Edward Moseley lived in several places throughout eastern North Carolina. In his will, he devised to his son Edward his plantation of two thousand acres, "where I formerly dwelt in Chowan County."[11] It has been said that in 1714 he bought the first lot sold in what was later to become known as Edenton, and that "within a year [he] built the first house in the future town."[12] There is no record of his personally occupying this structure as a "town house." Apparently he lived for a time in Bath.[13] He devised to his son John "my Lot and Houses in Brunswick where my Habitation usually is at Present."[14] He also devised to his son John "my plantation at Rockey Point, where I Frequently reside, on the West Side of the North East Branch of Cape Fear River."[15] In 1718 he was undoubtedly living in or near the present town of Edenton in Chowan Precinct (now County).

Maurice Moore was the son of Governor James Moore of South Carolina, who had married the stepdaughter of Sir John Yeamans, one of the early governors of what is now South Carolina. Maurice came into North Carolina as a major with a detachment of friendly Indians in 1713, to assist his older brother, Colonel James Moore, who had arrived earlier. Acting Governor Thomas Pollock had requested military aid from South Carolina in North Carolina's war against the Tuscarora Indians. Colonel James Moore returned to South Carolina, where in 1719 he was proclaimed by the people as their first royal governor, a position his father by the same name had held by appointment from the Lords Proprietors.

Maurice Moore remained in North Carolina, marrying the widow of Colonel Sam Swann (member of the Council, senior justice of the General Court, and Collector of the Customs), who was the daughter of Major Alexander Lillington and a sister of Edward Moseley's first wife. Upon her death, he married a Miss Porter.

In 1715 Colonel Maurice Moore was placed in command of an armed expeditionary force sent from North Carolina to assist South Carolina in its war against the Indians.

About 1725–1726 he laid off and established the town of Brunswick (now in historic ruins), approximately fourteen miles above the mouth of the Cape Fear River. During 1723 and 1724 he was a member of the Council. He was frequently a member of the Lower House of the Assembly, and in 1725 was elected its speaker. His principal plantation was at Rocky Point, near Brunswick, where he resided at the time of his death and where he was buried in 1743. He was the father of four children: Judge Maurice Moore; General James Moore of the Revolution; Rebecca, who became the wife of General John Ashe of the Revolution; and Elizabeth, who married Colonel Jones. His grandson, Alfred Moore (son of Judge Maurice Moore), was a member of the United States Supreme Court, succeeding James Iredell, the only other North Carolinian to sit on that bench.

Maurice Moore was the brother of Roger Moore ("King Roger," who established Orton Plantation, near the historic ruins of old Brunswick). Roger's first wife was Catherine, a child of Colonel William Rhett, who captured the notorious pirate, Stede Bonnet.[16]

On December 26, 1718, Colonel Moseley, Colonel Maurice Moore, Major Thomas Luten, Jr., Henry Clayton, and Joseph Moore unlawfully entered "with force and arms into a certain dwelling house then in possession of John Lovick, Deputy Secretary of and for this Province."[17] Lovick's rented home was located in Chowan Precinct at Sandy Point, on Albemarle Sound, about seven miles south of the present town of Edenton. It was being used as the Secretary's office and the Naval Office for the District of Roanoke. In it were kept the journal of the Council, the official seal of the colony, and the records of the province. The intruders fastened and nailed up the house during the space of the twenty hours they were there, and "with force and arms" riotously excluded Lovick from the possession of the house and the records of the province. Very likely they hoped to find information that would further link Eden and Knight with Blackbeard. But a search of the records by the intruders for almost a full day and night revealed nothing incriminating against the officials of the province. This must have been a bitter disappointment to them.

The next day the Provost Marshal arrested Edward Moseley and Maurice Moore. They were taken before John Blount, a Justice of the Peace, and before a large crowd there assembled Moseley attempted by seditious statements to stir the people into a rebellion.

According to an indictment subsequently drafted and found by a grand jury to be a true bill, the following is, in part, what Moseley said on that occasion:

"They could easily procure armed men to come and disturb quiett and honest men [referring to himself and others who had entered the home of John Lovick] but could not raise them to destroy Thack. But instead of that he [meaning Thack] was Suffered to go on in his vilaines. My Comittment is illegal. It is like the commands of a German Prince. I hope to see the Governor, who has so illegally committed me a Prisoner, himself putt in Irons and sent home to answer what he has done here. And I will endeavor to blacken his character as much as is in my power." And then of his further Malitious and seditious intent to stir up the people and procure the disturbance and ruin of the Kings Peace proceeded appealing to the People and by slanders in these seditious words and speeches. "Is not this a hard case—the Liberty and the property of the subject are taken away by these Illegall proceedings and you are as lyable to have yours destroy'd as ours now are?"[18]

The dramatic and seditious utterances of Moseley did not have the desired effect upon the inhabitants. There was no uprising of the people. They failed to follow him as they had years before in his leadership of Cary's Rebellion. Apparently the people were satisfied with the kind of government Eden and his Council had been furnishing.

If there had been a general disaffection with the government, this would have been an opportune time for an overthrow of proprietary rule. Governor Spotswood, ever loyal to the Crown, had long been hopeful that North Carolina could be converted from a proprietary to a royal colony. The land and naval forces that Spotswood had ordered into North Carolina were probably still in Bath or its vicinity. If Moseley and Moore had been successful in arousing the people in the Albemarle Sound area, then Virginia's forces in the Pamlico Sound area could have moved northward to sustain them; and, if necessary, additional forces could have been sent southward from Virginia to assist them— another of the two-pronged tactics in which Spotswood seemingly specialized.

A year later, on Monday morning, December 21, 1719, South Carolina overthrew its proprietary government and established a royal colony without bloodshed. The militia was drawn up in the market place of Charleston, and in the midst of beating drums, with the royal colors flying at the forts and on all ships in the harbor, Colonel James Moore was proclaimed a royal governor.[19] James Moore was the elder brother of Maurice, who collaborated with Governor Spotswood in his ordered invasion of North Carolina.

On December 30, 1718, Governor Eden convened the Council at the home of the newly appointed Chief Justice, Frederick

Jones, and informed its members of the actions of Moseley and Moore. The Council ordered the Attorney General to prosecute them for high crimes and misdemeanors at the next General Court. A bail bond of £3,000 was fixed for Moseley, and one of £2,000 for Moore.[20] The amount of the bail bonds was subsequently reduced by the General Court to £1,000 for each of the defendants. Being men of wealth, they were permitted to sign their own bail bonds.[21]

Governor Eden laid before a meeting of the Council held on April 3, 1719, a letter from Moseley directed to him and dated January 29, 1718/1719, which the Council members considered "a seditious and scandalous Libel containing several false and Villianous reflections on the Governor and Council's proceedings."[22] The letter was ordered placed in the hands of the Attorney General.

The defendants were indicted at a session of the General Court held "at the Court House at Queen Anne's Creek [now Edenton] in Chowan Precinct the 28th July 1719 and continued to the 1st of August following." The members of the court present were Frederick Jones, Chief Justice, John Blount, John Hardy, Thomas Miller, Thomas Harvey, John Worley, Major Robert West, Benjamin West, and Thomas Pollock, [Jr.].[23]

The Attorney General, Daniel Richardson, had prepared two separate indictments for the consideration of the grand jury. Edward Moseley, Maurice Moore, Thomas Luten, Jr., Henry Clayton, and Joseph Moore were charged with the incidents that occurred at the home of John Lovick on December 26, 1718.[24] All of the defendants, other than Joseph Moore, were prominent citizens of the province. Joseph Moore was identified as a laborer.

The other indictment, the more serious of the two, listed Edward Moseley only. It was for the "seditious words" uttered by Moseley on December 27, 1718.[25] The particular offense had been created by a statute of 1715 "for the more effectual observing of the King's Peace, and Establishing a good and lasting Foundation of Government in North Carolina"; and as the irony of events would have it, the law had been signed by Moseley as the speaker of the Assembly.[26]

Moseley's case attracted a great deal of attention from the public. As R. D. W. Connor states, "Moseley was the acknowledged leader of the popular party, and his contest with the governor assumed a political importance which lifted it above the ordinary criminal prosecution."[27]

The grand jury of sixteen persons, after being impaneled and sworn, returned true bills of indictment in both cases.[28] Colonel William Maule, the first of the three husbands of Penelope Golland, Governor Eden's stepdaughter, was the foreman. Moseley and Moore, who were present in court, pleaded not guilty. Moseley requested that the trial be postponed until the next term of court so that he might have more time to prepare his defense. The request was granted.

The next term of the General Court was held in the same place, beginning on October 29, 1719, and continuing through November 3, 1719. This time the members of the court present were Frederick Jones, Chief Justice, John Blount, John Polin, John Worley, Thomas Pollock, Jr., and Major Robert West.[29]

The first case tried was the one charging Moseley with the utterance of seditious statements on December 27, 1718. A trial jury of twelve persons found Moseley guilty of the charges contained in the indictment. The court ordered Moseley to "pay a fine of one hundred pounds and be incapable of bearing any office or place of Trust in this Government for three years and give bond with sufficient security in the sum of two hundred pounds for his good behavior a year and a day."[30]

When the second case, involving breaking into and entering the home of John Lovick at Sandy Point, was called for trial, the defendants pleaded guilty to the indictment and threw themselves upon the mercy of the court. After considering "the several aggravations of the persons" mentioned in the indictment and the fact that they had pleaded guilty and thrown "themselves upon the mercy of the court," the following fines were ordered: Colonel Maurice Moore, five pounds; Thomas Luten, Jr., twenty shillings; Colonel Edward Moseley and Henry Clayton, five shillings each. Apparently Joseph Moore was never found by the Provost Marshal. His name is not mentioned in the minutes of the October-November session of the General Court.[31]

The conviction and sentencing of Moseley and his followers in the General Court was effective in silencing the opposition to Governor Eden and his Council. Peace and tranquillity existed in the colony as long as Eden lived.

At a meeting of the Council held on November 10, 1719, it was agreed, at the suggestion of Eden, that "Edward Moseley should have Liberty to speak of any matters now lying before the Council that he was concerned in as an attorney before the sentence passed upon him by the General Court." At a subsequent meeting of the Council, held on April 4, 1720, Chief Justice Jones reported that a number of the inhabitants had been "injured and put to very great hardships and difficulty by reason of Colonel Edward Moseley's suspension" from the practice of law for three years. "Whereupon this Board unanimously agreed that the said Moseley might have Liberty to plead and Speake to such matters only as he can make appear to Mr. Chief Justice he was actually retained in before the sentence passed upon him by the General Court held in October 1719." Moseley, at this session of the Council, had himself submitted a written petition, which requested that all of his disabilities be removed. According to the minutes of the Council Journal, this petition referred to "Certain words spoken at Sandy Point which were uttered through inadvertency heat and passion and farr from any such sinister designs as in the Judgment was suggested and when in truth such words ought not to have been spoken or uttered and for which he is praying that his Sentence might be remitted promising for the future to behave himself with the greatest Care and Respect Imaginable." The Council took no action at this meeting in reference to Moseley's petition.[32]

Apparently Moseley subsequently adjusted his differences with Governor Eden and John Lovick. We find him testifying on November 21, 1723, to the validity of the Governor's will, which named Lovick the executor and residuary legatee. He stated that two months before Eden's death "he had occasion to wait on the Governor of North Carolina, concerning the proving of the Last Will and Testament of William Duckingfield, Esq., at which time the said Governor was weak and Languishing but of sound mind and memory," and that during the course of their conversation Governor Eden mentioned that he had executed a will giving all of his estate, except for some minor legacies, to Lovick.[33]

Upon the expiration of the three-year period prohibiting Moseley from practicing law and holding public office, and after the deaths of both Governor Eden and Colonel Thomas Pollock in 1722, Moseley and his associates who broke into the home of John Lovick rapidly gained positions of power and influence in the government of the colony. Edward Moseley was five or six times speaker of the Lower House of the Assembly. The Lords Proprietors appointed him Surveyor General of the Province, the oath of office being administered at a meeting of the Council held in Edenton on January 15, 1723/1724. Moseley became a member of the Council and George Burrington became Governor, both by appointments from the Lords Proprietors. The Council, on April 2, 1724, appointed Moseley Judge of the Court of Vice-Admiralty to fill the vacancy caused by the death of Daniel Richardson. In 1744 he became Chief Justice of North Carolina and continued to preside in that capacity until his death on July 11, 1749. He was one of the commissioners who ran the boundary line between Virginia and North Carolina, and years later he was appointed one of the commissioners to establish the boundary line between North Carolina and South Carolina. Few men have equaled his record, for variety and length of service, as a holder of public office.[34]

Chapter 16

End of Piracy

EDWARD TEACH, the famous knight of the black flag, and those whose lives he touched, lived during an era that has been called "the Golden Age of Piracy." The pirates of this period were strictly sea robbers; they did not plunder, burn, steal, or commit atrocious crimes on land. Many of their leaders belonged to a generation of intellectual vigor in matters relating to the sea. They acquired geographical and navigational knowledge which they passed on to others. Piracy was perhaps a necessary evil in the conquest of the rolling and turbulent oceans.

This can be said in favor of the pirates: they did their evil deeds openly, flourishing their black flags boldly; they were not petty thieves, as were their brother scoundrels on land.

Piracy for a long time was a way of life for the adventuresome. There was at first no really strong public sentiment to suppress it. Many colonists considered the pirate captains public benefactors. There were occasions when the English, ambitious for Britannia to become the mighty mistress of the seas, not only tolerated piracy but also actually encouraged it. When wars against Spain were no longer threatening, privateers and pirates were abandoned as important tools to be used in the development of a British empire. If England had not used the services of privateers and pirates during its long struggle with Spain, there is some likelihood that the people today in North America would be speaking Spanish rather than English. In judging historical personalities one must not compare their conduct invidiously with the human behavior of the present times.

They should be fairly judged in terms of their own environment.

The defeat and death of Blackbeard in his semiretirement prevented North Carolina from becoming a haven for pirates. Blackbeard himself must have known that the great days of piracy were over. Governor Woodes Rogers, operating out of Nassau, was doing an effective job of cleaning out the pirate nests in the West Indies. Pirates cannot exist if there are no bases from which to operate.

Yet the destruction of Blackbeard did not immediately end piracy along the Atlantic coastline. Virginia was plagued with pirates for a few years afterwards. William Byrd wrote in 1719, "These rogues swarm in this part of the world."[1] In 1720, the Council and House of Burgesses presented Governor Spotswood with an address which was concerned with the frequent plunderings of pirates and privateers off the coast and begged him to do something about them. Four pirates were convicted in 1720 and hanged in chains, as a warning to others. In 1721 Virginia established batteries on the James, York, and Rappahannock rivers and set up lookouts with beacons to watch for approaching pirates.[2]

Many factors, not the least of which were the objectionable Navigation Acts and the almost constant wars of England, had unfortunately combined to create piracy and make it an integer of the early colonial life of America. There were circumstances, as well, which ultimately led to the end of piracy.

The law has always been the major agency of social control. The enactment of statutes by Parliament, and their strict enforcement, in conjunction with the development of international law, were among the chief factors that eliminated piracy.

Order can be imposed upon chaos only by superior force. As England rebuilt and improved its navy, the chances of pirates being caught and punished became greater. The profits from piracy were not in keeping with the risks.

Sir William Blackstone, writing in his famous *Commentaries on the Laws of England*, in 1769, stated:

> The crime of piracy, or robbery and depredations upon the high seas, is an offense against the universal law of society; a pirate being, according to Sir Edward Coke, *hostis humani generis*. As therefore he has renounced all benefits of society and government, and has reduced himself afresh to the savage state of nature, by declaring war against all mankind, all mankind must declare war against him: so that every community hath a right, by the rule of self-defense, to inflict that punishment upon him, which every individual would in a state of nature have been otherwise entitled to do, for any invasion of his person or personal property. . . . By the statute of 8 Geo. I, c. 24, the trading with known pirates, or furnishing them with stores or ammunition, or fitting out any vessel for that purpose, or in any wise consulting, combining, confederating or corresponding with them; or the forcibly boarding any merchant vessel, though without seizing or carrying her off, and destroying or throwing any of the goods overboard, shall be piracy: and all accessories to piracy, are declared to be principal pirates, and felons without benefit of clergy. By the same statutes also, (to encourage the defence of merchant vessels against pirates) the commanders or seamen wounded, and the widows of such seamen as are slain, in any piratical engagement, shall be entitled to a bounty, to be divided among them, not exceeding one fiftieth part of the cargo on board; and such wounded seamen shall be entitled to the pension of Greenwich hospital; which no other seamen are, except only such as have served in a ship of war. And if the commander shall behave cowardly, by not defending the ship, if she carries guns or arms, or shall discharge the mariners from fighting, so that the ship falls into the hands of pirates, such commander shall forfeit all his wages, and suffer six months' imprisonment.[3]

Other factors that brought the end of piracy on the trackless oceans were power-driven ships and the telegraph.

The bold and picturesque pirate captains and their Brethren of the Coast belong to a vanished age. These villains, like our heroes, have enriched us, however, by making our history interesting. Blackbeard is one of those persons involved in the development of America who is worth remembering.

The night before he was killed at Ocracoke Inlet, knowing full well that two sloops were waiting to attack the next morning, a member of his crew asked Blackbeard whether Mrs. Teach knew where he had buried his money in case anything should happen to him in the battle. His reply was that "nobody but himself and the devil knew where it was and that the longest liver should take all."[4]

There are numerous places in northeastern North Carolina which Blackbeard frequented, and where he is said to have buried his treasure. These spots have been honeycombed by diggers seeking the fabulous hoards.

According to some stories, it was customary for the pirates to kill a prisoner where the treasure was buried, so that his ghost might guard the spot. If no prisoner was available, the pirate captain might facetiously ask for a volunteer from amongst his crew. Needless to say, the only volunteer ever buried with the stolen loot was an involuntary one.

Much of the Atlantic coastline is dotted with places where Blackbeard is said to have buried his gold and silver. Some of them are the storied "money islands."[5] While some diggings have resulted in the discovery of valuable coins, rumored to have been hidden by Blackbeard, no one has ever been able definitely to connect them with the notorious Teach. This was the situation a few years ago when a farmer plowed up a metal container near Bath and found a few very old foreign coins, far more likely to have been cached by some early settler fearful of an Indian attack, or by ordinary thieves, than by Blackbeard or some other notorious pirate.[6]

Buried treasure is one of the things people passionately want to believe in because they hope to find it. In the writer's opinion

Blackbeard never buried any substantial amount of gold, silver, precious stones, or jewelry. He was not a Red Sea pirate, and, in fact, never captured a ship that carried much gold or silver. Notoriously spendthrift and improvident, Teach was not temperamentally inspired to set aside for a rainy day.

Among the many places in North Carolina reputed to have been frequented by Blackbeard are the so-called "Teach's Oak," near Oriental, where he supposedly camped for relaxation; Holiday's Island in the Chowan River, where tradition says he buried some of his treasure;[7] and "The Old Brick House," near Elizabeth City, where it is said he once lived.

Teach's Oak is located almost at the water's edge on a peninsula farm lying between the Neuse River and two creeks, Smith and Gree. Large and ancient, and now gnarled and bent, the old tree was many years ago named after the infamous freebooter. Local tradition avers that Blackbeard posted a sentinel in its branches. There is evidence that the area has been dug up in the search for buried treasure, but none has been found.[8]

A few miles south of Elizabeth City, on the banks of the Pasquotank River, stands a quaint old two-story house known as "The Old Brick House." Sunk in the ground at the foot of the front steps is a small slab of stone, circular in shape, possibly an old corn grinding stone, bearing the carved inscription, "E.T. —1709."[9]

This house, about forty by thirty feet, is built mainly of wood, but has sides of brick and stone. A wide paneled entrance hall opens into a large room, also paneled, which had, until 1933, a fireplace surmounted by an intricately carved mantel that reached to the ceiling. "The original mantel and fireplace along with most of the pinewood floors were removed in 1933 when an antique dealer owned the home. The mantel and fireplace have been replaced with antique pieces from other old homes in the area."[10] On either side of the mantel is a closet, in one of which is a secret panel that can be slid back to gain access to the basement below. The stories say that there once existed a secret tunnel leading from the basement to the banks of the river. The house stands at a bend commanding a good view up and down the river.

And a better spot the pirate could not have found to keep a lookout for the avenging ship that should track him to his hiding place. And should a strange sail heave in sight, or one which he might have cause to fear was bringing an enemy to his door, quickly to the secret closet near the mantel in the banquet hall would Blackbeard slip, drop quietly down to the basement room beneath, bending low, rush swiftly through the underground tunnel, slip into the waiting sloop and be off and away up the river or down, whichever was safest, out of reach of the enemy.[11]

There is little doubt that Blackbeard visited many houses along the rivers emptying into Albemarle Sound, since this was the older and a more populated area of the colony; but it would have been impossible for him ever to have occupied the Old Brick House. The house was not built earlier than 1735. According to statements of descendants of the original owner, the place was built by the eldest son of Lord Murden, of England, who came to this country in that year. The brick, the stone, and the beautifully carved mantel and paneling were brought from England.[12]

It is thought that the house was intended to be entirely of brick; but the end walls of the massive chimneys having exhausted the supply, the building was finished with wood. The house was planned with the greatest care for defense against the Indian raids; hence the sliding panels, and the roomy and secret spaces in which the family plate and jewels brought from the old country could be quickly concealed, in case of sudden attack. With the same end in view, there were built in the basement, from the rich timber of the adjoining woods, stalls of cedar, the narrow windows of which can still be seen. In these stalls the ponies were kept for fear of Indian raids.[13]

As to who incised in the sunken stone "E.T.—1709," nothing is known. In any event, whoever did so did not know the dates of colonial history, if he intended some reference to Teach, who lived and married in North Carolina in 1718. There is no existing record of his having ever visited the colony as early as 1709.

Probably the most spectacular traces of Blackbeard remaining in North Carolina are the weird tales that have been told by the credulous, startled by strange sights and sounds, who believe that the headless ghost of Blackbeard can be seen and heard wandering about the coastal region in search of his head, severed at Ocracoke Inlet. Blackbeard, it is said, does not want to meet his partner, the Devil, without his awful head on his shoulders. He is afraid that neither the Devil nor any of his earthly friends in Hell would recognize him without it. It is mostly at night, when strong winds are blowing inland, that his restless spirit arises and renews its never-ending search for the most frightening head in history. Some say that they have heard weird and agonizing sounds; others claim that they have heard echoes of his bellowing voice and the thwacking of his heavy boots on the floor and steps; and there are some who say that they have heard the question, "Where is my head?" It is easy to imagine the headless ghost of Blackbeard making his rounds when the gale howls, shrieks, and flings sand against the window panes. Sometimes the headless ghost carries a lantern. It is common on the seacoast to identify any unexplainable light as simply "Teach's light." Some have seen it by both land and sea, on board ghostly ships, and even moving about houses along the sandy shores. "Some say the headless figure of Blackbeard can be seen in the dark of the moon as it swims around and around Teach's Hole [at Ocracoke Inlet], searching for its severed head. They aver that it gleams with a phosphorescent glow and is plainly visible just below the surface of the water."[14]

Notes*

CHAPTER 1
EARLY LIFE OF BLACKBEARD

1. Nearly all source materials have stated that Blackbeard was born in Bristol, a few of which are as follows: "Teach, Edward," *Encyclopedia Britannica*, 1973, XXI, 741; "Teach, Edward," *Dictionary of National Biography*, 1949–50, XIX, 481–82; Henry K. Brooke, *Book of Pirates* (Philadelphia: J. P. Perry, 1841), p. 118; Robert Carse, *The Age of Piracy* (New York: Holt, Rinehart & Winston, 1957), p. 215; Philip Gosse, *The Pirate's Who's Who* (Boston: Charles E. Lauriat Co., 1924), p. 291; Archibald Hurd, *The Reign of Pirates* (New York: Alfred A. Knopf, 1925), p. 60; Edward Rowe Snow, *Pirates and Buccaneers of the Atlantic Coast* (Boston: Yankee Publishing Co., 1944), p. 251; S. Wilkinson, *The Voyages and Adventures of Edward Teach, Commonly Called Blackbeard, the Notorious Pirate* (Boston: Book Printing Office, 1808), p. 3; Michael Craton, *A History of the Bahamas* (London: Collins, 1962), p. 97; Captain Charles Johnson, *A General History of the Robberies and Murders of the Most Notorious Pirates* (London: Routledge and Kegan Paul, Ltd., 1955), p. 45; Francis L. Hawks, *History of North Carolina* (Fayetteville, N.C.: E. J. Hale and Son, 1858), II, 558; Cyrus H. Karraker, *Piracy Was a Business* (Rindge, N. H.: Richard R. Smith, Publisher, 1953), p. 142.

A view to the contrary has been expressed, as follows: "It has always been believed that Teach was a Bristol man, but according to the anonymous author, probably Charles Leslie, of 'Thirteen Letters from a Gentleman to his Friend', published in 1740, it appears that Teach was a native of Jamaica. The account of him runs as follows: '. . . He was born in Jamaica, of very credible Parents; his Mother is alive in Spanish Town to this Day, and his Brother is at present Captain of the Train of Artillery'" (Philip Gosse, *The History of Piracy* [New York: Longmans, Green & Co., 1932], p.

*Sources, after first reference, are listed by author, except in the case of edited works, which are listed by title or short title, and in the case of several works by the same author, which are listed by author and title or short title.

193). Patrick Pringle checked on this statement, and, writing in 1953, stated: "Mr. Clinton Black, the archivist at Spanish Town, has kindly explored the registers and other records in Jamaica without finding any confirmation of this" (Patrick Pringle, *Jolly Roger: The Story of the Great Age of Piracy* [New York: W. W. Norton & Co., 1953], p. 190).

2. Marshall Delancey Haywood, "Governor Charles Eden," *N. C. Booklets*, III (December, 1903), p. 20; Wilkinson, p. 3; Johnson, p. 45; and Lloyd Haynes Williams, *Pirates of Colonial Virginia*, (Richmond: The Dietz Press, 1937), p. 83.

3. Thomas T. Upshur, in an address delivered on June 19, 1900, on the occasion of the dedication of a new courthouse at Accomac, on the eastern shore of Virginia, said: "You . . . have heard from your infancy of Blackbeard, the pirate; but you may not have heard that Blackbeard was a native of Accomack county, and that his name was Edward Teach. The rendezvous of his men was on Parramore's Beach, Revell's Island, Hog Island and Rogues' Island. The latter island received its name from the hiding-place of the band. His depredations became so frequent and his raids so daring that finally the Virginia authorities equipped vessels to put a stop to them. His Eastern-Shore haunts became too hot for his safety and he removed his headquarters to North Carolina, up in Albemarle Sound, whence he continued his excursions" (*Va. Magazine of History and Biography*, IX [1902], 95). To the same effect, W. H. T. Squires, *The Days of Yester-Year in Colony and Commonwealth: A Sketch Book of Virginia* (Portsmouth, Va.: Printcraft Press, Inc., 1928), p. 49; Leonora W. Wood, "Worst Cut-Throat," *Norfolk Virginian-Pilot*, February 4, 1951; Jennings Cropper Wise, *Ye Kingdom of Accawmacke or the Eastern Shore of Virginia in the Seventeenth Century* (Richmond: Bell Book and Stationery Co., 1911), pp. 186–87. It is true that there were a considerable number of pirates at one time operating in and out of the general area of Accomac; but this was in the 1680's, forty years before the time of Blackbeard's escapades. Lloyd Haynes Williams, in the preface of his *Pirates of Colonial Virginia*, says that "so far as the author has been able to ascertain, he [Blackbeard] made only one cruise off the Virginia Capes."

4. George Woodbury, *The Great Days of Piracy in the West Indies* (New York: W. W. Norton & Co., 1951), p. 81.

5. This is based upon pictures found in books published in Eng-

land shortly after his death and deductions from general accounts of his activities.

6. The basis of the claim that Blackbeard's real surname was Drummond apparently stems from the following statement, originally written in 1842: "I happen to know the fact that Blackbeard, whose family name was given as Teach, was in reality named Drummond, a native of Bristol. I have learned this fact from one of his family and name, of respectable standing, in Virginia, near Hampton. Captain Drummond was a half-crazed man, under high excitements, by his losses and imprisonment from the French. He had been a privateersman out of Liverpool, and had made several French captures, all of which he lost by their restoration at the peace. He then went again to sea and took all French vessels which he could, as a pirate, and eventually, being an outlaw, he captured all kinds which he came across. His surgeon, for a part of his time, was a Doctor Cabot, who became the ancestor of a family of respectability in Virginia. The name of Teach, it may be observed, seems to be a feigned name because no such name can be found in the Philadelphia or New York Directories" (John F. Watson, *Annals of Philadelphia and Pennsylvania* [Philadelphia: E. S. Stuart, 1898], II, 220).

The above, in the opinion of the present author, is merely a rash statement picked up by Watson a hundred and twenty-odd years after the death of Blackbeard. There have been innumerable false statements about Blackbeard, during the last hundred years or so, going the rounds of Virginia; some of those statements have reached print.

There was a family by the name of Teach living on the eastern shore of Virginia about the time that Watson wrote that the name of Teach seemed to be feigned (*Va. Magazine of History and Biography*, X [1903], 70–71; Squires, p. 49; *Norfolk Virginian-Pilot*, February 4, 1951; Wise, pp. 186–87). In fact, across the Chesapeake, in Lancaster County, there is at the present time a family by the name of Teach. The head of this family, Joseph Verne Teach, of Weems, Va., whose ancestors have been in this country for probably two hundred years, has written the author that in his travels he has looked up many people bearing the name Teach, and that neither they nor he have found any information which would tend to connect their ancestors with the notorious pirate.

Two Virginia historians, writing about the time that Watson

picked up the bit of information about the name Drummond, state that Blackbeard's name was Teach, and they give no reference to any fact that he had relatives in Virginia (Robert R. Howison, *History of Virginia* [Philadelphia: Carey and Hart, 1846], p. 420; Charles Campbell, *Introduction to the History of the Colony and Ancient Dominion of Virginia* [Richmond: B. B. Minor, 1847], p. 396).

Lake Drummond, in southeastern Virginia, was named in honor of William Drummond, a native of Scotland, who came to Virginia in 1660. In October, 1664, he was appointed the first governor of North Carolina, which at that time was confined chiefly to the waters of Albemarle Sound. Upon the completion of his three-year term, he retired to Jamestown, "where ten years later, having engaged in Bacon's rebellion, in January, 1677, he'fell into the hands of Governor Berkley and was summarily executed by that insensuate and exasperated tyrant" (Samuel A. Ashe, *History of North Carolina* [Greensboro, N.C.: Charles L. Van Noppen, 1908], I, 70, 89, 93).

Edmund H. Harding of Washington, N. C., who was president of the Beaufort County Historical Society at the time this volume was being written, informed the author that he requested duly qualified persons in Bristol to check the records of that place to determine whether any person with the surname of Teach or Thatch (or any variation of the name) was living there during the time of Blackbeard. The information he received was that no such records could be found.

7. Fleming MacLiesh and Martin L. Krieger, *The Privateers* (New York: Random House, 1962), p. 6. For a brief summary of Bristol's history, see "Bristol," *Encyclopedia Britannica*, 1966, IV, 220–22.

8. Hugh Williamson, *History of North Carolina* (Philadelphia: Thomas Dobson, 1812), p. 11.

9. Gosse, *The History of Piracy*, p. 115.

10. Pringle, p. 38.

11. Boies Penrose, *Tudor and Early Stuart Voyaging* (Washington: Folger Shakespeare Library, 1962), pp. 10–20; Hugh Talmage Lefler and Arthur R. Newsome, *North Carolina: The History of a Southern State* (Chapel Hill: University of North Carolina Press, 1954), p. 8; Ashe, pp. 7, 37; R. D. W. Connor, *History of North Carolina* (Chicago: Lewis Publishing Co., 1919), I, 12–13.

12. Gosse, *The History of Piracy*, p. 113. To the same effect, Pringle, p. 38.

13. Peter Gerhard, *Pirates of the West Coast of New Spain* (Glendale, California: A. H. Clark Co., 1960), p. 215; MacLiesh and Krieger, pp. 3, 310; Peter K. Kemp and Christopher Lloyd, *Brethren of the Coast* (New York: Macmillan Co., 1961), pp. 161–81.

14. MacLiesh and Krieger, p. 320; Kemp and Lloyd, p. 183; Carse, pp. 190–200.

15. MacLiesh and Krieger, p. 6.

16. *Ibid.*, p. 338.

17. Johnson, p. 45. To the same effect, Karraker, p. 142; Hugh F. Rankin, *The Pirates of Colonial N.C.* (Raleigh: N.C. State Dept. of Archives and History, 1963), p. 43; Carse, p. 215; Wilkinson, p. 3.

18. Pringle, p. 180; Addison B. C. Whipple, *Pirate Rascals of the Spanish Main* (New York: Doubleday & Co., 1957), pp. 74–80; Woodbury, pp. 70–74.

19. Woodbury, p. 73. To the same effect, Pringle, p. 180.

20. Woodbury, p. 80. To the same effect, Pringle, p. 180.

21. Woodbury, p. 80. To the same effect, Craton, p. 94; Pringle, p. 180.

22. Craton, p. 94.

23. Johnson, p. 45.

24. *Ibid.* Craton, p. 97, states, "After 1713, he joined up with Hornigold."

25. Whipple, p. 176.

26. Johnson, p. 45; Karraker, p. 142; Williams, p. 86; Carse, p. 215; Arthur L. Hayward, *Book of Pirates* (New York: Roy Publishers, 1956), p. 59.

27. Craton, p. 97.

28. Woodbury, p. 85.

29. Whipple, pp. 182–83.

30. Craton, p. 97.

31. Johnson, p. 45; Hayward, p. 60; Whipple, p. 183; Williams, p. 86; Wilkinson, p. 3. A letter of Captain Vincent Pearse, written on board the *Phenix*, at New Providence, dated March 4, 1717/1718, and addressed to the Lords of Admiralty, reported that Captain Teach had not been seen in the Bahama Islands for about

eight months (unpublished manuscript, Admiralty 1/2282, Public Record Office, London).

32. Johnson, p. 45; Williams, p. 86.

33. Johnson, p. 45; Williams, p. 87; Karraker, p. 142; Rankin, *The Pirates of Colonial N.C.*, p. 3; Hugh F. Rankin, *The Golden Age of Piracy* (New York: Holt, Rinehart & Winston, 1969), p. 116.

34. Williams, p. 87. The indictment of William Howard, which is set forth in detail in Chapter 8, accuses the defendant of being associated with Blackbeard when the sloops *Betty*, *Robert*, and *Good Intent* and the large ship *Concord* (subsequently renamed by Blackbeard the *Queen Anne's Revenge*) were piratically seized (Williams, pp. 79–82; *Tyler's Quarterly Historical and Genealogical Magazine*, I [1920], 36–39).

35. Williams, p. 87.

36. *Ibid.*; Johnson, p. 45; Karraker, p. 142; Hayward, pp. 60–61; Wilkinson, pp. 3–4.

37. Williams, p. 87.

38. Craton, p. 102.

39. *Ibid.*, p. 103; letter of Governor Woodes Rogers, dated October 31, 1718, addressed to the Council of Trade and Plantations, *Calendar of State Papers*, *Colonial Series*, *America and the West Indies*, ed. Cecil Headlam (London: Cassell & Co., 1930–1933), XXX (Aug. 1717–Dec. 1718), sec. 737 (hereafter referred to as *Cal. State Papers*).

40. MacLiesh and Krieger, p. 338; Craton, p. 102.

41. Craton, p. 103; MacLiesh and Krieger, p. 341; letter of Gov. Woodes Rogers, dated October 31, 1718, addressed to the Council of Trade and Plantations, *Cal. State Papers*, XXX (Aug. 1717–Dec. 1718), sec. 737, which the author has checked against a photostatic copy of the original (Public Record Office, London, Colonial Office 23, I [1717–1725], 14–36). The photostat is now in the Manuscript Division of the Library of Congress. The date of Rogers' arrival and Hornigold's surrender is that appearing in Rogers' letter.

42. Craton, p. 103. When the "Proclamation for the Suppressing of Pirates" (discussed in Chapter 5 and appearing in Appendix D of this work) was received in New York on January 4, 1717/1718, the Governor and Council immediately decided to send Cap-

tain Vincent Pearse, commander of the man-of-war *Phenix*, to New Providence with copies of the proclamation. Pearse reported to the Lords of Admiralty that when he arrived on February 23, 1717/ 1718, Captain Hornigold was among the pirate captains who voluntarily surrendered and accepted His Majesty's most gracious pardon, requesting certificates from him, for their protection, until they could get an official pardon from some governor. There was no governor as of this time in the Bahama Islands. There were about 500 pirates, all subjects of Great Britain, when Pearse arrived (see unpublished letters of Captain Vincent Pearse, addressed to the Lords of Admiralty, dated February 4, 1717/1718, March 4, 1717/1718, and June 3, 1718, Admiralty 1/2282, Public Record Office, London).

43. Johnson, pp. 107, 113, and 115–16. See also Gov. Rogers' letter dated October 31, 1718, addressed to the Council of Trade and Plantations, *Cal. State Papers*, XXX (Aug. 1717–Dec. 1718), sec. 737.

44. See Gov. Rogers' letter, dated October 31, 1718, addressed to the Council of Trade and Plantations, *Cal. State Papers*, XXX (Aug. 1717–Dec. 1718), sec. 737. To the same effect, Johnson, p. 116; Pringle, p. 187.

45. Johnson, pp. 556–92; Pringle, p. 211; MacLiesh and Krieger, p. 312. A photostatic copy of the record of the trial (Public Record Office, London, C.O. 23, Vol. I, A 28) may be found in the Manuscript Division of the Library of Congress.

46. *Cal. State Papers*, XXX (Aug. 1717–Dec. 1718), sec. 807.

CHAPTER 2
THE CREATION OF AN IMAGE

1. Hayward, pp. 60–61; Hawks, p. 558; Johnson, p. 45; Karraker, p. 142; Snow, p. 252; Rankin, *The Pirates of Colonial N.C.*, p. 45; Wilkinson, pp. 3–4; Williams, p. 87.

2. Johnson, p. 45; Rankin, *The Pirates of Colonial N.C.*, p. 45; Williams, p. 87; Wilkinson, p. 4; Carse, p. 216; Hayward, p. 62. Hayward is the only source which says that Captain Taylor surrendered without resistance; Carse and Rankin, especially, mention the fighting.

3. Whipple, p. 178.

4. Johnson, p. 45; Rankin, *The Pirates of Colonial N.C.*, p. 45; Williams, p. 87; Wilkinson, p. 4; Carse, p. 216; Hayward, pp. 63–64; Hurd, p. 62.

5. Johnson, p. 57.

6. Rankin, *The Pirates of Colonial N.C.*, p. 45.

7. Johnson, p. 57. For subsequent writers who have followed the classic description of Blackbeard, see Carse, p. 216; Hayward, pp. 61–62; Rankin, *The Pirates of Colonial N.C.*, p. 46; Williams, p. 83; Whipple, pp. 176–77; Karraker, p. 144; Woodbury, p. 85; Joseph Lewis French, *The Great Days of Piracy in the West Indies* (New York: Tudor Pub. Co., 1961), p. 151; Craton, p. 97; Snow, p. 259.

8. Johnson, p. 57.

9. Whipple, p. 177.

10. Woodbury, p. 123.

11. *Ibid.*

12. Robert W. Chambers, *The Rogues' Moon* (New York: A. L. Burt Co., 1928), p. 128.

13. Johnson, p. 58.

14. Rankin, *The Golden Age of Piracy*, p. 11.

15. Johnson, p. 56. To the same effect, Pringle, p. 200.

16. There is a paucity of materials dealing with Blackbeard's relations with women. The statements in this book have been based upon accounts found in Whipple, pp. 180–81.

17. Whipple, p. 181.

18. Letter of Governor Walter Hamilton to Council of Trade and Plantations, dated January 6, 1718, *Cal. State Papers*, XXX (Aug. 1717–Dec. 1718), sec. 298; Craton, p. 97; Johnson, p. 49.

19. Robert E. Lee, *North Carolina Family Law*, 3rd ed. (Charlottesville, Va.: The Michie Co., 1963), I, sec. 27.

20. *Ibid.*, sec. 35.

CHAPTER 3
SEARCHING FOR PRIZES

1. Pringle, p. 192.

2. Letter of Governor Walter Hamilton of St. Christopher's Island to Council of Trade and Plantations, dated January 6, 1718,

Cal. State Papers, XXX (Aug. 1717–Dec. 1718), sec. 298. See also Pringle, p. 192; Williams, p. 90.

3. Rankin, *The Golden Age of Piracy*, p. 109; Shirley Carter Hughson, *The Carolina Pirates and Colonial Commerce, 1670–1740* (Baltimore: Johns Hopkins Press, 1894), p. 69; Pringle, p. 192; Whipple, p. 183–84; Edward McCrady, *South Carolina under the Proprietary Government, 1670–1719* (New York: Macmillan, 1897), p. 589; *cf.* Thomas Pollock's letter to Governor Charles Eden, dated December 8, 1718, *Colonial Records of North Carolina*, ed. W. L. Saunders (Raleigh: P. M. Hale, State Printer, 1886–1890), II, 320 (hereafter referred to as *N.C. Col. Rec.*).

4. Included in Johnson, pp. 12–14; Williams, pp. 133–35; Woodbury, pp. 144–46.

5. Letter of Attorney General and Solicitor General to the Council of Trade and Plantations, dated Nov. 14, 1717, *Cal. State Papers*, XXX (Aug. 1717–Dec. 1718), sec. 201.

6. Johnson, p. 46.

7. For a general account of the meeting of Blackbeard and Bonnet, see Johnson, p. 46; Hughson, p. 70; Karraker, p. 143; Rankin, *The Pirates of Colonial N.C.*, p. 46; Whipple, pp. 183, 222–23; McCrady, p. 589; Carse, p. 216; Yates Snowden, *History of South Carolina* (New York: Lewis Publishing Co., 1920), pp. 173–74; Pringle, p. 191.

8. Johnson, p. 46.

9. Whipple, p. 223.

10. The account of the capture of the *Adventure* has been based upon that found in Johnson, p. 46; Rankin, *The Pirates of Colonial N.C.*, p. 46; Williams, pp. 90–91; Pringle, p. 193; Snow, p. 253; Hayward, p. 65.

11. Woodbury, p. 115.

12. *Ibid.*

13. *Ibid.*, p. 106.

14. *Ibid.*, pp. 109–10.

15. Woodbury, p. 120.

16. Johnson, pp. 482–83.

17. Johnson, p. 483. See also Woodbury, pp. 120–21.

18. Johnson, p. 46; Rankin, *The Pirates of Colonial N.C.*, pp. 46–47; Williams, p. 91; Snow, p. 253; Rankin, *The Golden Age of Piracy*, p. 110.

19. Johnson, p. 46; Rankin, *The Pirates of Colonial N.C.*, p. 48; Williams, pp. 92–93; Hayward, p. 66. In the Virginia indictment of William Howard during the fall of 1718, the defendant is accused of being with Blackbeard in the piratical taking of a vessel near Cuba in April, 1718. This indictment, which can be found in Chapter 8, fixes the date of the piracy of the brigantine of London, bound from Guinea to South Carolina, as being in May, 1718.

20. Johnson, p. 58.

21. *Cal. State Papers*, XXX (Aug. 1717–Dec. 1718), sec. 551.

CHAPTER 4

Blockade of Charleston

1. The account of Blackbeard's blockade of Charleston has been based upon Johnson, pp. 46–48, 59–64; letter of Governor Robert Johnson of South Carolina, dated June 18, 1718, addressed to Council of Trade and Plantations, *Cal. State Papers*, XXX (Aug. 1717–Dec. 1718), sec. 556; "Petition of Council and Assembly of the Settlements in South Carolina to King," dated February 3, 1720, *Cal. State Papers*, XXXI (Jan. 1719–Feb. 1720), sec. 541; abstract of unsigned letter from Charles Town, addressed to "Sir," dated June 13, 1718, *Cal. State Papers*, XXX (Aug. 1717–Dec. 1718), sec. 660; statements of Attorney General Richard Allen and witnesses in piracy trial of Stede Bonnet, *Trials of Stede Bonnet and Other Pirates* (London, 1719), and Thomas Bayly Howell, *State Trials* (London: Callaghan & Co., 1811), XV, 1231–302.

As being in general accord with the above, see Hawks, p. 274; Hughson, pp. 70–73; Karraker, pp. 144–50; Pringle, pp. 193–95; Williams, pp. 93–98; Whipple, p. 226; McCrady, pp. 589–92; Snowden, I, 174–75; Snow, pp. 254–55; David D. Wallace, *History of South Carolina* (New York: American Historical Society, 1934), I, 226; Herbert Ravenel Sass, "The Pirate Who Wanted to Be King," *American Magazine* (February, 1930), pp. 14–20; Rankin, *The Golden Age of Piracy*, pp. 110–12; Rankin, *The Pirates of Colonial N.C.*, pp. 48–49.

2. James Truslow Adams, *Provincial Society, 1690–1763* (New York: Macmillan Co., 1927), p. 195; Henry A. M. Smith,

"The Baronies of South Carolina," *South Carolina Hist. and Gen. Mag.*, XI (1910), 86.

3. Hughson, p. 73. To the same effect, McCrady, p. 590.

4. Most of the accounts indicate that there were only two pirates and a Mr. Marks who made the trip ashore. Some few list more. Judge Trott, in the questioning of witnesses in the trial of Stede Bonnet, implies that there were five persons who went ashore in Charleston; and the Attorney General in this same trial states there were three or four (see Howell, pp. 1214 and 1254). Hawks, p. 274, states there were four.

5. Johnson, p. 61.

6. Unsigned letter addressed to "Sir," from Charles Town, dated June 13, 1718, transcript found in *Records in the British Public Record Office Relating to South Carolina*, VII (1717–1720), 74 (S.C. Archives Dept., Columbia, S.C.), abstract of which is published in *Cal. State Papers*, XXX (Aug. 1717–Dec. 1718), sec. 660. To the same effect, Wallace, p. 226; Karraker, p. 147; Pringle, p. 194; Williams, p. 95.

7. Johnson, p. 62; Karraker, p. 148.

8. Johnson, p. 63.

9. *Ibid.* To the same effect, Hughson, p. 71; Karraker, p. 149; Williams, pp. 96–97; But *cf.* Snowden, p. 175; McCrady, p. 591.

10. Johnson, p. 63.

11. Hughson, p. 72.

12. McCrady, p. 591.

13. Johnson, p. 47.

14. *Ibid.*; speech of Attorney General Richard Allen, of South Carolina, on October 30, 1718, in the piracy trials of Stede Bonnet and others in Charleston, S.C., published in Howell, p. 1244. To the same effect, Rankin, *The Pirates of Colonial N.C.*, p. 49; Pringle, p. 194; Williams, p. 97.

15. Pringle, p. 195.

16. Whipple, p. 185.

17. Johnson, p. 48; speech of Attorney General Allen, of South Carolina, on October 30, 1718, in the piracy trials of Stede Bonnet and others in Charleston, published in Howell, p. 1244. To the same effect, Hawks, p. 274; Hughson, p. 72; Pringle, p. 194; Whipple, p. 185; Williams, p. 98; Snowden, p. 175; McCrady, p. 592; Wallace, p. 226.

CHAPTER 5
TREACHERY AT BEAUFORT INLET

1. Johnson, p. 48. For accounts of the Topsail Inlet (now Beaufort Inlet) incidents, see also Johnson, pp. 68–69; testimony of witnesses at the piracy trials of Stede Bonnet and others held at Charleston, S.C., October 28–November 12, 1718, Howell, pp. 1249, 1254, 1258, 1262, 1264. To the same effect, Karraker, p. 150; Williams, p. 99; Whipple, p. 187; Hayward, p. 68; Sass, p. 18; Rankin, *The Golden Age of Piracy*, p. 112; Rankin, *The Pirates of Colonial N.C.*, p. 50.

Governor Alexander Spotswood of Virginia, who is so often in error with statements of facts in his letters, fixes the place at Ocracoke Inlet rather than Topsail Inlet (letter of Gov. Spotswood to Council of Trade and Plantations, dated Dec. 22, 1718, *Cal. State Papers*, XXX [Aug. 1717–Dec. 1718], sec. 800).

Captain Ellis Brand, of the *Lyme*, reported on the incidents at Topsail Inlet in a letter, dated July 12, 1718, addressed to the Lords of Admiralty (unpublished manuscript, Admiralty 1/1472, Public Record Office, London).

Captain Vincent Pearse, commander of the man-of-war *Phenix*, stationed at New York, wrote to the Lords of Admiralty, on September 5, 1718, as follows: "I presume e're this comes to hand their Lordships will hear that one Teach, commander of a pirate, has lost his ship at Topsail Inlet in North Carolina, and that himself and the greater part of his Company, has surrendered themselves to the Governor there, and accepted his Majesty's most Gracious Pardon" (unpublished manuscript, Admiralty 1/2282, Public Record Office, London).

2. Johnson, pp. 68–69; Howell, pp. 1249, 1262, 1296.

3. Johnson, p. 48. Johnson states that there were seventeen marooned on the island; but Ned Patterson, of Aberdeen, Scotland, who was among those marooned, testified at his trial and that of Bonnet, in Charleston, S.C., on Oct. 30, 1718, that the number was twenty-five (Howell, p. 1254). The latter evidence would seem more authoritative.

4. Williams, pp. 99–100.

5. There is a minor discrepancy as to the number killed or wounded. This is probably due to the fact that some historians have

included as killed in battle a number of men whom others have listed as dying shortly thereafter from battle-inflicted wounds. In the letter addressed to the Lords Commissioners of Trade, dated October 21, 1718, the number killed is stated to be ten, with four others dying later from injuries. Judge Trott, in passing sentence upon Bonnet on November 12, 1718, said, "You killed no less than eighteen persons out of those sent by lawful authority to suppress you" (Howell, p. 1298).

6. Johnson, pp. 67–84; Hughson, pp. 94–110; Snowden, I, 173–82; McCrady, pp. 595–621; Wallace, I, 227–31; *Trials of Stede Bonnet and Other Pirates*; Howell, pp. 1231–302; letter addressed to Lords Commissioners of Trade, dated October 21, 1718, and signed by Governor Robert Johnson, Nicholas Trott, A. Skene, and three others (B.P.R.O.–Props. B.J., X, 174), a transcript of which may be found in *Records in the British Public Record Office Relating to South Carolina*, VII (1712–1720), 164–66 (S.C. Archives Dept., Columbia, S.C.); Rankin, *The Golden Age of Piracy*, p.101.

7. Johnson, pp. 264–70; Hughson, pp. 116–23; McCrady, pp. 606–21; Snowden, pp. 180–81; Wallace, pp. 231–33; letter of Governor Johnson and Council of South Carolina to Council of Trade, dated December 12, 1718, *Cal. State Papers*, XXX (Aug. 1717–Dec. 1718), sec. 787.

8. Wallace, pp. 232–33.

CHAPTER 6
BLACKBEARD SETTLES IN BATH TOWN

1. Johnson, p. 48; Ashe, p. 200; Hawks, p. 274; Karraker, p. 151; Williams, p. 100; Wilkinson, p. 9.

2. The statute recording the incorporation of Bath may be found in the famous 1715 revisal statutes, which, with minor revisions, re-enacted the statute of 1705 incorporating the town (Laws of N. C., 1715, ch. lii, *State Records of North Carolina*, ed. Walter Clark [Winston-Salem, Goldsboro, and Charlotte: M. O. Sherrill, State Lib., 1895–1905], XXIII, 73 [hereafter referred to as *N.C. State Rec.*]). The early origins of Bath have generally been based upon the accounts found in Paschal and Reed.

3. Letter of William Gordon, dated May 13, 1709, and addressed to Sec. of S.P.G., *N.C. Col. Rec.*, I, 715.

4. Paschal, p. 25; Reed, p. 69.

5. Ashe, p. 193; Connor, p. 124.

6. Paschal, p. 32.

7. Reed, pp. 47–48.

8. Council Journal, *N.C. Col. Rec.*, II, 314; J. R. B. Hathaway, ed., *North Carolina Historical and Genealogical Register* (Edenton, N.C., 1901), II, 191–92; Paul M. McCain, *The County Court in North Carolina Before 1750* (Durham, N.C.: Duke University Press, 1954), p. 100.

9. Council Journal, *N.C. Col. Rec.*, II, 314.

Chapter lxvi of the Laws of N.C., 1715, approved "An Act to provide for the building of a Court House to hold the Assembly in, at the fork of Queen Anne's Creek commonly called Matchacamak Creek in Chowan precinct" (*N.C. State Rec.*, XXIII, 95). The structure was probably built pursuant to this statute.

The original expenditure account for the construction of this building signed by Edward Moseley, on file in the Edenton Court House, has been printed in the *N.C. Historical and Genealogical Register*, II, 100–1.

10. See generally *N.C. Col. Rec.*; McCain, p. 100.

11. *N.C. Historical and Genealogical Register*, pp. 191–92; Herbert R. Paschal, "Proprietary North Carolina: A Study in Colonial Government" (unpublished Ph.D. dissertation, U.N.C., 1961), p. 605.

12. William K. Boyd, ed., *William Byrd's History of the Dividing Line Betwixt Virginia and North Carolina* (Raleigh: N.C. Historical Commission, 1929), p. 96.

13. Although a courthouse for Bath was authorized by the Assembly in 1715, it was probably not constructed until late 1722 or early 1723 (Paschal, p. 38). The first public building ever erected in North Carolina was built in Perquimans Precinct (now County) at some time prior to 1701. According to court records, there was a convening of court in "ye Gran Court House for the Precinct of Perquimans" on October 14, 1701. The structure was probably destroyed by fire, because there are no records of its use thereafter (Records of Perquimans Precinct Court, *N.C. Col. Rec.*, I, 550).

14. There has been a considerable variance in historians' accounts as to the population of the colony during this period. Hawks states that the total population of the province in 1714 was but 7,500, not indicating whether this figure included Negroes and Indians (p. 89). Pollock estimated that in 1717 there were "2,000 tithables in the colony from whom taxes could be collected." This would seem to indicate a population of about 9,000, black and white (*N.C. Col. Rec.*, II, xvii). Boone and Barnwell, in a report to their Lordships on the Council of Trade and Plantations, in England, dated November 23, 1720, wrote: "The number of inhabitants we can't positively tell but their Tithables or those paying taxes are about 1,600, they are mostly whites, having not 500 blacks in the Government" (*N.C. Col. Rec.*, II, 396). The final report of the Council of Trade and Plantations to the King, dated September 8, 1721, is in general accord with the last statement (*N.C. Col. Rec.*, II, 419, 421; *Cal. State Papers*, XXXII [March 1720–December 1721], sec. 656).

15. Paschal, p. 23.

16. *N.C. Col. Rec.*, II, 235–36.

17. Paschal, pp. 38–39.

18. Paschal, p. 41.

19. Paschal, p. 47.

20. *Ibid.*, p. 41. See also *American Guide Series: North Carolina* (Chapel Hill: University of North Carolina Press, 1939), p. 554.

21. B.P.R.O. B.T. Properties, XXX, 386, printed in *N.C. Col. Rec.*, II, 50–51; Council Journal, dated Feb. 11, 1714/1715, *N.C. Col. Rec.*, II, 170; Council Journal, dated Mar. 30, 1722, *N.C. Col. Rec.*, II, 450.

22. Governor Eden's instructions may be found in manuscript form in Council Journal, 1712–1728, pages 84–100, N.C. Dept. of Archives, Raleigh. The handwriting is extremely difficult to read. Governor Hyde's instructions are printed in *N.C. Col. Rec.*, I, 844–46. They are signed by the Lords Proprietors and dated Jan. 24, 1711/1712.

23. Council Journal, dated Feb. 11, 1714/1715, *N.C. Col. Rec.*, II, 170; *ibid.*, dated Mar. 30, 1722, p. 450.

The statutory fee schedule for the governor and other colonial officials is set forth in Chapter lviii, Laws of N.C., 1715, printed in

N.C. State Rec., XXIII, 83. For example, the governor received 10/ for a marriage license and £4 for an ordinary keeper's license at general court and £2 for the same at a precinct court.

24. Biographical sketches of Eden may be found in *Biographical History of North Carolina*, ed. Samuel A. Ashe (Greensboro, N.C.: C. L. Van Noppen, 1905), I, 262–64; Beth G. Crabtree, *North Carolina Governors* (Raleigh: State Dept. of Archives and History, 1958), p. 29; Haywood, p. 20.

25. B.P.R.O. B.T. North Carolina, VI, 29, printed in *N.C. Col. Rec.*, II, 58.

26. Council Journal, dated May 28, 1714, *N.C. Col. Rec.*, II, 129. For a description of Hecklefield's farm, see Catherine Albertson, *In Ancient Albemarle* (Raleigh: Commercial Printing Co., 1914), pp. 31–35.

27. B.P.R.O. B.T. North Carolina, VII, 96, printed in *N.C. Col. Rec.*, II, 298.

28. For a copy of the charter, see Mattie Erma Edwards Parker, ed., *North Carolina Charters and Constitutions, 1578–1698* (Raleigh: Carolina Charter Tercentenary Commission, 1963), p. 100. The book is Volume I of a contemplated new series of *The Colonial Records of North Carolina*. The charter of 1665 was the second of two charters. The earlier one was granted in 1663.

29. *North Carolina Charters and Constitutions, 1578–1698*, p. 236. For a copy of a patent granted by the Lords Proprietors appointing Thomas Smith, of Charleston, S.C., a landgrave, see *N.C. Booklets*, VII, No. 1 (July, 1907), 47–48.

30. "Landgrave," *Webster's Unabridged Dictionary*, 1967, p. 1268.

31. Reed, pp. 49–50; *American Guide Series: North Carolina*, p. 553.

According to the minutes of the Council Journal, a meeting was held at "the house of the honorable Charles Eden Esq. Governor Captain General and Admiral" on December 17, 1714; at "the Governor's house in Chowan" on July 5, 1715; at "the Governor's house at Sandy Point" on September 13, 1715; at "the house of ye honorable Governor's" on August 4, 1716; at "Sandy Point in Chowan" on July 31, 1718; at "the house of the Honorable Governor" on December 3, 1720. The Sandy Point referred to is apparently a place about seven miles south of the present town of Edenton, a site then within Chowan Precinct. The above would seem to indicate that Governor Eden's first home was at Sandy Point (see generally the Council Journal, *N.C. Col. Rec.*, II, 147, 182, 199, 242, 307, 396).

In 1722 Governor Eden owned property at what is now the southeast corner of King and Court Streets, in Edenton. There apparently were no structures on the property at the time. Subsequently there were erected thereon the Edmund Hatch House, the Old Bond House, and the East Custom House, all of which are presently historic homes of Edenton (see a current, but undated, pamphlet entitled "Historic Edenton and Countryside," published by the Edenton Woman's Club).

32. Reed, p. 50; *American Guide Series: North Carolina*, p. 553.

33. In 1718 Eden owned lots numbers 9, 10, 22, and 23 on Water (Bay) Street, with waterfront privileges down to the bay, plus lots numbers 67 and 68 on King Street, which did not face the bay. Paschal states that Blackbeard had a house on Bay Street (Paschal, pp. 26–27, 32; Reed, p. 49. Both cited books contain early maps of Bath Town).

34. *N.C. Col. Rec.*, II, 229. In a letter of John Urmstone, missionary, to the Secretary of S.P.G., dated June 22, 1717, it is stated that Governor Eden has "since gone to live in the County of Bath" (*N.C. Col. Rec.*, II, 287).

35. *N.C. Col. Rec.*, II, 242.

36. Reed, p. 49. As indicating that Knight was living in Pasquotank in 1715, see *N.C. Col. Rec.*, II, 208.

37. Albertson, p. 36.

38. Letter from church warden and vestry of Pasquotank Precinct to Secretary of S.P.G., dated August 10, 1717, *N.C. Col. Rec.*, II, 292; *N.C. Historical and Genealogical Register*, I, 56, and III, 276.

39. Knight was appointed Secretary of the Colony by a commission of the Lords Proprietors. He was appointed Collector of Customs for the District of Currituck by a commission under the hand and seal of Robert Quarry, Surveyor General for Her Majesty's Customs in the Southern District of the Continent in America (Council Journal, dated May 9, 1712, *N.C. Col. Rec.*, I, 842–43). His commission and instructions from the Lords Proprietors bear the

date of Jan. 24, 1711/1712 (Council Journal, 1712–1718, in N.C. Dept of Archives, Raleigh, N.C.). This is the same date as that of Governor Hyde's instructions (*N.C. Col. Rec.*, I, 844–46).

40. Connor, p. 97.

41. *N.C. Col. Rec.*, II, 291.

42. Reed, p. 50. *American Guide Series: North Carolina*, p. 553. The author was directed to the spot during the summer of 1966 by the Rev. Alexander C. D. Noe, who was born in 1881 and was Rector of St. Thomas Church, Bath, between 1936 and 1953, and by Mrs. John A. Tankard, a native of Bath, who is an employee of the N.C. Department of Archives and History and was then in charge of the Bath Historic Site.

43. Albertson, p. 57.

44. Reed, p. 50; Albertson, pp. 58–59; *American Guide Series: North Carolina*, p. 553.

45. To the effect that Governor Eden had no child, only a step-child, see Hawks, pp. 562–63; *Biographical History of North Carolina*, I, 263–64; *N.C. Historical and Genealogical Register, III*, 152; Blackwell P. Robinson, *The Five Royal Governors of North Carolina, 1729–1775* (Raleigh: Carolina Charter Tercentenary Commission, 1963), p. 25; Haywood, p. 17; Bill Sharp, *A New Geography of North Carolina* (Raleigh: Sharp Pub. Co., 1958), IV, 1734.

46. Haywood, p. 17; *Biographical History of North Carolina*, I, 263–64. Sometimes the name appears in the printed records as "Galland" or "Gollond," rather than "Golland," which is undoubtedly due to the inability of the transcriber to distinguish the handwritten "o" from an "a."

47. Tombstone inscription in Edenton.

48. John Lovick, who married Penelope Golland, the widow of William Maule, mentions his wife's brother John Golland (J. Bryan Grimes, *North Carolina Wills and Inventories in the Office of the Secretary of State* [Raleigh: Edwards & Broughton, 1912], pp. 291–94. Hereafter referred to as *North Carolina Wills*).

49. Haywood, p. 17; *Biographical History of North Carolina*, I, 263–64; *ibid.*, IV, 192–93.

50. In *N.C. Col. Rec.*, I, 728, there is a letter, dated May 27, 1710, written by Thomas Pollock, which introduces William Maule to John Lawson as a young man who had been twice captured by

the French, upon whom fortune had frowned, and who was "very capable of surveying."

A complaint was filed in the General Court on the "last Tuesday October 1720" by Governor Eden against William Maule, Surveyor General, for £160, alleged to be due in connection with fees to which the Governor was entitled when a purchase right was surveyed. The complaint alleged that the nonpayment of these fees began the first of 1715 and had continued ever since (*N.C. Historical and Genealogical Register*, III, 151). To the effect that Maule was Surveyor General, see letter dated August 16, 1716, *N.C. Col. Rec.*, II, 239.

On October 28, 1724, Governor Burrington appointed Maule as a member of the Council in the place of Christopher Gale, who was then on a trip to England for the purpose of having Burrington removed. On November 7, 1724, the Council appointed Maule as Judge of Admiralty in the place of Edward Moseley, who had resigned (Council Journal, *N.C. Col. Rec.*, II, 535, 542).

Having departed from the Council upon the return of Gale during the spring of 1725, we find Maule on November 1, 1725, a prominent member of the Lower House of the Assembly (Journal of Lower House, *N.C. Col. Rec.*, II, 575–76).

Colonel Maule, who lived in Bertie Precinct, died shortly thereafter. In a will dated February 21, 1725, and probated March 30, 1726, he gave "[his] plantation called Scott's Hall, and allso [his] plantation called Mount Galland" to his wife; and to his daughter, Penelope Maule, he gave the residue of his estate. His brother, Dr. Patrick Maule, a plantation owner on the Pamlico River, was named executor and guardian of his daughter (Grimes, *North Carolina Wills*, p. 303).

51. Incidents involving John Lovick may be found throughout the rest of this chapter, as well as in Chapter 15, "The Aftermath in North Carolina."

In 1718 Lovick was living at Sandy Point, in Chowan Precinct, which is a spot about seven miles south of the town of Edenton on the shores of Albemarle Sound (Council Journal, dated December 10, 1718, *N.C. Col. Rec.*, II, 321).

Shortly after Blackbeard's death, probably in 1719, Lovick was granted the whole of Ocracoke Island (David Stick, *Outer Banks of North Carolina* [Chapel Hill: University of North Carolina Press, 1958], p. 32).

Lovick apparently acquired ownership of Roanoke Island in 1723 and resold it in 1729 to Richard Sanderson. There is no evidence that he ever lived on the historic island (William S. Powell, *Paradise Preserved* [Chapel Hill: University of North Carolina Press, 1965], p. 21).

Captain John Lovick married twice. There were no children from either of these marriages. His first wife was Sarah Blount, daughter of John Blount and Elizabeth Davis Blount (*N.C. Historical and Genealogical Register*, I, 57).

His second marriage to the widow of William Maule occurred at some time between the probate of Maule's will on March 30, 1726, and the signing of his own will on August 21, 1727. His will was drafted by William Little, the Attorney General, and was probated on November 10, 1733. After making some devises and bequests to friends, including John Lovick, son of his brother, Thomas Lovick, he left his entire estate to his wife Penelope. His wife was named the sole executrix (Grimes, *North Carolina Wills*, pp. 291–94).

52. George Phenney was Governor of the Bahama Islands from 1721 to 1727. His term of office was in between the two administrations of the famous Woodes Rogers. Many of the documents and letters of the administration of Governor Phenney may be found in the Public Record Office, London, Colonial Office 23, Vols. I and II (photostatic copies of which may be found in the Manuscript Division, Library of Congress). *Cf. N.C. Col. Rec.*, III, 477, 517; Karraker, pp. 196–97; Craton, p. 110.

The dates of his arrival in North Carolina and his marriage thereafter to Penelope are unknown. In his will, dated June 23, 1736, and probated June 23, 1737, he identified himself as "Surveyor General of His Majesties Customs in the Southern District, on the Continent of America." Property was therein willed to his wife Penelope, who was stated at the time to be pregnant (Grimes, *North Carolina Wills*, pp. 331–32). As to his appointment on August 31, 1731, as Surveyor General of Customs in the district including Pa., Md., Va., N.C., S.C., the Bahama Islands, and Jamaica, succeeding Richard Fitzwilliams, see *Calendar of Treasury Books and Papers*, ed. William A. Shaw (London: Her Majesty's Stationery Office, 1898), II (1731–34), 93, 204.

53. Robinson, pp. 12–26; Haywood, p. 15; *Biographical His-*

tory of North Carolina, V, 192–93; Griffin J. McRee, *Life and Correspondence of James Iredell* (New York: Appleton, 1857), p. 35.

Governor Gabriel Johnston, a native of Scotland, studied medicine at the University of St. Andrews, and was a political writer and man of letters before coming to North Carolina in 1734. He was Governor of North Carolina for eighteen years, 1734–1752, a period longer than that of any other governor, proprietary, royal, or state. Notwithstanding the fact that the Crown owed him over £13,000 sterling in back salary as Governor at the time of his death, he had accumulated an extensive and valuable estate. We do not know at what time his first wife, Penelope, died, but a second wife, Frances, survived him. Under a will written at Eden House on May 16, 1751, and probated on April 16, 1753, he devised much of the land inherited from his wife, Penelope, to their daughter, Penelope Johnston. His widow, Frances, in 1754 married John Rutherford, Esq., of New Hanover County. A notation in the final accounting of Governor Johnston's estate states that Eden House was burned between the date of the preliminary inventory, taken in May, 1753, and the final accounting on February 20, 1756 (Boyd, p. 104; Grimes, *North Carolina Wills*, pp. 269–70, 501–6).

54. Council Journal, dated March 30, 1722, *N.C. Col. Rec.*, II, 449–50.

55. *Ibid.*, III, 1–8; *cf.*, *ibid.*, II, 679.

56. See copy of Governor Eden's will recorded in Will Book II, page 299, Office of the Secretary of State, Raleigh, N.C. Also printed in Grimes, *North Carolina Wills*, pp. 176–77.

57. Lovick's will is found in Grimes, *North Carolina Wills*, pp. 291–94.

58. Among those stating that Governor Eden had a child named Penelope without designating her a stepchild, see John H. Wheeler, *Reminiscences and Memoirs of North Carolina and Eminent North Carolinians* (Columbus, Ohio: Columbus Printing Works, 1884), p. 118; John W. Moore, *History of North Carolina* (Raleigh: A. Williams, 1880), I, 56; McRee, pp. 31 and 400, ftns.

59. That Governor Johnston made his home at Eden House, see *N.C. Col. Rec.*, IV, 1120; *ibid.*, V, 771; Haywood, p. 19; Borinson, pp. 25–26.

60. McRee, p. 33.

61. Reed, p. 49. As to Eden's death, see Council Journal, dated March 30, 1722, *N.C. Col. Rec.*, II, 449; Hawks, p. 562; and the inscription on his tombstone in Edenton. The date of Pollock's death is from *N.C. Col. Rec.*, II, 460.

62. Haywood, p. 20.

63. *Ibid.*, p. 21. Verified by actual inspection in 1967 by the author.

CHAPTER 7

REFUGE IN NORTH CAROLINA

1. Johnson, p. 50; Rankin, *Pirates of Colonial North Carolina*, p. 52; Williams, p. 104.

2. S. A. Ashe, "Our Own Pirates," *N.C. Booklets*, II, No. 2 (1902), p. 10.

3. Hughson, p. 39; Karraker, pp. 66–82; Hamilton Cochran, *Freebooters of the Red Sea: Pirates, Politicians and Pieces of Eight* (New York: Bobbs Merrill, 1965), pp. 69–74; letter of Governor Cranfield of New Hampshire, dated Aug. 25, 1684, *Cal. State Papers*, XI (1681–1685), sec. 1845; Adams, pp. 53–54.

4. Karraker, p. 91; see also Snow, pp. 114–16.

5. Hughson, p. 39; Karraker, pp. 69–82; Pringle, pp. 128, 166; Cochran, pp. 69–74; Snow, pp. 120–21; Herbert L. Osgood, *The American Colonies in the Eighteenth Century* (New York: Columbia University Press, 1924), I, 205.

6. Karraker, p. 70 (citing *New York Colonial Documents* [Albany, 1853, 1854], IV, 447). To the same effect, Snow, p. 121.

7. Hughson, p. 39; Karraker, pp. 93–99; Pringle, p. 171; William M. Mervine, "Pirates and Privateers in the Delaware Bay and River," *The Pennsylvania Magazine*, XXXII (1908), 459.

8. Karraker, p. 93.

9. Hughson, p. 39.

10. Pringle, p. 166.

11. Karraker, pp. 93–94. See also Charles M. Andrews, *The Colonial Period of American History* (New Haven: Yale University Press, 1938), III, 318, ftn.

12. Watson, II, 216, 224; Hughson, p. 39.

13. Karraker, p. 96. For an account of Portlock and Brandenham, see Karraker, pp. 96–99.

14. For a detailed account see Williams, pp. 31–45, 129–30; *William and Mary College Quarterly* (1st series), VIII (1900), 166; *ibid*. (2nd series), VIII (1928), 220; Randolph Manuscript, printed in *Virginia Magazine of History and Biography*, XX (1912), 5; Lyon Gardiner Tyler, *Williamsburg, the Old Colonial Capital* (Richmond: Whittet & Shepperson, 1907), pp. 118–19.

The first fiscal accounting of the College of William and Mary, down to April 16, 1697, records the fact that among the college's original receipts there was "300 pounds representing money received from the pirates Davies, Hinson, and Delawafer" (*William and Mary College Quarterly* [1st series], VIII [1900], 166; *ibid*. [2nd series], VIII [1928], 220).

15. The entire court order is set forth in Williams, pp. 129–30; *William and Mary College Quarterly* (1st series), VII (1899), 165.

16. Williams, p. 36. To the effect that it was the handiwork of the Rev. James Blair, see Randolph Manuscript, *Virginia Magazine of History and Biography*, XX (1912), 5; "Founding of Virginia's First College," *Virginia Cavalcade*, VII, No. 1 (Summer, 1957), 16.

17. Lefler and Newsome, pp. 62–63.

18. In 1714, "after the expenses of government were paid, there remained for each proprietor a dividend of net profit of about twenty pounds only" (Hawks, p. 89).

19. Hugh F. Rankin, *Upheaval in Albemarle: The Story of Culpepper's Rebellion, 1675–1689* (Raleigh: Carolina Charter Tercentenary Commission, 1962), p. 4.

20. Archibald Henderson, *North Carolina: The Old North State and the New* (Chicago: Lewis Publishing Co., 1941), I, 93.

21. McCain, p. 4.

22. See letter of Lords Proprietors to Governor Eden, dated Sept. 15, 1714, *N.C. Col. Rec.*, II, 175.

23. Hughson, p. 27.

24. *N.C. Col. Rec.*, II, x, xi.

25. *Ibid*.

26. Johnson, p. 50.

27. Johnson, p. 49; Rankin, *Pirates of Colonial North Carolina*, pp. 51–52; Paschal, p. 34; Williams, p. 101; Wilkinson, p. 9.

28. Laws of North Carolina, 1715, ch. 1, printed in *N.C. State Rec.*, XXIII, 1.

29. Several statements in eastern Carolina that certain families were descendants of this marriage were found by the author to be without any historical foundation. This does not, however, preclude the possibility of a considerable number of descendants of Blackbeard's illegitimate children, conceived both before and after his final marriage.

In the first official census, conducted in 1790, there were no persons living in North Carolina with the surname of Teach or Thack. There were four males residing in Perquimans County with the surname of Thatch and two males in the New Bern District of Hyde County with the surname of Keach (*First Census of the United States, 1790: North Carolina* [Washington, 1908], pp. 32, 139; also reprinted with an index in *N.C. State Rec.*, XXVI, 643, 900).

There are no persons with the surname of Teach, Thack, Thatch, or Keach in the official list of freeholders (males owning fifty acres or more and subject to be called for jury service) prepared for all North Carolina precincts in the year 1723 (Hawks, pp. 61–67).

30. This letter, written from Route 1, Pinetown, N.C. (about five miles from Bath), on June 16, 1947, signed by Mrs. Ada S. Bragg, and addressed to a relative, Mrs. E. P. White of Buxton, N.C., stated that Mrs. White's great-great-aunt, Mary Ormond, became Teach's last wife. Mrs. Bragg is now deceased. During August, 1966, the author read this letter while interviewing Mrs. White at her home in Buxton, where, up until December, 1965, she had been postmaster for thirty-five years. Mrs. White's mother before her marriage to Lindley Tyer, Mrs. White's father, was Anne Elizabeth Ormond. Mrs. White stated that she was unable personally to trace her ancestors beyond great-grandparents.

31. Reed, pp. 217, 224.

32. Paschal, p. 57. For Wyriott Ormond's will, see Grimes, *North Carolina Wills*, p. 323.

One of the signers of the famous resolution at the Edenton Tea Party on October 25, 1774, (the first known political activity of women on American soil) was Mrs. Elizabeth P. Ormond, who later married Dr. Samuel Dickinson and occupied the Cupola House in Edenton (*Historical Edenton and Countryside*).

For an account of how the news of the Battles of Lexington and Concord was transmitted, see *N.C. Col. Rec.*, IX, 1229, ff. (reprinted from the *American Archives*, II, 363). The message was received in the following towns on the dates designated: Williamsburg, May 2; Edenton, May 4; Bath, May. 6.

33. Kemp and Lloyd, p. 1.

34. Ashe, II, 454–55; Stick, *Outer Banks of North Carolina*, pp. 279–80. See also Charles Christopher Crittenden, *The Commerce of North Carolina, 1763–1789* (New Haven, Conn.: Yale University Press, 1936), pp. 1–20.

35. Johnson, p. 48; Karraker, p. 151; Williams, p. 101.

36. *N.C. Col. Rec.*, II, 322, 347.

CHAPTER 8

SEAFARING ACTIVITIES OF A PARDONED PIRATE

1. Watson, II, 223; *Minutes of Provincial Council, Pennsylvania*, III, 45; Hughson, p. 75; Pringle, p. 199; Rankin, *Pirates of Colonial N.C.*, p. 53; Whipple, p. 188; McCrady, p. 592; Sass, p. 19.

2. Watson, II, 224.

3. Watson, II, 216–17, 219, 223.

4. Johnson, p. 49; Williams, p. 103.

5. Accounts of the incident may be found in Johnson, p. 49; Hughson, pp. 74–75; Karraker, p. 151; Pringle, p. 199; Rankin, *Pirates of Colonial N.C.*, p. 52; Williams, p. 103; Whipple, p. 188; Minutes of N.C. Council Journal, dated May 27, 1719, *N.C. Col. Rec.*, II, 341; letter of Governor Spotswood to Lords of Trade and Plantations, dated May 26, 1719, *Official Letters of Alexander Spotswood*, ed. R. A. Brock (Richmond: Virginia Historical Society, 1885), II, 324 (hereafter referred to as Spotswood) and *N.C. Col. Rec.*, II, 338–40; letter of Governor Spotswood to Secretary Craggs, dated May 26, 1719, Spotswood, p. 317; letter of Governor Spotswood to Council of Trade and Plantations, dated Aug. 11, 1719, *Cal. State Papers*, XXXI (Jan. 1719–Feb. 1720), sec. 357, at p. 207.

Johnson, p. 49, gives the date as June, 1718; but, according to the deposition in the Virginia trial of Israel Hands, who was with Blackbeard at the time of the capture of the ship, the capture occurred in August, 1718 (see *N.C. Col. Rec.*, II, 341), and, according to the letter of Governor Spotswood dated May 26, 1719, the capture is expressly fixed as having occurred on August 22, 1718. August seems more nearly correct.

Some of the accounts state that the vessels were bound for Martinique from France; others state that the vessels were bound for France from Martinique. It would seem more logical that they were departing from the West Indies if they were transporting sugar and cocoa.

6. Johnson, p. 49. To the same effect, Hughson, pp. 74–75; Rankin, *Pirates of Colonial N.C.*, p. 52; Pringle, p. 199; Williams, p. 103.

7. Johnson, p. 49; Karraker, p. 151; Rankin, *Pirates of Colonial N.C.*, p. 52; Williams, p. 103.

8. Hughson, p. 75.

9. William S. Holdsworth, *History of English Law* (Boston: Little, Brown and Co., 1926), VIII, 269; *Corpus Juris Secundum* (Brooklyn, 1936), II, title "Admiralty," secs. 21–22; Erastus Benedict, *Law of American Admiralty*, 6th ed. (New York: Arnold W. Knouth, 1940), I, secs. 117–26; Gustavus H. Robinson, *Handbook of Admiralty Law in the United States* (St. Paul, Minn.: West Pub. Co., 1939), secs. 98–102; Andrews, IV, 251–54; Thomas L. Mears, "The History of Admiralty Jurisdiction," reprinted in *Select Essays in Anglo-American History* (Boston: Little, Brown and Co., 1908), p. 312; James D. Dewell, Jr., "The Laws of Salvage," 21 *Yale Law Journal* 493 (1912); Note, "The Nature of Salvage Services," 33 *Harvard Law Review* 453 (1920); Salvage Act of August 1, 1912, c.268, 37 Stat. at Large 242, 46 *U.S. Code Annotated* (St. Paul, Minn., 1958), sec. 727 *et seq*; *The Blackwall*, 10 Wall. 1, 19 L.Ed. 870 (U.S. Supreme Court, 1870); *cf.* William Blackstone, *Commentaries on the Laws of England* (Oxford, England: Clarendon Press, 1769), III, 106.

10. Blackstone, III, 106.

11. *The Blackwall*, 10 Wall. 1, at p. 12, 19 L.Ed. 870 (U.S. Supreme Court, 1870; *Vernicos Shipping Co. v. U.S.*, 349 F.2d 465 (C.A.N.Y. 1965).

12. Benedict, I, sec. 121; *Nolan v. Rederiaktieselkab*, 267 F.2d 584 (C.A. Pa. 1959).

13. *Re Moneys in Registry of District Court*, 170 F. 47 (E.D., Pa. 1909).

14. Holdsworth, VIII, 269.

15. *Ibid.*

16. L. Kinvin Worth, "The Massachusetts Vice Admiralty Court and the Federal Admiralty Jurisdiction," *American J. of Legal History*, VI (1962), 265.

17. Crittenden, p. 8. In January, 1698, His Majesty's ship, *Swift Advice*, was deserted by all of her own crew in the Capes of Virginia and from there was driven by the wind and the sea and finally came to rest upon the sand banks of North Carolina. The inhabitants came and plundered her of what they could carry away (*North Carolina Historical and Genealogical Register*, III, 33–36).

18. *Graveyard of the Atlantic* (Chapel Hill: University of North Carolina Press, 1952).

19. *Ibid.*, pp. 5–8.

20. *Ibid.*, pp. 209–12; Carl Goerch, *Ocracoke* (Winston-Salem: John F. Blair, Publisher, 1958), pp. 80–84; Charles Harry Whedbee, *Legends of the Outer Banks* (Winston-Salem: John F. Blair, Publisher, 1966), pp. 121–34.

21. Johnson, p. 65.

22. Johnson, p. 49. To the same effect, Karraker, p. 151; Pringle, p. 199; Rankin, *Pirates of Colonial N.C.*, pp. 52–53; Williams, pp. 103–4.

23. Johnson, pp. 49–50; Williams, p. 104.

24. Jonathan Price, *A Description of Occacock Inlet*, a pamphlet originally published in New Bern, 1795, reprinted in *N.C. Historical Review*, III (1926), 624–33.

25. *Cal. State Papers*, XXX (Aug. 1717–Dec. 1718), sec. 800, p. 430; Spotswood, II, 274, 305.

26. Stick, *Outer Banks of North Carolina*, pp. 33–34, 299.

27. *Ibid.*, pp. 33–34, 299; Grimes, *North Carolina Wills*, p. 390.

28. See minutes of Council Journal, *N.C. Col. Rec.*, II, 296, 311, 500, 724, *passim.*

29. Stick, *Outer Banks of North Carolina*, p. 299.

30. Stick, *Graveyard of the Atlantic*, p. 4.

31. For references to Vane's visit with Blackbeard at Ocracoke Inlet, see Johnson, pp. 107–8; Brooke, p. 133; Carse, p. 241; Charles Ellams, ed. *Pirates Own Book* (Salem, Mass.: Marine Research Dept., 1924), p. 132.

32. Letter of Gov. Woodes Rogers to the Council of Trade and

Plantations, dated Oct. 31, 1718, printed in *Cal. State Papers*, XXX (Aug. 1717–Dec. 1718), sec. 737. For an account of Vane's daring exploit in the harbor of Nassau, see Johnson, pp. 112–13; MacLiesh and Krieger, p. 340; Craton, p. 103.

33. Johnson, pp. 113–16.

34. *Ibid.*, pp. 106–7.

35. *Ibid.*, pp. 67–84; Hughson, pp. 94–110; Snowden, pp. 173–82; McCrady, pp. 597–604; Wallace, pp. 227–31.

36. Johnson, p. 108.

37. *Ibid.*

38. Whipple, p. 189; Pringle, p. 202.

39. Johnson, p. 108.

40. *Ibid.*

41. *Ibid.*, pp. 108–10, 118; Craton, p. 103.

42. Johnson, p. 123.

43. *Ibid.*, pp. 118–41.

44. *Ibid.*, p. 140. For a thorough account of the life of Anne Bonny, see Johnson, pp. 125–41.

45. For an account of the life of Mary Read, see Johnson, pp. 130–41.

46. *The Tryals of Captain John Rackham and Other Pirates*, a pamphlet printed in Jamaica by Robert Baldwin, a printer, in 1721. The authenticity of this pamphlet is substantiated by the fact that Sir Nicholas Lawes, Governor of Jamaica, who presided at the Court of Admiralty, sent a copy of it to the Council of Trade and Plantations in lieu of an official report. For references to the capture and trial of Captain John Rackham, Anne Bonny, and Mary Read, see the letters of Governor Lawes addressed to the Council of Trade and Plantations, dated Nov. 13, 1720, June 12, 1721, and Aug. 28, 1721, which have been printed in *Cal. State Papers*, XXXII (Mar. 1720–Dec. 1721), secs. 288, 523i, 634iii.

47. *The Tryals of Captain John Rackham and Other Pirates.* The author has a photostatic copy of the proceedings in the trial of Anne Bonny and Mary Read, including the detailed testimony of the witnesses. This physical examination was pursuant to the ancient writ *de ventre inspiciendo*. See *Black's Law Dictionary* (4th ed., 1957).

48. Johnson, p. 136.

49. Johnson, p. 141.

CHAPTER 9

THE VIRGINIA TRIAL OF BLACKBEARD'S QUARTERMASTER

1. Governor Spotswood's letter, dated August 14, 1718, addressed to Council of Trade and Plantations, Spotswood, II, 286, at 294. Also printed in *Cal. State Papers*, XXX (Aug. 1717–Dec. 1718), sec. 657.

2. The proclamation can be found in *Executive Journals, Council of Colonial Virginia*, ed. H. R. McIlwaine (Richmond: Virginia State Library, 1928), III, 612.

3. Leonidas Dodson, *Alexander Spotswood* (Philadelphia: University of Pennsylvania Press, 1932), p. 3; Spotswood I, viii, ix; Richard L. Morton, *Colonial Virginia* (Chapel Hill: University of North Carolina Press, 1960), II, 409–18.

4. Dodson, pp. 304–5; Spotswood, I, viii; Percy Scott Flippin, *The Royal Government of Virginia* (New York: Columbia University Press, 1919), pp. 60–61.

5. Osgood, II, 216; Dodson, p. v.

6. Osgood, II, 229.

7. Dodson, p. 16.

8. William Best Hesseltine and David L. Smiley, *The South in American History* (Englewood Cliffs, N.J.: Prentice-Hall, 1960), p. 42.

9. That this was recommended by the Council of Trade and Plantations in a report to the King on September 8, 1721, see *Cal. State Papers*, XXXII (Mar. 1720–Dec. 1721), sec. 656; *N.C. Col. Rec.*, II, 419–20.

10. *N.C. Col. Rec.*, I, xxii, 628.

11. *Ibid.*, II, xv–xvi.

12. *Ibid.*, II, xvii–xviii.

13. Dodson, pp. 304–5; Spotswood, II, 333. Spotswood's annual salary of £2,000 sterling was fixed by par. 123 of his Royal Instructions, dated April 15, 1715 (Public Record Office, London, Colonial Office 5: 190, pp. 128–76, a copy of which may be found in the Manuscript Division, Library of Congress).

14. Dodson, pp. 281–92; Morton, pp. 422, 482. Paragraph 78 of Spotswood's Royal Instructions, dated April 15, 1715, expressly stated there were to be no further exemptions of quitrent payments for the first seven years and that any previously issued should be

"taken to be void and of none effect" (Public Record Office, London, Colonial Office 5: 190, pp. 128–76).

15. Dodson, p. 278, n. 3; Spotswood, II, 217.

16. Spotswood, II, 220.

17. Flippin, p. 120.

18. Hugh Jones, *The Present State of Virginia* (Richmond: Virginia State Library, 1912), p. 238. See also Ashe, pp. 141–46; Hawks, pp. 492–96.

19. Spotswood, II, 284.

20. Phillip Alexander Bruce, *History of Virginia* (Chicago and New York: American Historical Society, 1924), I, 301.

21. Letter of Governor Spotswood, dated December 22, 1718, addressed to Council of Trade and Plantations, *Cal. State Papers*, XXX (Aug. 1717–Dec. 1718), sec. 800; letter of Governor Spotswood, dated July 28, 1721, addressed to Secretary Craggs, Spotswood, II, 351–54. See also Williams, pp. 77–82.

22. Letter of Governor Spotswood, dated December 22, 1718, addressed to Council of Trade and Plantations, *Cal. State Papers*, XXX (Aug. 1717–Dec. 1718), sec. 800; letter of Governor Spotswood, dated July 28, 1721, addressed to Secretary Craggs, Spotswood, II, 351–54.

23. *Cal. State Papers*, XXX (Aug. 1717–Dec. 1718), secs. 215, 403–5, 449, 471, 614, 648, 669iii, 703, 713.

24. *Ibid.*, p. xviii.

25. For a brief account of John Holloway, see Spotswood, II, 57 ftn.; Morton, II, 475, 486 ftn.; Tyler, *Williamsburg, the Old Colonial Capital*, p. 26.

26. Governor Eden's will is recorded in Will Book II, p. 299, Office of the Secretary of State, Raleigh, N.C. Also printed in Grimes, *North Carolina Wills*, pp. 176–77.

27. Letter of Governor Spotswood, dated December 22, 1718, addressed to Council of Trade and Plantations, *Cal. State Papers*, XXX (Aug. 1717–Dec. 1718), sec. 800; letter of Governor Spotswood, dated July 28, 1721, addressed to Secretary Craggs, Spotswood, II, 351–54. See also Pringle, p. 201; Williams, p. 78; letter of Captain Ellis Brand, commander of H.M. Ship, the *Lyme*, dated July 4, 1719, addressed to Josiah Burchett, the Secretary of Lords Commissioners of the Admiralty, Public Record Office, London, Treasury I, Vol. 223, folios 7, 7a (transcript of which may be found in N.C. Dept. of Archives and History, Raleigh).

28. See Spotswood's letter, dated December 22, 1718, *Cal. State Papers*, XXX (Aug. 1717–Dec. 1718), sec. 800.

29. *Ibid.*; Dodson, p. 217 ftn.; *Executive Journals, Council of Colonial Virginia*, III, 484.

30. Letter of Sir H. Penrice (Judge of Admiralty), dated August 16, 1718, *Cal. State Papers*, XXX (Aug. 1717–Dec. 1718), sec. 658; letter of Sir H. Penrice to Mr. Burchett, dated August 22, 1718, *ibid.*, XXX (Aug. 1717–Dec. 1718), sec. 669ii.

31. Williams, pp. 64–68.

32. Johnson, pp. 74–75; Howell, XV, 1231–302.

33. The original copy has been preserved by the Virginia State Library, where this writer examined it. Printed copies of it may be found in Williams, pp. 79–82; *Tyler's Quarterly Historical and Genealogical Magazine*, I (1920), 36–39; *Calendar Virginia State Papers, 1652–1781*, ed. William Palmer (Richmond: R. F. Walker, Supt. Public Printing, 1875), I, 196 (first 2 paragraphs only).

34. Williams, p. 78.

35. Letter of Governor Spotswood, dated July 28, 1721, addressed to Secretary Craggs, Spotswood, II, 351–54.

36. Flippin, p. 307.

37. Letter of Governor Spotswood, dated July 28, 1721, addressed to Secretary Craggs, Spotswood, II, 351–54.

38. See letter of Captain Ellis Brand, dated July 4, 1719, addressed to Josiah Burchett, the Secretary of Lords Commissioners of the Admiralty, Public Record Office, London, Treasury I, Vol. 223, folios 7, 7a (transcript of which may be found in N.C. Dept. of Archives and History, Raleigh).

39. *Cal. State Papers*, XXX (Aug. 1717–Dec. 1718), secs. 640, 642, 713, 800; Williams, p. 79; Johnson, p. 57.

Whether Howard returned to piracy we do not know. The chances are that he did not linger long in Virginia after receiving his pardon. According to British records, he gave testimony at the piracy trial of Dr. William Howell, held in Nassau on December 22, 1721, and his testimony was to the effect that Dr. Howell had been impressed by Captain Benjamin Hornigold as a surgeon four or five years previously and that the physician had steadfastly refused to accept any of the spoils of piracy. Respectable citizens of Nassau, where Dr. Howell had been a highly regarded official of the government for the past three years, similarly testified. Dr. Howell was acquitted of the piracy charges (Public Record Office, London, Colonial Office 23, Vol. I, Bahamas [1717–1725], pp. 192–97, a photostatic copy of which may be found in the Manuscript Division, Library of Congress).

CHAPTER 10
PREPARATIONS IN VIRGINIA FOR THE CAPTURE OF BLACKBEARD

1. Johnson, pp. 264–70; Hughson, pp. 116–23; McCrady, pp. 606–21: Snowden, pp. 180–81; Wallace, pp. 231–33; letter of Governor Johnson and Council of South Carolina to Council of Trade, dated December 12, 1718, printed in *Cal. State Papers*, XXX (Aug. 1717–Dec. 1718), sec. 787.

2. Letter of Governor Spotswood, dated October 22, 1718, addressed to Secretary Craggs, Spotswood, II, 305; letter of Governor Spotswood, dated December 22, 1718, addressed to Council of Trade and Plantations, *Cal. State Papers*, XXX (Aug. 1717–Dec. 1718), sec. 800, p. 430; Johnson, p. 50; Williams, p. 107.

Captain Ellis Brand, commander of the man-of-war *Lyme*, stationed in Virginia, on July 12, 1718, wrote as follows to the Lords of Admiralty: "I am to acquaint you for Your Lordship's information that on the 10 June or thereabouts a large pyrate ship of forty guns with three sloops in her company came upon the coast of North Carolina where they endeavored to goe in to a harbour, called Topsail Inlett, the ship stuck upon the bar at the entrance of the harbour and is lost, as is one of the sloops, the other two sloops being still in there possession with two hundred and 30 of the pyrats. They continue together, given out they design for Cureico and other of the Islands. When they first came on the coast there number consisted of three hundred and twentie, whites and Negroes, the rest having been to surrender, some to the governor of N. Carolina and several are come into Virginia. I am told by a man that left them, about seventeen days since that the two sloops are fallen out and it was expected they would engage each other if there disputes are not reconciled amongst them; I have enquired of severall people that are acquainted with the place they are in att, and they all agree they are not to be come att with a ship. I shall use my utmost endeavours to inform myself of them and what part of the coast, they most, cruise upon and if it is possible for me to destroy them notwithstanding they are soe much superior to me, in number as one hundred and thirtie men, I shall not fail of doing my endeavour" (unpublished manuscript, Admiralty 1/1472, Public Record Office, London).

3. Letter of Governor Spotswood, dated December 22, 1718, addressed to Council of Trade and Plantations, *Cal. State Papers*, XXX (Aug. 1717–Dec. 1718), sec. 800, p. 432; Morton, p. 461. See also Osgood, p. 248; Hughson, p. 78; Johnson, p. 52; Karraker, p. 153; Rankin, *Pirates of Colonial N.C.*, p. 54; Williams, p. 107.

4. *Cal. State Papers*, XXX (Aug. 1717–Dec. 1718), sec. 800, p. 431.

5. *N.C. Col. Rec.*, II, 319. Captain Ellis Brand, in a letter addressed to the Admiralty, dated February 6, 1718/1719, mentions that Colonel Moseley and Colonel Moore assisted him and his horses in crossing Albemarle Sound (unpublished manuscript, Admiralty 1/1472, Public Record Office, London).

6. Letter of Governor Spotswood, dated May 26, 1719, addressed to Lords of Trade, Spotswood, II, 324.

7. Letter of Governor Spotswood, dated May 26, 1719, addressed to Lords of Trade, Spotswood, II, 324. See also a similar letter of the same date addressed by Spotswood to Secretary Craggs, p. 317.

8. Johnson, p. 50; Rankin, *Pirates of Colonial N.C.*, p. 54; Pringle, p. 200; Whipple, p. 189. That Brand was captain of the *Lyme*, see letter of Governor Spotswood, dated May 26, 1719, addressed to Secretary Craggs, Spotswood, II, 317; letter of Captain Brand, dated February 6, 1718/1719, addressed to Admiralty, unpublished manuscript, Admiralty 1/1472, Public Record Office, London.

9. Dodson, p. 211.

10. Rankin, *Pirates of Colonial N.C.*, p. 55; Karraker, p. 153; Pringle, p. 203; letter of Thomas Pollock, dated December 8, 1718, addressed to Governor Eden, *N.C. Col. Rec.*, II, 319. A letter of Captain Brand, dated February 6, 1718/1719, addressed to Admiralty (unpublished manuscript, Admiralty 1/1472, Public Record Office, London), tells of the plans that he, Governor Spotswood, and Captain Gordon made for the capture of Blackbeard. Since July, Brand had been employing persons to go to North Carolina and bring back information to him about Blackbeard. Incidents and events of his travel overland into North Carolina are set forth in this

letter. As a confirmation of the fact that Captain Brand went into North Carolina by land, see letter of Captain George Gordon, addressed to the British Admiralty, dated September 14, 1721 (unpublished manuscript, Admiralty 1/1826, Public Record Office, London).

11. Johnson, p. 50; Karraker, p. 153; Williams, p. 107; abstract of letter of Lieutenant Maynard, dated December 17, 1718, addressed to Lieutenant Symonds, from *The Weekly Journal or British Gazetteer*, April 25, 1719, reprinted in Arthur L. Cooke, "British Newspaper Accounts of Blackbeard's Death," *Virginia Magazine of History and Biography*, LXI (July, 1953), 306. The letter can be found in Appendix A of this work.

12. Johnson, p. 50; Williams, pp. 107–8; Governor Spotswood's letter dated December 28, 1718, addressed to Council of Trade and Plantations, *Cal. State Papers*, XXX (Aug. 1717–Dec. 1718), sec. 800, p. 431; letter of Lieutenant Maynard, dated December 17, 1718, addressed to Lieutenant Symonds, in Appendix A of this work.

13. Governor Spotswood's letter, dated October 22, 1718 (obviously misdated), addressed to Secretary Craggs, Spotswood, II, 306; written message of Governor Spotswood to House of Burgesses on November 13, 1718, *Journals of the House of Burgesses of Virginia, 1718*, ed. H. R. McIlwaine (Richmond: Virginia State Library, 1912), 223–24.

14. Johnson, p. 55. It was not unusual for members of the Royal Navy to desert their ship and to join the crew of a pirate vessel. Captain Vincent Pearse, commander of the man-of-war *Phenix*, stationed in New York, in a letter addressed to the Lords of Admiralty, and dated June 3, 1718, tells of three members of his own crew who deserted and became associated with Charles Vane, the notorious pirate captain (unpublished manuscript, Admiralty 1/2282, Public Record Office, London).

15. *Journals of the House of Burgesses of Virginia, 1718*, pp. 224–28, 233.

16. *Ibid.*, pp. 228, 230, 231; Morton, pp. 458–60; Dodson, pp. 183–88.

17. Morton, p. 481.

18. Johnson, pp. 51–52; Whipple, pp. 189–90; Williams, pp. 113–15; Snow, pp. 260–61.

19. Letter of Captain Brand, dated February 6, 1718/1719, addressed to Admiralty, unpublished manuscript, Admiralty 1/1472, Public Record Office, London; Johnson, p. 52; Karraker, p. 153; Williams, p. 108. Kecoughtan is an Indian name sometimes spelled "Kicquotan" or "Kicquetan."

20. Letter of Captain Brand, dated Feb. 6, 1718/1719, addressed to Admiralty, unpublished manuscript, Admiralty 1/1472, Public Record Office, London.

21. Rankin, *Pirates of Colonial N.C.*, p. 55; Karraker, p. 153; Pringle, p. 203; letter of Thomas Pollock, dated December 8, 1718, addressed to Governor Eden, *N.C. Col. Rec.*, II, 319.

22. Letter of Captain Brand, dated Feb. 6, 1718/1719, addressed to Admiralty, unpublished manuscript, Admiralty 1/1472, Public Record Office, London.

23. *Ibid.*; letter of Captain Brand, dated March 12, 1718/1719, addressed to Admiralty, unpublished manuscript, Admiralty 1/1472, Public Record Office, London.

24. Letter of Governor Spotswood, dated November 7, 1718, addressed to Governor Eden, unpublished manuscript, Lee–Ludwell Papers, Archives of the Virginia Historical Society, Richmond, Va. See letter of Tobias Knight, dated November 17, 1718, found in the possession of Blackbeard, which has been set forth in Chapter 14 of this work, "Trial of Tobias Knight"; it states that Governor Eden was expected in Bath that night or the following day. A letter of Captain Brand, dated March 12, 1718/1719, addressed to Admiralty (unpublished manuscript, Admiralty 1/1472, Public Record Office, London), states that when Brand returned to Virginia, Governor Eden accompanied him to the next county (which was, of course, Albemarle County, wherein he had built his "Eden House").

25. Letter of Captain Brand, dated February 6, 1718/1719, addressed to Admiralty, unpublished manuscript, Admiralty 1/1472, Public Record Office, London.

CHAPTER 11
BATTLE OF OCRACOKE INLET

1. Johnson, p. 52; letter of Governor Spotswood, dated December 22, 1718, addressed to Council of Trade and Plantations, *Cal.*

State Papers, XXX (Aug. 1717–Dec. 1718), sec. 800, p. 431 (further references in this chapter will be to letter of Governor Spotswood, dated December 22, 1718); abstract of letter of Lieutenant Maynard, dated December 17, 1718, addressed to Lieutenant Symonds, from *The Weekly Journal or British Gazetteer*, April 25, 1719, reprinted in Arthur L. Cooke, "British Newspaper Accounts of Blackbeard's Death," *Virginia Magazine of History and Biography*, LXI (July, 1953), 306. The letter can also be found in Appendix A of this work (further references in this chapter will be to letter of Lieutenant Maynard, dated December 17, 1718). Letter of Captain Ellis Brand, dated February 6, 1718/1719, addressed to the Admiralty, unpublished manuscript, Admiralty 1/1472, Public Record Office, London (further references in this chapter will be to letter of Captain Brand, dated February 6, 1718/1719).

2. Johnson, p. 56; letter of Captain Ellis Brand, dated February 6, 1718/1719.

3. Johnson, p. 52.

4. Letter of Governor Spotswood, dated December 22, 1718. To the same effect, letter of Governor Spotswood, dated February 14, 1718/1719, addressed to Lord Cartwright (Carteret), *N.C. Col. Rec.*, II, 325 (further references in this chapter will be to letter of Governor Spotswood, dated February 14, 1718/1719).

The letter of Lieutenant Maynard, dated December 17, 1718, avers that Blackbeard "had on board twenty-one men." This number could have included Samuel Odell and three other visitors from a trading sloop, who had spent the preceding night at a drinking party aboard the *Adventure* (Johnson, p. 53). Captain Ellis Brand, reporting the battle to the British Admiralty, stated that "the Pyrate had nineteen men, thirteen white and six Negros" (letter of Captain Ellis Brand, dated February 6, 1718/1719). Later writers have also disagreed as to the number of Teach's crew. Williamson, p. 7, says that Teach had only seventeen men with him. Ashe, p. 201, says that Teach had a crew of eighteen men. Lefler and Newsome, p. 64, say that Teach had a crew of eighteen. Hughson, p. 77, states that Teach had "not more than twenty men."

5. Letter of Captain Ellis Brand, addressed to the Admiralty, dated February 6, 1718/1719.

6. This letter may be found in Chapter 14, "Trial of Tobias Knight," at p. 146.

7. Woodbury, p. 95.

8. Whipple, p. 205.

9. Johnson, pp. 53, 55–56; Karraker, p. 154; Rankin, *Pirates of Colonial N.C.*, p. 55; Williams, p. 108.

10. Johnson, p. 53; Ashe, p. 200; letter of Governor Spotswood, dated December 22, 1718; letter of Lieutenant Maynard, dated December 17, 1718.

11. Rankin, *Pirates of Colonial N.C.*, p. 55. See also Williams, p. 109; Johnson, p. 53.

12. Johnson, pp. 54–55, mentions by name only the *Ranger*, and indicates that Maynard was not on board that vessel. Since Lieutenant Maynard, in his letter, dated December 17, 1718, states that Hyde was in command of the "little Sloop with 22 Men, and I had 32 in my Sloop," it follows that the *Ranger* was the smaller of the two sloops.

13. Letter of Lieutenant Maynard, dated December, 1718; Johnson, p. 50; Karraker, p. 153; Williams, p. 107.

14. Letter of Captain George Gordon, dated September 17, 1721, addressed to the Admiralty, unpublished manuscript, Admiralty 1/1826, Public Record Office, London (further references in this chapter will be to letter of Captain Gordon, dated September 14, 1721).

15. Letter of Captain Ellis Brand, dated February 6, 1718/1719. And, of course, there were the employed pilots.

16. Donald Barr Chidsey, *The American Privateers* (New York: Dodd, 1962), p. 36.

17. *The History of the Most Noted Pirates* (New York: Empire State Book Co., 1926), p. 62.

18. Whipple, p. 199.

19. Johnson, p. 53; Rankin, *Golden Age of Piracy*, p. 120; *id.*, *Pirates of Colonial N.C.*, pp. 54–55; Hayward, pp. 73–74.

20. Spotswood, in a letter dated December 22, 1718, and a number of others have stated that Blackbeard's *Adventure* carried eight mounted guns. The letter of Lieutenant Maynard, dated December 17, 1718, states that there were nine mounted. Newspaper accounts in the *Boston News-Letter*, which are set forth in Appendix

A of this work, stated that Blackbeard had ten great guns. It is strange that Maynard should have said there were nine mounted guns. Vessels generally carried, for purpose of balancing the craft, an even, rather than an odd, number of mounted cannons.

21. Johnson, p. 53. The letter of Governor Spotswood, dated December 22, 1718, states that this broadside "killed and wounded twenty of the King's men." The letter of Lieutenant Maynard, dated December 17, 1718, states that he "had 20 Men killed and wounded"; the letter of Captain Gordon, dated September 14, 1721, states that this broadside killed and wounded twenty-one men.

22. Rankin, *Pirates of Colonial N.C.*, p. 56; Pringle, p. 203; Whipple, p. 201; letter of Lieutenant Maynard, dated December 17, 1718; letter of Captain Brand, dated February 6, 1718/1719; letter of Captain Gordon, dated September 14, 1721.

23. Letter of Captain Gordon, dated September 14, 1721.

24. *Ibid.*; letter of Lieutenant Maynard, dated December 17, 1718. According to Johnson, fourteen of Blackbeard's men entered Maynard's sloop (p. 54).

25. Johnson, p. 54.

26. *Ibid.*

27. *Ibid.*, pp. 54–55.

28. *Ibid.*, p. 54; letter of Lieutenant Maynard, dated December 17, 1718; Rankin, *Pirates of Colonial N.C.*, p. 58; Williams, p. 111.

29. Johnson, p. 55.

30. *Ibid.*

31. Letter of Captain Gordon, dated September 17, 1721.

32. Johnson, p. 55; letter of Lieutenant Maynard, dated December 17, 1718.

33. Letter of Captain Gordon, dated September 14, 1721.

34. Johnson, p. 55.

35. See *N.C. Col. Rec.*, II, 341–49. See generally, Johnson, pp. 55–56.

36. Johnson, pp. 53, 59. See, in this connection, comment of Williams, p. 117.

37. Letter of Governor Spotswood, dated December 22, 1718. This letter was written before the return of Lieutenant Maynard and his crew to Virginia. In the subsequent letter, dated February 14, 1718/1719, Governor Spotswood listed the casualties as "being

no less than 12 killed and 22 wounded of the King's Men." It is apparent that during this interval of time another of the wounded men aboard the King's vessels had died.

38. Letter of Lieutenant Maynard, dated December 17, 1718. Since Maynard mentioned that Hyde, who commanded the smaller sloop, was killed and that five of Hyde's men were wounded, these casualties could have been in addition to his statement "I had eight Men killed and 18 wounded." And, of course, some of the wounded could have subsequently died of their wounds.

39. Letter of Captain Brand, dated February 6, 1718/1719.

40. Letter of Governor Spotswood, dated February 14, 1718/1719.

41. Letter of Captain Gordon, dated September 14, 1721.

42. Johnson, p. 59.

43. Johnson, pp. 55–56; letter of Lieutenant Maynard, dated December 17, 1718; Pringle, p. 203; Williams, p. 111; Whipple, pp. 210–11; Alice K. Rondthaler, *The Story of Ocracoke* (Ocracoke, 1966), p. 3, a pamphlet sold to tourists in the Town of Ocracoke.

44. Johnson, p. 56; Rankin, *Pirates of Colonial N.C.*, p. 60; letter of Lieutenant Maynard, dated December 17, 1718; newspaper accounts in *Boston News-Letter*, which are set forth in Appendix A of this work; Campbell, p. 108; Order of Privy Council, unpublished manuscript, Privy Council Register 2/87, page 293, Public Record Office, London.

45. Watson, II, 221; Squires, pp. 58–59; William H. Gaines, Jr., "Pursuit of a Pirate—How an Expedition from Virginia Tracked Down the Notorious Blackbeard," *Virginia Cavalcade*, II, No. 2 (Autumn, 1952), 16; Campbell, p. 108; Williams, p. 113. J. E. Davis, *Round About Jamestown* (Hampton, Va., 1907), p. 49.

On April 11, 1719, there appeared accounts in two London newspapers, which are set forth in Appendix A of this work, stating that Blackbeard's head had been fixed on a pole near the harbor's mouth.

46. Watson, II, 221. See also Haywood, p. 16; John Esten Cooke, *Virginia: A History of the People* (New York: Houghton, Mifflin and Co., 1911), p. 307. The skull cannot be found in Virginia at the present time. A well-known New England writer on pirates and a collector of pirate memorabilia has a skull reputedly that of Blackbeard. It has been offered for sale to persons in Vir-

ginia and North Carolina; but because of insufficient existing proof
of its authenticity, the offers have been rejected.

47. Johnson, p. 55; Williams, p. 112.

48. Letter of Captain Gordon, dated September 14, 1721.

49. Johnson, p. 59. According to the letter of Captain Brand,
dated February 6, 1718/1719, Maynard and his men "found at a
tent on shore about one hundred and forty baggs of cocoa and ten
cask of sugar which were belonging to Thach." The letter of Captain Gordon, dated September 14, 1721, mentions goods of Blackbeard found by Maynard in a tent on Ocracoke Island.

Johnson states that sixty hogsheads of sugar were seized in the
storehouse of Governor Eden and twenty hogsheads of sugar from
Knight (p. 56). The letter of Captain Brand, dated February 6,
1718/1719, tells of some sugar he found in or around Bath Town
which he believed to be the effects of Teach. See also the testimony
given at the trial of Tobias Knight, *N.C. Col. Rec.*, II, 344, 346.

50. Letter of Governor Spotswood, dated May 26, 1719, addressed to Lords of Trade, Spotswood, II, 324. See also a similar
letter of Spotswood, of the same date, addressed to Secretary Craggs,
Spotswood, II, 317. Maynard informed the Privy Council that
Blackbeard's "sloop and cargo was sold for above two thousand five
hundred pounds" (unpublished manuscript, Privy Council Register,
2/87, page 293, Public Record Office, London).

51. Johnson, p. 56; Rankin, *Colonial Pirates of N.C.*, pp. 60–61;
Pringle, p. 204; Williams, pp. 114, 117; letter of Captain Brand,
dated February 6, 1718/1719.

52. Letter of Lieutenant Maynard, dated December 17, 1718.
Spotswood's letter, dated December 22, 1718, stated: "I also expect
from North Carolina a considerable quantity of sugar and cocoa,
wch. were in the possession of Tach and his crew."

53. Spotswood's letter, dated December 21, 1718, addressed to
Governor Eden, stated: "I have no news from Captain Brand since
he went from here, nor do I know any thing of the success of the
men of Warr sloops, further than the common report of their taking
Tache's sloop and killing himself" (unpublished manuscript, Lee–
Ludwell Papers, Archives of the Virginia Historical Society, Richmond, Va.).

54. *Cal. State Papers*, XXX (Aug. 1717–Dec. 1718), sec. 800.

CHAPTER 12

DISPUTE OVER JURISDICTION

1. In a letter written by Knight from Bath, dated November 17, 1718, and addressed to Captain Teach, Knight stated that he was expecting Governor Eden to arrive the following day (*N.C. Col. Rec.*, II, 343–44). See also letter of Captain Ellis Brand, dated March 12, 1718/1719, addressed to the British Admiralty, unpublished manuscript, Admiralty 1/1472, Public Record Office, London.

2. Colonel Thomas Pollock, an attorney, once the wealthiest man of the colony, owned land throughout the province. It is said that he owned one plantation of 40,000 acres and nearly a hundred slaves. Pollock's home was on the west side of the Chowan River at the mouth of the Salmon River and was called "Ball-Gra" (sometimes spelled "Balgroy"), which was the name of the home of his father, Thomas Pollock, in Scotland. When Edward Hyde, cousin of Queen Anne, arrived as Governor in 1710, he accepted the hospitality of the homes of Pollock and others in the community. The first Assembly called by Governor Hyde met in Pollock's home. Pollock was buried at his beloved Ball-Gra, but at some time during the 1800's his remains were exhumed and placed in the cemetery of St. Paul's Church in Edenton. He was born on May 6, 1654, and died on August 30, 1722. Despite many descendants, there are none now who bear his name ("Thomas Pollock," *Biographical History of North Carolina*, I, 411–12; *The Chronicle of the Bertie County Historical Association*, No. 2 [October, 1953], p. 4; John E. Tyler, "Governor Pollock and Ball-Gra," in "Bertie County's Colonial and State Governors of North Carolina" [typed manuscript in N.C. Dept. of Archives and History, 1949]. For family references, see *N.C. Col. Rec.*, II, 217, 241, 276–78. For some idea of Pollock's landholdings and other wealth, see his will printed in Grimes, *North Carolina Wills*, pp. 342–47).

3. *N.C. Col. Rec.*, II, 318–20.

4. Public Record Office, London, Colonial Office, Class 5, Vol. 190, beginning p. 116 (Plantations 1714 to 1716), copy of which is in Manuscript Division, Library of Congress.

5. *Ibid.*, pp. 128–76, 280.

6. Reprinted in *Virginia Magazine of History and Biography*, XXII (1914), 414–15.

7. Letters of Governor Spotswood to Secretary Craggs and Lords of Trade, both dated May 26, 1719, printed in Spotswood, II, 316–26 and *N.C. Col. Rec.*, II, 333–40. See also letter of Captain Ellis Brand, dated March 12, 1718/1719, addressed to the British Admiralty, unpublished manuscript, Admiralty 1/1472, Public Record Office, London.

8. Letter of Governor Spotswood to Lord Cartwright (Carteret), dated Feb. 14, 1718/1719, Spotswood, II, 272–75.

9. *Ibid.*

10. The letters of Governor Spotswood, addressed to Governor Eden, dated November 7, 1718, December 21, 1718, and January 28, 1718/1719, may be found in the Lee–Ludwell Papers, in manuscript form, in the Archives of the Virginia Historical Society. Photostatic copies are in the possession of the writer.

11. Letter of Governor Spotswood, dated January 28, 1718/1719, addressed to Governor Eden, unpublished manuscript, Lee–Ludwell Papers, Archives of Virginia Historical Society.

12. See letter of Governor Edmund Andros to Council of Trade and Plantations, dated March 14, 1698, *Cal. State Papers*, XVI (Oct. 1697–Dec. 1698), sec. 291; *William and Mary College Quarterly* (1st series), V (1896), 129.

13. Letter of Governor Spotswood, dated January 28, 1718/1719, addressed to Governor Eden, unpublished manuscript, Lee–Ludwell Papers, Archives of Virginia Historical Society.

14. Proclamation can be found in Appendix D of this work.

15. *Ibid.*

16. *N.C. Col. Rec.*, II, 318–20.

CHAPTER 13

The Virginia Trial of the Captured Pirates

1. *Colonial Williamsburg: Official Guidebook* (Williamsburg, 1965), p. 74.

2. *Executive Journal of the Council of Colonial Virginia*, III, 496; also printed in *N.C. Col. Rec.*, II, 327.

3. *N.C. Col. Rec.*, II, 341.

4. The writer personally made trips to Williamsburg and Richmond in 1966, seeking these court records, but to no avail. He was informed by archivists and researchers in both places that the records of both the Vice-Admiralty Court and the General Court of this period had become lost by fire.

"The great mass of the records of the General Court of Virginia, both for the colonial period and a later period, was destroyed by the burning of the State court building in the southeastern corner of the capitol square on the night of April 2/3, 1865, when Richmond was evacuated by the troops of the Southern Confederacy" (*Minutes of the Council and General Court of Colonial Virginia, 1622–1632, 1670–1676*, ed. H. R. McIlwaine [Richmond, 1927], I, Preface).

The original Capitol in Williamsburg was gutted by fire in 1747 and the reconstructed second Capitol was destroyed by fire in 1832.

5. *N.C. Col. Rec.*, II, 328, 341–49.

6. Governor Spotswood probably presided at the Court of Vice-Admiralty that tried the pirate prisoners under a special commission. The General Court, which was the highest court in Virginia, was composed of the members of the Governor's Council, any five of whom formed a quorum, with the Governor as the presiding officer (Hugh F. Rankin, *Criminal Trial Proceedings in the General Court of Colonial Virginia* [Williamsburg: University Press of Virginia, 1965], pp. 48, 52). A recent writer on the colonial courts of Virginia has stated: "A court of vice-admiralty was composed of seven persons, one of whom, the presiding officer, was to be the governor, the lieutenant-governor, or a member of the Council; the remaining six to be selected from among merchants, planters, military or naval officers, or officers serving aboard merchant vessels" (*ibid.*, pp. 218–19). It would have been wholly unlike Spotswood to yield the presidency of the commissioners to another in this very special case.

7. Johnson, in his text, at p. 56, states that there were taken to Virginia "fifteen prisoners, thirteen of whom were hanged." Samuel Odell was acquitted and Israel Hands was later pardoned. On p. 59, Johnson lists the names of those hanged, as follows: John Carnes; Joseph Brooks, Jr.; James Blake; John Gills; Thomas Gates; James White; Richard Stiles; Caesar; Joseph Philips; James Robbens; John Martin; Edward Salter; Stephen Daniel; and Richard Greensail. Since there are fourteen names on this list, Williams, at p. 117,

has suggested that Johnson probably erroneously placed on the list of those hanged at Williamsburg the name of one of the pirates killed at Ocracoke. Both lists appear on the same page of Johnson's book.

8. Johnson, pp. 56, 59; Williams, p. 115.

9. Johnson, p. 57. To the same effect, Williams, p. 115. *Cf.* Minutes of Executive Council, dated May 28, 1719, *Executive Journal of the Council of Colonial Virginia*, III, 506.

10. Gaines, p. 16; Williams, p. 115.

11. Rankin, *Criminal Trial Proceedings in the General Court of Colonial Virginia*, pp. 116–17.

12. Letter of Governor Spotswood, dated May 20, 1720, addressed to the Board of Trade, Spotswood, II, 338; *Executive Journal of the Council of Colonial Virginia*, III, 521–22; Williams, p. 122; Jones, p. 269.

13. *Executive Journal of the Council of Virginia*, III, 489–90, 522; Dodson, p. 218.

Henry Irvin petitioned the Governor and the Virginia Council for £20 in current money to reimburse him for two horses supplied to the Governor and used for transporting William Bell and his son, of Currituck Precinct, North Carolina, who gave evidence against the prisoners (*Calendar Virginia State Papers*, I, 200; Jones, p. 242).

14. Letter of Governor Spotswood, dated May 26, 1719, addressed to Secretary Craggs, Spotswood, pp. 316–23; letter of Governor Spotswood, dated May 26, 1719, addressed to Lords of Trade, *ibid.*, pp. 324–26. Both letters can also be found in *N.C. Col. Rec.*, II, 333–38. To the effect that Lieutenant Maynard had filed a petition with the King's Privy Council stating that Blackbeard's "sloop and cargo were sold for above two thousand five hundred pounds," see Privy Council Register 2/87, page 293 (unpublished manuscript, Public Record Office, London).

15. Spotswood's proclamation can be found in Johnson, pp. 51–52; Williams, pp. 113–15. Concerning the payment of the rewards, see Johnson, p. 59; Pringle, p. 206; Williams, p. 117.

16. "Teach, Edward," *Dictionary of National Biography*, 1922, XIX, 481–82.

17. Johnson, p. 59; Pringle, p. 206; Williams, p. 117.

18. Order of Privy Council, dated August 24, 1721, unpub-

lished manuscript, Privy Council Register 2/87, page 293, Public Record Office, London.

19. Letter of Captain George Gordon, dated September 14, 1721, addressed to Lords Commissioners of Admiralty, unpublished manuscript, Admiralty 1/1826, Public Record Office, London.

20. *Ibid.*

21. *Ibid.*

22. "Blackbeard," *Encyclopedia of Virginia Biography*, ed. Lyon Gardiner Tyler (New York: Lewis Historical Publishing Co., 1915), I, 186–87.

23. If a person during the first half of the eighteenth century obtained the rank of captain in the Royal Navy, he was nearly always promoted to the rank of rear-admiral, on seniority. Beginning with 1718, the Royal Navy published an official seniority list, ranking captains, commanders, and lieutenants according to the dates of their first commission in those ranks. Ellis Brand is listed as having been made captain in 1715 and a "superannuated rear-admiral in 1747." The name Maynard does not appear on a list that excluded all persons who had died before their positions on the list entered "the promotional zone" (Daniel C. Baugh, *British Naval Administration in the Age of Walpole* [Princeton, N.J.: Princeton University Press, 1965], pp. 130–33).

24. Johnson, pp. 64–66. Since the members of the Eden family were influential in England, it is possible, and even probable, that they pressured Charles Johnson to change his evaluation of Governor Eden.

CHAPTER 14
TRIAL OF TOBIAS KNIGHT

1. Council Journal, April 4, 1719, *N.C. Col. Rec.*, II, pp. 329–30.

2. *Ibid.*

3. All information and quotations concerning Knight's Trial are from the Council Journal, May 27, 1719 (*N.C. Col. Rec.*, II, 341–49).

4. John H. Russell, *The Free Negro in Virginia, 1619–1865* (Baltimore: Johns Hopkins Press, 1913), p. 117.

See also John Spencer Bassett, *Slavery and Servitude in the Colony of North Carolina* (Baltimore: Johns Hopkins Press, 1896), p. 29; John Hope Franklin, *The Free Negro in North Carolina* (Chapel Hill: University of North Carolina Press, 1943), p. 82; Rankin, *Criminal Trial Proceedings in the General Court of Colonial Virginia*, p. 98; George M. Stroud, *A Sketch of the Laws Relating to Slavery* (Philadelphia: H. Longstreth, 1856), p. 44.

5. Laws of North Carolina, 1746 (second session), ch. 2, sec. 50, *N.C. State Rec.*, XXIII, 262.

6. Laws of North Carolina, 1762, ch. 1, sec. 45, *N.C. State Rec.*, XXIII, 559; Laws of North Carolina, 1773, ch. 1, sec. 42, *N.C. State Rec.*, XXIII, 882; Laws of North Carolina, 1777, ch. 2, sec. 42, *N.C. State Rec.*, XXIV, 61 (changed to fourth generation). See also Bassett, *Slavery and Servitude*, p. 29.

7. See Stroud, p. 45; Russell, p. 117.

8. Bassett, *Slavery and Servitude*, p. 30.

9. Haywood, p. 7; Minutes of Board of the Lords Proprietors of Carolina, dated July 31, 1719, *N.C. Col. Rec.*, II, 350; *cf* Johnson, p. 66.

10. Minutes of Council Journal, August 1, 1717, *N.C. Col. Rec.*, II, 291 and *passim*.

11. Karraker, p. 163; Treasury I, Vol. CCXXIII, folios 7, 7a, and Vol. CCXXXVI, folio 92, transcripts of which may be found in the Dept. of Archives and History, Raleigh, N.C.

12. *Executive Journal of the Council of Colonial Virginia*, III, 466–67.

13. As to Fitzwilliam's appointment as Surveyor General, see *Calendar of Treasury Books and Papers*, I (1729–1730), 470–71; as to his appointment as Governor of the Bahama Islands, *ibid.*, II (1898), 489, 632, 657, 677.

14. Boyd, p. 15.

CHAPTER 15
Aftermath in North Carolina

1. Letter from Colonel Thomas Pollock to the Governor of South Carolina, dated February 20, 1712/1713, *N.C. Col. Rec.*, II, 20; Hawks, p. 415. See also Hugh T. Lefler, *History of North Carolina*

(New York: Lewis Historical Publishing Co., 1956), I, 66; Ashe, pp. 166–78; Connor, pp. 94–99; Hawks, p. 556. For an interesting account of Cary's Rebellion, see Reed, pp. 59–64.

2. Ashe, p. 166.

3. Reed, pp. 58–60.

4. Connor, p. 94.

5. For Moseley's will, see Grimes, *North Carolina Wills*, pp. 313–19.

6. Ashe, p. 162; Reed, p. 35; *N.C. Historical and Genealogical Register*, III (April, 1903), p. 258.

7. Ashe, pp. 53, 158, 162; Reed, p. 35. For tombstone record of Henderson Walker, see John H. Wheeler, *Historical Sketches of North Carolina from 1584 to 1854* (Philadelphia: Columbus Printing Works, 1851), p. 34.

8. Ann died on November 18, 1712, at the age of 55 years and 5 months. Wheeler, *Historical Sketches*, p. 34; Spotswood, p. 72.

9. *N.C. Historical and Genealogical Register*, I (January, 1900), 58. See also Reed, p. 35.

10. For copy of Moseley's will, see Grimes, *North Carolina Wills*, pp. 313–19. He gave a small remembrance in his will to "my mother-in-law Mrs. Susannah Hasell" (*ibid.*, p. 316).

11. *Ibid.*

12. Blackwell P. Robinson, ed., *North Carolina Guide* (Chapel Hill: University of North Carolina Press, 1955), pp. 177–79.

13. Reed, pp. 35, 87, 152.

14. Grimes, *North Carolina Wills*, p. 314.

15. *Ibid.*

16. As to Maurice Moore generally, see "Maurice Moore," *Biographical History of North Carolina*, II, 293–98; Lawrence Lee, *The Lower Cape Fear in Colonial Days* (Chapel Hill: University of North Carolina Press, 1965), pp. 91–92; and the indices to Ashe, Connor, Lefler, and *N.C. Col. Rec.*

17. Indictment of Moseley and others, General Court Records, dated July 28, 1719; *N.C. Col. Rec.*, II, 359–60; Minutes of Council Journal, dated December 30, 1718, *N.C. Col. Rec.*, II, 321–22.

18. *N.C. Col. Rec.*, II, 359–60. See also *ibid.*, II, 321–22.

19. McCrady, pp. 654–55; Snowden, I, 186.

20. Minutes of Council Journal, Dec. 30, 1718, *N.C. Col. Rec.*, II, 321–22.

21. General Court Records, July 31, 1719, *N.C. Col. Rec.*, II, 361–62.

22. Minutes of Council Journal, April 3, 1719, *N.C. Col. Rec.*, II, 329–30.

23. General Court Records, July 28, 1719–July 31, 1719, *N.C. Col. Rec.*, II, 357–63.

Colonel Thomas Pollock, twice Acting Governor of North Carolina, sat almost continuously in the Council from the time of his arrival in the colony in 1683 until the time of his death on August 30, 1722. His son, Thomas Pollock, Jr., during the latter days of the Colonel's life, was a justice on the General Court. Subsequent to his father's death, the son became a member of the Council and later Chief Justice of North Carolina. Colonial records did not always record the suffix "Jr." to his name. The son was undoubtedly the one attending the session of the General Court from July 28 to August 1, 1719, though there was no "Jr." attached to his name in the minutes of the General Court, as there was at the next session of the General Court held from October 29 through November 3, 1719.

24. *Ibid.*

25. *Ibid.*

26. N.C. Laws of 1715, ch. xxxi, *N.C. State Rec.*, XXIII, 39–40. See also minutes of Council Journal, Dec. 30, 1718, *N.C. Col. Rec.*, II, 321.

27. Connor, I, 129.

28. General Court Records, July 28, 1719–July 31, 1719, *N.C. Col. Rec.*, II, 357–63.

29. General Court Records, October 29, 1719–November 3, 1719, *N.C. Col. Rec.*, II, 364–69.

30. *Ibid.*

31. *Ibid.*

32. Minutes of Council Journal, November 10, 1719, *N.C. Col. Rec.*, II, 351; minutes of Council Journal, April 4, 1720, *N.C. Col. Rec.*, II, 379, 380.

33. Minutes of Council Journal, November 21, 1723, *N.C. Col. Rec.*, II, 503–4.

34. Ashe, on pp. 53–54, lists Moseley as speaker of the Assembly in 1708, 1715, 1722, and 1731; and on pp. 237 and 246, he states that Moseley was chosen the speaker during the 1733 and 1734 sessions, but that no statutes were passed during these latter

two years. D. H. Hill, "Edward Moseley: Character Sketch," *N.C. Booklets*, V, No. 3 (January, 1906), 205, and *N.C. Col. Rec.*, III, 361, state that Moseley was chosen speaker of the Assembly "five or six times."

Regarding Moseley's serving as Surveyor General, see minutes of Council Journal, November 16, 1723, *N.C. Col. Rec.*, II, 503; as member of the Council, minutes of Council Journal, January 15, 1723/1724, *N.C. Col. Rec.*, II, 515; as judge of the Vice-Admiralty Court, minutes of Council Journal, April 2, 1724, *N.C. Col. Rec.*, II, 520. Moseley resigned from the Vice-Admiralty Court on November 7, 1724, and William Maule was appointed in his place (*ibid.*, p. 542). Ashe, pp. 54, 260, 276, mentions Moseley as Chief Justice.

Moseley's will was probated in August, 1749 (Grimes, *North Carolina Wills*, pp. 313–19).

Concerning commissioners for N.C.–Va. boundary, see Hawks, pp. 94, 96–97; *N.C. Col. Rec.*, II, 724, 735–44. For N.C.–S.C. boundary, see Marvin L. Skaggs, *North Carolina Disputes Involving Her Southern Line* (Chapel Hill: University of North Carolina Press, 1941), pp. 43, 46; *N.C. Col. Rec.*, V, 375; *ibid.*, VI, 793.

CHAPTER 16

THE END OF PIRACY

1. Jones, pp. 268–69.

2. *Ibid.*; Dodson, pp. 219–21; *Journals of the House of Burgesses of Virginia, 1712–1726*, pp. 310–13; Williams, p. 122.

3. Blackstone, IV, 71–73.

4. Johnson, p. 58.

5. Watson, I, 271; *ibid.*, II, 223.

There is located near Wilmington, N.C., a beautiful islet of several acres called "Money Island." It is situated about one mile southwest of Wrightsville Beach, about eight miles east of Wilmington, in the waters of a sound. A fringe of beach now separates the waters of the sound and the ocean. The islet is heavily wooded and privately owned. Although Blackbeard is sometimes associated with this particular "Money Island," most of the legends of the area are to the effect that Captain William Kidd is the one who buried a large portion of his stolen loot there around 1698. Diggings, however, have not revealed any buried treasure (Louis T. Moore, "Pirate Treasure Remains Buried on Money Island?" *Charlotte* [N.C.] *Observer*, October 10, 1926, sec. 5, p. 4; Louis T. Moore, *Stories Old and New of the Cape Fear Region* [Wilmington, 1956], pp. 38–42; S. A. Ashe, "Our Own Pirates," *N.C. Booklets*, II, No. 2 [1902], p. 6).

Located off the Georgia coast, in McIntosh County, is Blackbeard Island. According to legend, this was a refuge of Blackbeard and, of course, a place where he buried his treasure ("Pirate Blackbeard's Island to Become Refuge for Birds," *Greensboro* [N.C.] *Daily News*, September 26, 1933).

6. Whedbee, p. 56.

In 1938, a Negro farmer, Dallas Gordon, plowed up on his ten-acre farm, which he had twenty-one years earlier purchased for $500, two or three ingots of melted gold. The farm was located about fifteen miles east of Bath, near the mouth of Pamlico River (Charles Parker, "A Plow Turns Up Buried Treasure," *News and Observer* [Raleigh, N.C.], June 26, 1938, p. 1).

7. Wheeler, p. 117; Whedbee, pp. 55–56; F. Roy Johnson, *Legends and Myths of North Carolina's Roanoke-Chowan Area* (Murfreesboro, N.C., 1966) pp. 81–82. Holiday's Island is located near where Bennet and Catherine creeks empty into the Chowan River.

8. There apparently are other legends of trees associated with Blackbeard. This writer has found no historical records to sustain a recently developing legend that Blackbeard had a sister, Susie Whitefield, who lived near the present town of Grimesland, in Pitt County, North Carolina, on what is now known as the "Grimes Plantation," and that the pirate captain visited her and posted a sentinel in a tall cypress tree on the banks of the Tar River to keep a lookout and to warn of any surprise attack (Whedbee, p. 55; Roy Hardee, "Grimes Plantation a State Historic Site," *News and Observer* [Raleigh, N.C.], November 5, 1967, sec. 3, p. 9).

In a distant part of the State, near the mouth of the Cape Fear River, there once existed a legend of still another "Blackbeard Tree." A letter received by the writer, dated February 28, 1967, from Helen F. Taylor, Secretary and Treasurer of the Brunswick County Historical Society, Winnabow, N.C., states, "On my grandparents' plantation here at Winnabow there was an oak tree called the 'Blackbeard Tree' but I can't recall the story told me. I do know that the tree had that name as far back as 1840."

9. For accounts of the Old Brick House, see Albertson, pp. 55–56, 62–65; Squires, p. 58; G. W. Brothers, "A Trip to Blackbeard's Castle," *Wake Forest Student*, XXX, No. 2 (November, 1910), 112; Jesse F. Pugh, "A Pirate and His House," *U. of North Carolina Magazine* (April, 1913), pp. 195–98; Charles Haskett, "Blackbeard Legends Giving Way to Fact," *News and Observer* (Raleigh, N.C.), December 14, 1952, sec. 4, p. 12, reprinted as "Blackbeard Legend Is Giving Way," *Year Book of Pasquotank Historical Society* (Elizabeth City, N.C., 1955), pp. 66–67; "Notorious Pirate Teach Built Treasure House for Housing Gold and Wives," *Charlotte* (N.C.) *Observer*, March 27, 1927, sec. 3, p. 6.

10. Haskett, "Blackbeard Legend Is Giving Way," *Yearbook of Pasquotank Historical Society*, p. 67.

11. Albertson, p. 56.

12. Albertson, pp. 64–65. See also Haskett, "Blackbeard Legend Is Giving Way," *Yearbook of Pasquotank Historical Society*, p. 67.

13. Albertson, pp. 64–65.

14. Whedbee, p. 56. See also Richard Powell Carter, "Teach's Light and Teach's Gold Flicker in Old Bath," *News and Observer* (Raleigh, N.C.), September 10, 1933, sec. 1, p. 3.

Appendix A

Contemporary newspaper accounts of the Battle of Ocracoke Inlet appeared in both American and English newspapers.

The *Boston News-Letter* was America's first—and at the time the only—regularly issued newspaper (Clarence G. Brigham, *History and Bibliography of American Newspapers, 1690–1820* [Worcester, Mass., 1947], I, 327). Although *Public Occurrences*, published in 1690, might technically be called a newspaper, except for its having been suppressed after its first issue, the *Boston News-Letter* was the first newspaper in America continuously published. It was a weekly, established by John Campbell and printed by Bartholomew Green. Its first issue appeared on April 24, 1704, and it continued to be published until 1776, a period of seventy-two years. Campbell, in 1723, transferred the paper to Green, who became both publisher and printer. The newspaper in 1719 was a two-columned sheet about eight by twelve inches, printed on both sides, and promising to furnish the subscribers "with all the most remarkable occurrences of Europe in the Public Prints of London, besides those of this and the Neighboring Provinces" (*Boston News-Letter*, Number 775, dated "From Monday Feb. 16 to Monday Feb. 23, 1719," back page, photostatic copy of which was obtained from Massachusetts Historical Society, Boston, Mass.).

The back page of the *Boston News-Letter* referred to above carried the following belated account of the capture of Blackbeard:

"Boston, By Letters of the 17th of December last from North Carolina, we are informed, That Lieutenant Robert Maynard of His Majesty's Ship Pearl (Commanded by Capt. Gordon) being fitted out at Virginia, with two Sloops, mann'd with Fifty Men, and small Arms, but no great Guns, in quest of Capt. Teach the Pirate, called Blackbeard, who made his Escape from thence, was overtaken at North Carolina, and had ten great Guns and Twenty one Men on board his Sloop. Teach when he began the Dispute Drank Damnation to Lieutenant Maynard if he gave Quarters, Maynard replyed he would neither give nor take Quarters, whereupon he boarded the Pirate and fought it out, hand to hand, with Pistol and Sword; the Engagement was very desperate and bloody on both sides wherein Lieutenant Maynard had Thirty five of his Men killed and wounded in the Action, himself slightly wounded. Teach and most of his Men were killed, the rest carryed Prisoners to Virginia, by Lieut. Maynard, to be tryed there; who also carrys with him Teach's Head which he cut off, in order to get the Reward granted by the said Colony."

In its next issue, Number 776, dated "From Monday Feb. 23 to Monday March 2, 1719," on the unnumbered last page, there appeared a more detailed account of the event, as follows:

"Rhode-Island, February 20. On the 12th Currant arrived here . . . Humphry Johnson in a Sloop from North Carolina, bound to Amboy who sailed the next Day, and informs that Governour Spotswood of Virginia fitted out two Sloops, well manned with Fifty pickt Men of His Majesty's Men of War lying there, and small Arms, but not great Guns, under the Command of Lieutenant Robert Maynard of His Majesty's Ship *Pearl* in pursuit of that Notorious and Arch Pirate Capt. Teach, who made his escape from Virginia, when some of his Men were taken there, which Pirate Lieutenant Maynard came up with at North Carolina, and when they came in hearing of each other, Teach called to Lieutenant Maynard and told him he was for King GEORGE, desiring him to hoist out his boat and come aboard. Maynard replyed that he designed to come aboard with his sloop as soon as he could, and Teach understanding his design, told him that if he would let him alone, he would not meddle with him; Maynard answered that it was him he wanted, and that he would have him dead or alive, else it would cost him his life; whereupon Teach called for a Glass of Wine, and swore Damnation to himself if he either took or gave Quarter.

"Then Lieutenant Maynard told his Men that now they knew what they had to trust to, and could not escape the Pirates hands if they had a mind, but must either fight and kill, or be killed; Teach begun and fired several great Guns at Maynard's Sloop, which did but little damage, but Maynard rowing nearer Teach's Sloop of Ten Guns, Teach fired some small Guns, loaded with Swan shot, spick Nails and pieces of old Iron, in upon Maynard, which killed six of his Men and wounded ten, upon which Lieutenant Maynard, ordered all the rest of his Men to go down in the Hould: himself, Abraham Demelt of New York, and a third at the Helm stayed above Deck.

"Teach seeing so few on the Deck, said to his Men, the Rogues were all killed except two or three, and he would go on board and kill them himself, so drawing nearer went on board, took hold of the fore sheet and made fast the Sloops; Maynard and Teach themselves then begun the fight with their Swords, Maynard making a thrust, the point of his Sword went against Teach's Cartridge Box, and bended it to the Hilt, Teach broke the Guard of it, and wounded Maynard's Fingers but did not disable him, whereupon he Jumpt back, threw away his Sword and fired his Pistol, which wounded Teach. Demelt struck in between them with his Sword and cut Teach's Face pretty much; in the Interim both Companies ingaged in Maynard's Sloop, one of Maynard's Men being a Highlander, ingaged Teach with his broad Sword, who gave Teach a cut on the Neck, Teach saying well done Lad, the Highlander reply'd, if it be not well done, I'll do it better, with that he gave him a second stroke, which cut off his Head, laying it flat on his Shoulder, Teach's Men being about 20, and three or four Blacks were all killed in the Ingagement, excepting two carried to Virginia: Teach's body was thrown overboard, and his Head put on the top of the Bowsprit."

Benjamin Franklin, having become apprenticed in 1717 at the age of twelve years to his older half-brother, James Franklin, says in his *Autobiography* that he wrote and printed "a sailor's song, on the taking of Teach (or Blackbeard) the pirate" and that he went through the streets of Boston selling the same (*The Autobiography of Benjamin Franklin*, ed. Frank Woodworth Pine [Garden City, N.Y., 1916], p. 23). Franklin wrote: "This flattered my vanity; but my father discouraged me by ridiculing my performances, and telling me verse-makers were generally beggars. So I escaped being a poet, most probably a very bad one" (*ibid.*). Franklin was thirteen years old at the time he composed the ballad.

No authenticated copy of Franklin's famous sailor's song exists. There is, however, to be found in Leonard W. Laboree's *The Papers of Benjamin Franklin* ([New Haven, 1959], I, 7) one stanza which George Hayward, a Boston physician, recalled at some time before the War Between the States, and which he thought to be a part of Franklin's ballad:

So each man to his gun,
For the work must be done,
   With cutlass, sword, or pistol.
And when we no longer can strike a blow,
Then fire the magazine, boys, and up we go!
It's better to swim in the sea below
Than to swing in the air and feed the crow,
   Says jolly Ned Teach of Bristol.

Edward Everett Hale discovered in *Some Real Sea-Songs*, a volume printed by John Ashton in London during the 1890's, a sailor's ballad entitled "The Downfall of Piracy" (Edward Everett Hale, "Ben Franklin's Ballads," *New England Magazine* [new series], XVIII [June, 1898], pp. 505–7). Hale was of the opinion that this is the song written by the youthful Franklin. Perhaps so. This ditty, as reprinted in the *New England Magazine*, June, 1898 (*ibid.*), is as follows:

THE DOWNFALL OF PIRACY

Will you hear of a bloody Battle,
   Lately fought upon the Seas,
It will make your Ears to rattle,
   And your Admiration cease;
Have you heard of Teach the Rover,
   And his Knavery on the Main;
How of Gold he was a Lover,
   How he lov'd all ill got Gain.

When the Act of Grace appeared,
   Captain Teach with all his Men,
Unto Carolina steered,
   Where they kindly us'd him then;
There he marry'd to a Lady,
   And gave her five hundred Pound,
But to her he prov'd unsteady
For he soon march'd off the Ground.

And returned, as I tell you,
    To his Robbery as before,
Burning, sinking Ships of value,
    Filling them with Purple Gore;
When he was at Carolina,
    There the Governor did send,
To the Governor of Virginia,
    That he might assistance lend.

Then the Man of War's Commander,
    Two small Sloops he fitted out,
Fifty Men he put on board, Sir,
    Who resolv'd to stand it out:
The Lieutenant he commanded
    Both the Sloops, and you shall hear,
How before he landed,
    He suppress'd them without fear.

Valiant Maynard as he sailed,
    Soon the Pirate did espy,
With his Trumpet he then hailed,
    And to him they did reply:
Captain Teach is our Commander,
    Maynard said, he is the Man,
Whom I am resolv'd to hang, Sir,
    Let him do the best he can.

Teach replyed unto Maynard,
    You no Quarter here shall see,
But be hang'd on the Mainyard,
    You and all your Company;
Maynard said, I none desire,
    Of such Knaves as thee and thine,
None I'll give, Teach then replyed,
    My Boys, give me a Glass of Wine.

He took the Glass, and Drank Damnation
    Unto Maynard and his Crew;
To himself and Generation,

Then the Glass away he threw;
Brave Maynard was resolv'd to have him,
Tho' he'd Cannons nine or ten;
Teach a broadside quickly gave him,
Killing sixteen valiant Men.

Maynard boarded him, and to it
They fell with Sword and Pistol too;
They had Courage, and did show it,
Killing of the Pirate's Crew.
Teach and Maynard on the Quarter,
Fought it out most manfully,
Maynard's Sword did cut him shorter,
Losing his head, he there did die.

Every Sailor fought while he, Sir,
Power had to wield the Sword,
Not a Coward could you see, Sir,
Fear was driven from aboard;
Wounded Men on both Sides fell, Sir,
'Twas doleful Sight to see,
Nothing could their Courage quell, Sir,
O, they fought courageously.

When the bloody Fight was over,
We're informed by a Letter writ,
Teach's Head was made a Cover,
To the Jack Staff of the Ship:
Thus they sailed to Virginia,
And when they the Story told,
How they kill'd the Pirates many,
They'd Applause from young and old.

Two rival London newspapers on the same day, April 11, 1719, published accounts of the capture and death of Blackbeard, based on letters apparently just received from Virginia (Arthur L. Cooke, "British Newspaper Accounts of Blackbeard's Death," *Virginia Magazine of History and Biography*, LXI [July, 1953], 304). The item appearing in the *Weekly Journal or British Gazetteer* (*ibid.*, p. 305) follows:

"Extract of some Letters from Virginia.

"Capt. Teach; alias Blackbeard, the famous Pyrate, came within the Capes of this Colony in a Sloop of six Guns and twenty Men; whereof our Governor having Notice, order'd two Sloops to be fitted out, which fourtunately met with him. When Teach saw they were resolv'd to fight him, he leap'd upon the Round-House of his Sloop, and took a Glass of Liquor, and drank to the Masters of the two Sloops, and bid Damnation seize him that should give Quarter; but notwithstanding his Insolence, the two Sloops soon boarded him, and kill'd all except Teach, and one more, who have been since executed. The Head of Teach is fix'd on a Pole erected for that Purpose."

On the same day a fuller account appeared in the *Weekly Journal or Saturday's Post* (Reprinted in Cooke, p. 304):

"Letters from James-Town in Virginia give an Account, that on the 16th of February they were alarmed there with the News of three Pirate Ships, which were seen off the Capes; whereupon all merchant Ships and Sloops that were in the Road or in our Rivers up the Bay had immediate notice to hale in to the shore, for their Security, or else to prepare for their Defence, if they thought themselves in a Condition to fight; soon after two Boats, who were sent out to get Intelligence, came crowding in, and brought an Account that one of the Pirates was come into the Bay, being a small Sloop of six Guns; our Governor expecting the rest would have followed, and having no sufficient Force to fight them at Sea, expected they would make some Attempt to land, for the sake of Plunder; but being quickly informed that there was no more than that one Sloop, manned out two Sloops immediately to attack him. The Pirate boldly prepared to fight them both, having obliged all his Men to swear to fight to the last Gasp, and take no Quarter, and accordingly hoisted their black Ensign with a Death's Head; however our Sloops attacked them vigorously, and after an obstinate Fight, in which the Pirates were as good as their Words in refusing Quarter, they entered the Sloop and cut them all to pieces, except the Capt. and another, whom they reserved for the Gallows. This Captain proved to be the famous Teach, alias Black Beard; they brought him ashoar in Chains, very much wounded, and made short Work with him; for the day after they hanged both him and his Companion, and he is now set upon a Pole near the harbour's Mouth."

These English accounts are full of inaccurate history (See Chapter 11 of this work). Professor Arthur L. Cooke, in an article written in 1953, commented: "Certainly it is strange that such a completely garbled account of the affair should have reached the London press. It would seem almost impossible that any correspondent in Virginia could have been so thoroughly misinformed about an event which had excited such interest in the colony. Yet it does not seem likely, on the other hand, that the London journalists were responsible for distorting the account; the two papers agreed on most points and apparently had taken their reports from the same letters. Perhaps it is just an extreme example of the unreliability of the news which the British press reported from the colonies" (Cooke, p. 305).

The Weekly Journal or British Gazetteer, on April 25, 1719, sought to correct its errors of two weeks before by publishing a letter credited to Lieutenant Robert Maynard (reprinted in Cooke, p. 306).

"North-Carolina, December 17.

"Abstract of a Letter from Mr. Maynard, first Lieutenant of His Majesty's Ship the *Pearl*, the Station-Ship at Virginia, to Mr. Symonds, Lieutenant of His Majesty's Ship the *Phoenix*, the Station-Ship at New-York.

"Sir,

"This is to acquaint you, that I sail'd from Virginia the 17th past, with two Sloops, and 54 Men under my Command, having no Guns, but only small Arms and Pistols. Mr. Hyde commanded the little Sloop with 22 Men, and I had 32 in my sloop. The 22d I came up with Captain Teach, the notorious Pyrate, who has taken, from time to time, a great many English Vessels on these Coasts, and in the West-Indies; he went by the name of Blackbeard, because he let his Beard grow, and tied it up in black Ribbons. I attack'd him at Cherhock in North-Carolina, when he had on Board 21 Men, and nine Guns mounted. At our first Salutation, he drank Damnation to me and my Men, whom he stil'd Cowardly Puppies, saying, He would neither give nor take Quarter. Immediately we engag'd, and Mr. Hyde was unfortunately kill'd, and five of his Men wounded in the little Sloop, which, having no-body to command her, fell a-stern, and did not come up to assist me till the Action was almost over. In the mean time, continuing the Fight, it being a perfect Calm, I shot away Teach's Gib, and his Fore-Halliards, forcing him ashoar, I boarded his Sloop, and had 20 Men kill'd and wounded. Immediately thereupon, he enter'd me with 10 Men; but 12 stout Men I left there, fought like Heroes, Sword in Hand, and they kill'd every one of them that enter'd, without the loss of one Man on their Side, but they were miserably cut and mangled. In the whole, I had eight Men killed, and 18 wounded. We kill'd 12, besides Blackbeard, who fell with five Shot in him, and 20 dismal Cuts in several Parts of his Body. I took nine Prisoners, mostly Negroes, all wounded. I have cut Blackbeard's head off, which I have put on my Bowspright, in order to carry it to Virginia. I should never have taken him, if I had not got him in such a Hole, whence he could not get out, for we had no Guns on Board; so that the Engagement on our Side was the more Bloody and Desperate."

This letter varies in some particulars from other contemporary accounts of the battle (See Chapter 11). These differences are not, on the whole, substantial. One may, however, infer from this account that Maynard boarded Blackbeard's ship and that Blackbeard and ten of his men immediately counterattacked by entering upon Maynard's sloop, which is clearly contrary to all the other contemporary accounts. It is possible that Maynard used the term "boarded" here with a meaning different from that ordinarily used. Perhaps he did not intend to imply that he and his men actually went aboard Blackbeard's sloop and there engaged in hand-to-hand fighting, but rather that he rammed or came up beside Blackbeard's sloop, or that the wooded hulls of the two vessels scraped or "boarded" each other, or that he engaged in a tactical maneuver in coming up alongside Blackbeard's sloop. If this is the meaning of the word "boarded," as used by Maynard, then his report of the particular incident is not inconsistent with other contemporary accounts. Indeed, there are dictionary definitions giving this nautical meaning to the word ("Board," *Webster's New International Dictionary* [Springfield, Mass., 1944] "Naut. The side of a ship; as, board and board, board on board, board to board, side by side. . . . v. Transitive. 1. To come up against or alongside of [a ship], as for the purpose of attacking." *American College Dictionary* [New York and London, 1948] has among its definitions of "board" the following: "Naut. the side of a ship; to come up alongside of [a ship], as to attack or to go on board . . . obs. to approach; accost." See also "Naval Strategy and Tactics," *Encyclopedia Britannica* [London, 14th ed., 1940]).

Perhaps the best explanation of the discrepancy in Maynard's letter is that found in a letter written by George Gordon, Maynard's superior officer, dated September 14, 1721, and addressed to the Lords Commissioners of Admiralty (unpublished manuscript, Admiralty 1/1826, Public Record Office, London). Gordon, in this letter, positively denies that Maynard went upon Blackbeard's sloop before Blackbeard was killed, concluding as follows: "This, Sirs, is the true and real steps of that action, given in upon oath at his Majesty's Court of Admiralty in Virginia, by himself and people, the truth of which if need by Lt. Governor Spotswood can judge as also Capt. Brand: there being no such thing given out there of his boarding Thatch sword in hand; as he is pleased to tell" (*ibid.*).

It should be observed that Blackbeard is identified as Teach in all these contemporary newspaper accounts.

Appendix B

LETTER OF COLONEL THOMAS POLLOCK TO
GOVERNOR CHARLES EDEN

(Referred to in Chapter 12, Entitled "Dispute Over Jurisdiction")

The letter, which follows, was written only sixteen days after the capture of Blackbeard. It was in reply to a letter which Colonel Thomas Pollock had received, along with other papers, by messenger from Governor Charles Eden. The document has been preserved in *North Carolina Colonial Records*, II, 318–20.

"Dec. 8th 1718

"Hon^d Sir:

"I have herewith enclosed my real sentiments as to the queries proposed by Mr. Knight, but must needs acknowledge my weakness in such high matters, and want of time, being unwilling to detain the messenger too long: and to answer to what you desire in the postscript of Mr. Knight's letter, I declare that I never heard any thing of any applications to Verginia concerning Captn Thach, nor nothing of any intended expedition out of Verginia, until I heard that Capt Brand was come in, and that he and Col. Moore and Captn Veall were gone to Pamplico.

"There seems to be a great deal of malice and design in their management of this affair: wherefore I hope your Honor will be very cautious, and not to give them any opportunity to take advantage, which you no some people are ready and willing to do. And the Statute 11 and 12 King William being that all Governors in the said plantations under proprietors shall assist the commissioners, as is before expressed in the answer, and believing that Governor Spottswood would not act as he does by that old commission to Governor Nicholson; wherefore it is good, in my opinion, to be easy in the matter, and ready to do as the law directs, that they may be disappointed if they expect any advantages by your refusal. And as for the trial of the men, if they will have it in Verginia, it [will] ease your Honor of a great deal of trouble, and take off the odium of it from this government.

"I hope your Honor will pardon my freedom, and take it in good part, and if I have erred any way in my opinion, please to attribute it to my weakness and want of a right apprehension of the matter, and not to be the want of sincerity of him who is [there is a break here in the *Colonial Records*].

"As for the sugars or other goods delivered, or landed to be delivered, to the Governor, to be secured for those that can make appear a right to them it seems to me that they can not be seized or carried out of the government, until by Judgment and condemnation the property be determined to be in the King, the Lords Proprietors or recovered by due course of law by the owner, and it seems to me the goods being in this government, or in some superior government, which is only in England, unless the government of Verginia have a commission from our present King thereanent according to the statute the 11 and 12 King William, which statute was only for seven years, and in the fifth of Queen Anne continued for seven years more and lastly in the first of our present King revived and continued for five years more and to the end of the next session of Parliament.

"Then as for Governor Spottswood sending in forces here to apprehend Capt[n] Theach and his men, it seems very dark and strange to me for by the foresaid Statute 11 and 12 of King William the power of trying pirates is only given commissioners to be appointed by the King under the great seal of England or the seal of admiralty. So that unless the Governor of Verginia be appointed by Commissioners as aforesaid from our present King thereanent, I know not by what authority he could send in warlike forces into this Government without the consent of the Government. And I should think if he had a commission from our present King to act in this manner, it would have been easy to have expressed it more fully in his power given to Captain Brand, and it would have been reasonable (as I take it) to have sent in a copy of it to the Governor here, that he might have had some guide and directions how to proceed in this matter. For as for King Williams commission to Governor Nicholson, (as I take it) it was determined at farthest in six months after his death, and so I believe can be no sufficient authority for any other Governor of Verginia to act by: and also by the same commission the Governor of Carolina seemed to be of equal power with the Governor of Verginia in the trial of pirates.

"And whereas by the King's proclamation all admirals, Captains, Governors, & cet. are commanded only to seize on and take such of the pirates who shall refuse or neglect to surrender themselves according to the proclamation:

"Now abeit that Theach and his men have come in and surrendered themselves, according to the proclamation, yet if they have been guilty of piracy after the 5th of January last, whether this may not be accounted a refusing or neglecting to surrender themselves according to the Law intent and meaning of the proclamation.

"And as for carrying out such person to be tried in Verginia, unless as is said the Governor of Verginia has a particular commission from the present King, I cannot see how he can legally do it, for, if the act by virtue of the commission to Governor Nicholson, by the same commission the Governor here hath the same power, and the persons being inhabitants of this government ought to be tried here, for where two persons have equal rights, he that hath the possession ought to have the preferance.

"I have given my opinion and true sentiments in the matter proposed, according to the best of my knowledge impartially, but must acknowledge my weakness and unacquaintedness in affairs of such high concern, and also want of time, having but little time to peruse the papers and return. . . ."

Appendix C

JURISDICTION OF COLONIAL COURTS OF VICE-ADMIRALTY

(Referred to in Chapter 12, Entitled "Dispute Over Jurisdiction")

An act of the English Parliament in 1696 created the first admiralty courts in America (Charles M. Andrews, *The Colonial Period of American History* [New Haven, 1937], IV, 225–26; David S. Lovejoy, "Rights Imply Equality: The Case Against Admiralty Jurisdiction in America, 1764–1776," *William and Mary Quarterly* [3d Series], XVI [1959], 460). Maritime cases before then were tried in the established common-law courts (Carl W. Ubbelohde, Jr., "The Vice-Admiralty Court of Royal North Carolina," *North Carolina Historical Review*, XXXI [1954], 519). On June 20, 1697, Sir Edmund Andros, then Governor of Virginia, was commissioned under the Great Seal of the High Court of Admiralty of England to appoint officers for an Admiralty Court in Virginia, Carolina, and the Bahama Islands (letter of Governor Andros to Council of Trade and Plantations, dated March 14, 1698, *Cal. State Papers*, XVI [Oct. 1697–Dec. 1698], sec. 291; see also *William and Mary College Quarterly* [1st series], V [1896], 129). The commission was accompanied by a letter from the English Admiralty nominating the first officers (*ibid.*). By virtue of this authority, Governor Andros on March 8, 1697/1698, drafted a commission appointing Edward Hill, a member of Virginia's Council, the judge of the Court of Admiralty for Virginia and North Carolina (*North Carolina Historical and Genealogical Register*, ed. J. R. B. Hathaway [Edenton, January, 1903], III, 39–40; *William and Mary College Quarterly* [1st series], V [1896], 129). Governor Andros sent to Deputy Governor Thomas Harvey, of North Carolina, a copy of the Hill commission, saying in an accompanying letter that he, Andros, had authority to fill any vacancy occurring (letter from Deputy Governor Thomas Harvey to Governor John Archdale, dated July 10, 1698, *North Carolina Historical and Genealogical Register*, III, 35–39). According to a letter to Governor John Archdale, who was then either in Charleston or on a trip to England, Harvey had handled the matter by communicating to Andros that there was no vacancy, since Captain Henderson Walker was serving in that capacity in North Carolina (*ibid.*; Ashe, 146–47). Apparently the Lords Proprietors in London were informed, and they very much approved the way he had answered the letter of Andros (*N.C. Col. Rec.*, I, 491). Walker had been in the colony for over sixteen years, had served as Attorney General, Justice of the General Court, and a member of the Council, and was later, from 1699 through 1704, to be President of the Council and *ex officio* Acting Governor (Ashe, 150, 158; Connor, 75; Hawks, 498).

Governor Francis Nicholson, returning on December 9, 1698, for his second administration as Governor of Virginia, sought to inform Deputy Governor Harvey, by letter of May 3, 1699, that in consequence of the commission received by Governor Andros, his predecessor, he had authority to appoint officers for the admiralty courts of Virginia, Carolina, and the Bahama Islands (letter of Governor Nicholson to Deputy Governor Harvey, dated May 3, 1699, *N.C. Col. Rec.*, I, 510). Governor Nicholson apparently received a royal commission under the Great Seal of England and directions relating to the trial of pirates in Virginia and "our Province of North and South Carolina" (see proclamation issued to Nicholson, dated February 2, 1700/1701, signed by John Fermon, by His Majesty's Command, as printed in Williams, pp. 132–33 and *The Virginia Magazine of History and Biography*, XXII [1914], 122–23. For copy of Nicholson's commission, dated August 4, 1702, giving him authority to pursue and prosecute pirates outside the limits of Virginia, see *ibid.*, XX [1912], 230).

Governor Spotswood suggested to the Lords of Admiralty and to the Lords Commissioners of Trade, by letters of July 3, 1716, that owing to the commission under the Great Seal of Admiralty issued to a former governor under an earlier sovereign, he might "in some measure" be entrusted with the care of the Bahama Islands, and expressed the hope that if his actions at the time with respect to pirates in the Bahamas did not come within his authority he would "not be judged too officious or impertinent" (Spotswood, pp. 168–72).

The Lords Proprietors of Pennsylvania, Carolina, and the Bahama Islands during this period were protesting in England that their charters gave them the authority to establish an Admiralty Court (*N.C. Col. Rec.*, I, 471–72, 491, 632; Ubbelohde, p. 519).

Rhode Island refused to recognize the King's commission appointing a judge of the Admiralty Court within the province (*Cal. State Papers*, XVI [Oct. 1697–Dec. 1698], sec. 282 and xiii).

North Carolinians consistently ignored the Virginians' contention that the latter's Court of Admiralty had jurisdiction over admiralty matters arising in the Province of North Carolina (Ubbelohde, p. 520; J. S. Bassett, *The Constitutional Beginnings of North Carolina* [Baltimore, 1894], pp. 70–71). "It is possible that no ordinary admiralty case from North Carolina was ever tried in the Virginia Court" (Ubbelohde, p. 520). North Carolinians maintained their own Court of Vice-Admiralty, the officials of which were appointed by the English Admiralty, but any temporary vacancies on which were filled by the Governor and his Council (Council Journal, *N.C. Col. Rec.*, II, 520, 765; Bassett, p. 71).

The Statute of 11 and 12 William III, c. 7, entitled "An Act for the more effectual Suppression of Piracy," was enacted in 1698. Originally limited to a period of seven years, it was subsequently extended from time to time. It was under this statute that all acts of piracy were tried throughout the second decade of the eighteenth century. The statute provided that pirates could not be tried in America unless the colonial governor had a special commission authorizing him to appoint persons to conduct the trial in a Court of Vice-Admiralty. Otherwise, the captured pirates were to be sent to England for trial. Commissions automatically expired six months after the death of the sovereign who issued them.

The colonial governors, possessed of the required commission, appointed seven or more commissioners to conduct the trials of pirates. The presiding judge, sometimes referred to as the president of the court, collected the votes of the other commissioners, beginning with the junior member and ending with himself. It was not unusual for the Governor to be the presiding judge, but more often it was the Judge of the Court of Vice-Admiralty or Chief Justice of the Colony. The procedure for the trial of pirates in the Court of Vice-Admiralty under a Royal Commission by designated commissioners was quite different from that for the trial of an ordinary case in the Court of Vice-Admiralty. An indictment, or articles of piracy, was read to the accused. There were detailed forms and procedures to be used under the Statute of 11 and 12 William III, c. 7, copies of which are still extant (Erwin C. Surrency, "The Procedure for the Trial of a Pirate," *American Journal of Legal History*, **VIII** [1957], 251). A Mr. Lackin was sent from England to Philadelphia, under a special commission, to direct the manner in which pirates were to be tried there (*ibid.*; see also Percy Scott Flippin, *The Royal Government in Virginia* [New York, 1919], p. 332).

Appendix D

PROCLAMATION UNDER WHICH BLACKBEARD,
BONNET, HORNIGOLD, AND HUNDREDS OF
OTHER PIRATES SURRENDERED

(This proclamation appears in Johnson, pp. 12–14; Williams, pp. 133–35; and Woodbury, pp. 144–46.)

By the King
A PROCLAMATION for Suppressing of PYRATES

Whereas we have received information, that several Persons, Subjects of Great Britain, have, since the 24th Day of June, in the Year of our Lord, 1715, committed divers Pyracies and Robberies upon the High-Seas, in the West-Indies, or adjoyning to our Plantations, which hath and may Occasion great Damage to the Merchants of Great Britain, and others trading into those Parts; and tho' we have appointed such a Force as we judge sufficient for suppressing the said Pyrates, yet the more effectually to put an End to the same, we have thought fit, by and with the Advice of our Privy Council, to Issue this our Royal Proclamation; and we do hereby promise, and declare, that in Case any of the said Pyrates, shall on, or before, the 5th of September, in the Year of our Lord 1718, surrender him or themselves, to one of our Principal Secretaries of State in Great Britain or Ireland, or to any Governor or Deputy Governor of any of our Plantations beyond the Seas; every such Pyrate and Pyrates so surrendering him, or themselves, as aforesaid, shall have our gracious Pardon, of, and for such, his or their Pyracy, or Pyracies, by him or them committed, before the fifth of January next ensuing. And we do hereby strictly charge and command all our Admirals, Captains, and other Officers at Sea, and all our Governors and Commanders of any Forts, Castles, or other Places in our Plantations, and all other our Officers Civil and Military, to seize and take such of the Pyrates, who shall refuse or neglect to surrender themselves accordingly. And we do hereby further declare, that in Case any Person or Persons, on, or after, the 6th Day of September, 1718, shall discover or seize, or cause or procure to be discovered or seized, any one or more of the said Pyrates, so refusing or neglecting to surrender themselves as aforesaid, so as they may be brought to Justice, and convicted of the said Offense, such Person or Persons, so making such Discovery or Seizure or causing or procuring such Discovery or Seizure to be made, shall have and receive as a Reward for the same, viz. for every Commander of any private Ship or Vessel, the Sum of 100£ and for every Lieutenant, Master, Boatswain, Carpenter, and Gunner, the Sum of 30£ and for every private Man, the sum of 20£. And if any Person or Persons, belonging to, and being Part of the Crew, of any Pyrate Ship and Vessel, shall, on or after the said sixth Day of September, 1718, seize and deliver, or cause to be seized and delivered, any Commander or Commanders, of such Pyrat Ship or Vessel, so as that he or they be brought to Justice, and convicted of the said Offence, such Person or Persons, as a Reward for the same, shall receive for every such Commander, the sum of 200£ which said Sums, the Lord Treasurer, or the Commissioners of our Treasury for the time being, are hereby required, and desired to pay accordingly.

Given at our Court, at Hampton-Court, the fifth Day of September, 1717, in the fourth Year of our Reign.

George R.

God save the King.

Bibliography

BOOKS

Adams, James Truslow. *Provincial Society, 1690–1763*. New York: Macmillan Co., 1927.

Albertson, Catherine. *In Ancient Albemarle*. Raleigh: Commercial Printing Co., 1914.

American Guide Series: North Carolina. Chapel Hill: U. of N.C. Press, 1939.

Andrews, Charles M. *The Colonial Period of American History*. New Haven: Yale University Press, 1938.

Ashe, Samuel A. *History of North Carolina*, Vol. I. Greensboro: Charles L. Van Noppen, 1908.

Bassett, John Spencer. *The Constitutional Beginnings of North Carolina*. Baltimore: Johns Hopkins Press, 1894.

————. *Slavery and Servitude in the Colony of North Carolina*. Baltimore: Johns Hopkins Press, 1896.

Baugh, Daniel C. *British Naval Administration in the Age of Walpole*. Princeton: Princeton University Press, 1965.

Benedict, Erastus. *Law of American Admiralty* (6th ed. by Arnold W. Knouth). New York: Bender, 1940.

Blackstone, William. *Commentaries on the Laws of England*, Vol. IV. Oxford, England: Clarendon Press, 1769.

William Byrd's History of the Dividing Line Betwixt Virginia and North Carolina. Edited by William K. Boyd. Raleigh: N.C. Historical Commission, 1929.

Biographical History of North Carolina. Edited by Samuel A. Ashe. Greensboro: C. L. Van Noppen, 1905.

Brigham, Clarence G. *History and Biography of American Newspapers, 1690–1820*. Worcester, Mass., 1947.

Brooke, Henry K. *Book of Pirates*. Philadelphia: J. P. Perry, 1841.

Bruce, Phillip Alexander. *History of Virginia*. Chicago and New York: American Historical Society, 1924.

Calendar of State [British] *Papers, Colonial Series, America and the West Indies, Preserved in the Public Record Office*, Vols. XXIX–XXXII. Edited by Cecil Headlam. London: Cassell & Co., Ltd., 1930–1933.

Calendar of Treasury Books and Papers, 1720–1730, Vol. I. Edited by William A. Shaw. London: Her Majesty's Stationery Office by Eyre and Spottiswoode, 1897.

Calendar Virginia State Papers, Vol. I. Edited by William P. Palmer. Richmond: R. F. Walker, Supt. Public Printing, 1875.

Campbell, Charles. *Introduction to the History of the Colony and Ancient Dominion of Virginia.* Richmond: B. B. Minor, 1847.

Carse, Robert. *The Age of Piracy.* New York: Holt, Rinehart & Winston, 1957.

Chambers, Robert W. *The Rogues' Moon.* New York: A. L. Burt Co., 1928.

Chidsey, Donald Barr. *The American Privateers.* New York: Dodd, 1962.

Cochran, Hamilton. *Freebooters of the Red Sea: Pirates, Politicians and Pieces of Eight.* New York: Bobbs-Merrill, 1965.

Colonial Records of North Carolina, Vols. I–X. Edited by W. L. Saunders, 1958. Raleigh: P. M. Hale, State Printer, 1886–1890.

Colonial Williamsburg: Official Guidebook. Williamsburg, Va., 1965.

Connor, R. D. W. *History of North Carolina.* Chicago: Lewis Publishing Co., 1919.

Cooke, John Esten. *Virginia: A History of the People.* New York: Houghton, Mifflin and Co., 1911.

Corpus Juris Secundum. Brooklyn, 1936.

Crabtree, Beth G. *North Carolina Governors.* Raleigh: State Dept. of Archives and History, 1958.

Craton, Michael. *A History of the Bahamas.* London: Collins, 1962.

Crittenden, Charles Christopher. *The Commerce of North Carolina, 1763–1789.* New Haven: Yale University Press, 1936.

Davis, J. E. *Round About Jamestown.* Hampton, Va., 1907.

Dictionary of National Biography. Edited by Sir Leslie Stephen and Sir Sidney Lee. London: Oxford University Press, 1949–50.

Dodson, Leonidas. *Alexander Spotswood.* Philadelphia: U. of Pa. Press, 1932.

Executive Journal of the Council of Colonial Virginia. Edited by H. R. McIlwaine. Richmond: Virginia State Library, 1928.

First Census of the United States, 1790: North Carolina. Washington, D.C., 1908.

Flippin, Percy Scott. *The Royal Government of Virginia*. New York: Columbia University Press, 1919.

Franklin, Benjamin. *Autobiography*. Edited by Frank Woodworth Pine. Garden City, N.Y.: Holt & Co., 1916.

Franklin, John Hope. *The Free Negro in North Carolina*. Chapel Hill: U. of N.C. Press, 1943.

French, Joseph Lewis. *The Great Days of Piracy in the West Indies*. New York: Tudor Pub. Co., 1961.

Gerhard, Peter. *Pirates of the West Coast of New Spain*. Glendale, Calif.: A. H. Clark Co., 1960.

Goerch, Carl. *Ocracoke*. Winston-Salem: John F. Blair, 1958.

Gosse, Philip. *The History of Piracy*. New York: Longmans, Green & Co., 1932; Tudor Publishing Co., 1946.

————. *The Pirates' Who's Who*. Boston: Charles E. Lauriat Co., 1924.

Grimes, J. Bryan. *North Carolina Wills and Inventories in the Office of the Secretary of State*. Raleigh: Edwards and Broughton, 1912.

Hawks, Francis L. *History of North Carolina*, Vol. II. Fayetteville, N.C.: E. J. Hale and Son., 1858.

Hayward, Arthur L. *Book of Pirates*. New York: Roy Publishers, 1956.

Henderson, Archibald. *North Carolina: The Old North State and the New*, Vol. II. Chicago: Lewis Publishing Co., 1941.

Hesseltine, William Best, and Smiley, David L. *The South in American History*. Englewood Cliffs, N.J.: Prentice-Hall, 1960.

History of the Most Noted Pirates. New York: Empire State Book Co., 1926.

Holdsworth, William S. *History of English Law*, Vol. VIII. Boston: Little, Brown and Co., 1926.

Howell, Thomas Bayly. *State Trials*, Vol. XV. London: Callaghan & Co., 1811.

Howison, Robert R. *History of Virginia*. Philadelphia: Carey and Hart, 1846.

Hughson, Shirley Carter. *The Carolina Pirates and Colonial Commerce, 1670–1740*. Baltimore: Johns Hopkins Press, 1894.

Hurd, Archibald. *The Reign of Pirates*. New York: Alfred A. Knopf, 1925.

Johnson, Captain Charles. *A General History of the Robberies and Murders of the Most Notorious Pirates.* Originally published in London, 1724; numerous editions; cited herein is the 1726 fourth edition, edited by Arthur L. Haywood, London, 1926, and again reprinted 1955. London: Routledge and Kegan Paul Ltd., 1955.

Johnson, F. Roy. *Legends and Myths of North Carolina's Roanoke-Chowan Area.* Murfreesboro, N.C., 1966.

Jones, Hugh. *The Present State of Virginia.* Edited by Richard L. Morton. Original ed., London, 1724. Chapel Hill: U. of N.C. Press, 1956.

Journals of the House of Burgesses of Virginia, 1718. Edited by H. R. McIlwaine. Richmond: Virginia State Lib., 1912.

Karraker, Cyrus H. *Piracy Was A Business.* Rindge, N. H.: R. R. Smith, 1953.

Kemp, Peter K., and Lloyd, Christopher. *Brethren of the Coast.* New York: Macmillan Co., 1961.

Labaree, Leonard Woods. *Royal Government in America.* New Haven and London: Yale University Press, 1931.

———. *The Papers of Benjamin Franklin,* Vol. I. New Haven: Yale University Press, 1959.

Lawson, John. *History of North Carolina.* Originally published under this title in London, 1714; numerous editions; cited herein is edition edited by Frances Lathan Harris, Richmond: Garrett, 1937.

Lee, Lawrence. *The Lower Cape Fear in Colonial Days.* Chapel Hill: U. of N.C. Press, 1965.

Lee, Robert E. *North Carolina Family Law* (3rd ed.) Charlottesville, Va.: The Michie Co., 1963.

Lefler, Hugh Talmage, and Newsome, Arthur R. *North Carolina: The History of a Southern State.* Chapel Hill: U. of N.C. Press, 1954.

Lefler, Hugh Talmage. *History of North Carolina.* New York: Lewis Historical Pub. Co., 1956.

McCain, Paul M. *The County Court in North Carolina before 1750.* Durham: Duke University Press, 1954.

McCrady, Edward. *South Carolina under the Proprietary Government, 1670–1719.* New York: Macmillan Co., 1897.

MacLiesh, Fleming, and Krieger, Martin L. *The Privateers.* New York: Random House, 1962.

McRee, Griffin J. *Life and Correspondence of James Iredell.* New York: Appleton, 1857.

Mears, Thomas L. "The History of Admiralty Jurisdiction," reprinted in *Select Essays in Anglo-American History.* Boston: Little, Brown & Co., 1908.

Minutes of the Council and General Court of Colonial Virginia, 1622–1632, 1670–1676. Edited by H. R. McIlwaine. Richmond, 1927.

Moore, John W. *History of North Carolina*, Vol. I. Raleigh: A. Williams, 1880.

Moore, Louis T. *Stories Old and New of the Cape Fear Region.* Wilmington, N.C., 1956.

Morton, Richard L. *Colonial Virginia.* Chapel Hill: U. of N.C. Press, 1960.

North Carolina Charters and Constitutions, 1578–1698. Edited by Mattie Erma Edwards Parker. Raleigh: Carolina Charter Tercentenary Commission, 1963.

North Carolina Guide. Edited by Blackwell P. Robinson. Chapel Hill: U. of N.C. Press, 1955.

North Carolina Historical and Genealogical Register. Edited by J. R. B. Hathaway. Edenton, N.C., 1901.

Osgood, Herbert L. *The American Colonies in the Eighteenth Century.* New York: Columbia University Press, 1924.

Paschal, Herbert R. *A History of Colonial Bath.* Raleigh: Edwards and Broughton Co., 1955.

Penrose, Boies. *Tudor and Early Stuart Voyaging.* Washington: Folger Shakespeare Library, 1962.

Pirates Own Book. Edited by Charles Ellams. Salem, Mass.: Marine Research Dept. [1924].

Powell, William S. *Paradise Preserved.* Chapel Hill: U. of N.C. Press, 1965.

Pringle, Patrick. *Jolly Roger: The Story of the Great Age of Piracy.* New York: W. W. Norton & Co., 1953.

Rankin, Hugh F. *Golden Age of Piracy.* New York: Holt, Rinehart & Winston, 1969.

———. *The Pirates of Colonial North Carolina.* Raleigh: N.C. State Dept. of Archives and History, 1963.

———. *Criminal Trial Proceedings in the General Court of Co-*

lonial Virginia. Williamsburg, Va.: University Press of Virginia, 1965.

――――. *Upheaval in Albemarle: The Story of Culpepper's Rebellion, 1675–1689.* Raleigh: Carolina Charter Tercentenary Commission, 1962.

Reed, C. Wingate. *Beaufort County: Two Centuries of Its History.* Raleigh, 1962.

Robinson, Blackwell P. *The Five Royal Governors of North Carolina, 1729–1775.* Raleigh: Carolina Charter Tercentenary Commission, 1963.

Robinson, Gustavus H. *Handbook of Admiralty Law in the U.S.* St. Paul, Minn.: West Publishing Co., 1939.

Russell, John H. *The Free Negro in Virginia, 1619–1865.* Baltimore: John Hopkins Press, 1913.

Sharp, Bill. *A New Geography of North Carolina,* Vol. IV. Raleigh: Sharp Pub. Co., 1958.

Skaggs, Marvin L. *North Carolina Disputes Involving Her Southern Line.* Chapel Hill: U. of N.C. Press, 1941.

Snow, Edward Rowe. *Pirates and Buccaneers of the Atlantic Coast.* Boston: Yankee Pub. Co., 1944.

Snowden, Yates. *History of South Carolina,* Vol. I. New York: Lewis Publishing Co., 1920.

Spotswood, Alexander. *Official Letters of Alexander Spotswood,* Vol. II. Edited by R. A. Brock. Richmond: Virginia Historical Society, 1885.

Squires, W. H. T. *The Days of Yester-Year in Colony and Commonwealth: A Sketch Book of Virginia.* Portsmouth, Va.: Printcraft Press, Inc., 1928.

State Records of North Carolina, Vols. XI–XXVI. Edited by Walter Clark. Winston-Salem, Goldsboro, Charlotte: M. O. Sherrill, State Lib., 1895–1905.

Stick, David. *Graveyard of the Atlantic.* Chapel Hill: U. of N.C. Press, 1952.

――――. *Outer Banks of North Carolina.* Chapel Hill: U. of N.C. Press, 1958.

Stroud, George M. *A Sketch of the Laws Relating to Slavery.* Philadelphia: H. Longstreth, 1856.

Trials of Stede Bonnet and Other Pirates. London, 1719.

Tyler, Lyon Gardner. *Encyclopedia of Virginia Biography*, Vol. I. New York: Lewis Historical Publishing Co., 1915.

————. *Williamsburg, the Old Colonial Capital*. Richmond: Whittet & Shepperson, 1907.

Verrill, A. Hyatt. *The Real Story of the Pirates*. New York: D. Appleton Co., 1923.

Wallace, David D. *History of South Carolina*, Vol. I. New York: American Historical Society, 1934.

Watson, John F. *Annals of Philadelphia and Pennsylvania*, Vol. II. Edited by Willis P. Hazard. Philadelphia: E. S. Stuart, 1898.

Whedbee, Charles Harry. *Legends of the Outer Banks*. Winston-Salem: John F. Blair, 1966.

Wheeler, John H. *Historical Sketches of North Carolina from 1584 to 1854*. Philadelphia: Columbus Printing Works, 1851.

————. *Reminiscences and Memoirs of North Carolina and Eminent North Carolinians*. Columbus, Ohio: Columbus Printing Works, 1884.

Whipple, Addison B. C. *Pirate Rascals of the Spanish Main*. New York: Doubleday & Co., 1957.

Wilkinson, S. *The Voyages and Adventures of Edward Teach, Commonly Called Blackbeard, the Notorious Pirate*. Boston: Book Printing Office, 1808.

Williams, Lloyd Hanes. *Pirates of Colonial Virginia*. Richmond: The Dietz Press, 1937.

Williamson, Hugh. *History of North Carolina*, Vol. I. Philadelphia: Thomas Dobson, 1812.

Wise, Jennings Cropper. *Ye Kingdom of Accawmacke or the Eastern Shore of Virginia in the Seventeenth Century*. Richmond: Bell Book and Stationery Co., 1911.

Woodbury, George. *The Great Days of Piracy in the West Indies*. New York: W. W. Norton & Co., 1951.

Newspapers, Periodicals, and Pamphlets

"Accounts of the College," *William and Mary College Quarterly* (1st series), VIII (1900), 166.

"Anidmaversions on a Paper Entituled [*sic*] Virginia Addresses,

Printed in Philadelphia," *Virginia Magazine of History and Biography*, XXII (1914), 414–15.

Ashe, Samuel A. "Our Own Pirates," *North Carolina Booklets*, II, No. 2 (1910), pp. 6–10.

"Blackbeard Legend Is Giving Way," *Yearbook of the Pasquotank Historical Society, 1955* (Elizabeth City, N.C.), pp. 66–67.

"Blackbeard Legends Giving Way to Fact," *News and Observer* (Raleigh, N.C.), Dec. 14, 1912, sec. 4, p. 12.

Boston Newsletter, No. 775, dated "From Monday Feb. 16 to Monday Feb. 23, 1719" and No. 776, dated "From Monday Feb. 23 to Monday March 2, 1719." A photostatic copy can be obtained from Massachusetts Historical Society, Boston, Mass.

Brothers, G. W. "A Trip to Blackbeard's Castle," *Wake Forest Student*, XXX, No. 2 (November, 1910), p. 112.

Chronicle of the Bertie County (N.C.) *Historical Association*, No. 2 (October, 1953).

Cooke, Arthur L. "British Newspaper Accounts of Blackbeard's Death," *Va. Magazine of History and Biography*, LXI (July, 1953), 304.

"Copy of Patent to Landgrave," *N.C. Booklets*, VII, No. 1 (July, 1907), pp. 47–48.

Dewell, James D., Jr. "The Laws of Salvage," *Yale Law Journal*, XXI (1919), 493.

"Founding of Virginia's First College," *Virginia Cavalcade*, VII, No. 1 (Summer, 1957), p. 16.

Gaines, William H., Jr. "Pursuit of a Pirate—How an Expedition from Virginia Tracked Down the Notorious Blackbeard," *Va. Cavalcade*, II, No. 2 (Autumn, 1952), 15.

Grimes, J. Bryan. "Some Notes on Colonial North Carolina," *N.C. Booklets*, V, No. 2 (October, 1905), 90.

Hale, Edward Everett. "Ben Franklin's Ballads," *New England Magazine* (new series), XVIII (June, 1898), 505–7.

Hardee, Roy. "Grimes Plantation a State Historic Site," *News and Observer* (Raleigh, N.C.), Nov. 5, 1967, sec. 3, p. 9.

Haywood, Marshall DeLancey. "Governor Charles Eden," *N.C. Booklets*, III, No. 8 (December, 1903), 20.

Hill, D. H. "Edward Moseley: Character Sketch," *N.C. Booklets*, V, No. 3 (January, 1906), 205.

Historic Edenton and Countryside. Edenton Woman's Club. A recent but undated pamphlet.

Lovejoy, David S. "Rights Imply Equality: The Case Against Admiralty Jurisdiction in America, 1764–1766," *William and Mary College Quarterly* (3rd series), XVI (1959), 460.

Mervine, William M. "Pirates and Privateers in the Delaware Bay and River," *The Pa. Magazine*, XXXII (1908), 459.

Moore, Louis T. "Pirate Treasure Remains Buried on Money Island?" *Charlotte* (N.C.) *Observer*, October 10, 1926, sec. 5, p. 4.

"Notorious Pirate Teach Built Treasure House for Housing Gold and Wives," *Charlotte* (N.C.) *Observer*, March 27, 1927, sec. 3, p. 6.

"Papers Relating to the Founding of the College," *William and Mary College Quarterly* (1st series), VII (1899), 165.

Parker, Charles. "A Plow Turns Up Buried Treasure," *News and Observer* (Raleigh), June 26, 1938, p. 1.

"Pirate Blackbeard's Island to Become Refuge for Birds," *Greensboro* (N.C.) *Daily News*, Sept. 26, 1933.

Price, Jonathan. *A Description of Ocracoke Inlet.* A pamphlet originally published in New Bern, N.C., 1795, and reprinted in *N.C. Historical Review*, III (1926), 624–33.

Pugh, Jesse F. "A Pirate and His House," *University of N.C. Magazine*, April, 1913, pp. 195–98.

"Randolph Manuscript," *Va. Magazine of History and Biography*, XX (1912).

Rondthaler, Alice K. *The Story of Ocracoke.* Ocracoke, 1966.

Sass, Herbert Ravenel. "The Pirate Who Wanted to Be King," *American Magazine*, February, 1930, pp. 14–20.

Smith, Henry A. M. "The Baronies of South Carolina." *South Carolina History and Gen. Mag.*, XI (1910), 86.

"Some Notes on the Four Forms of the Oldest Building of William and Mary College," *William and Mary College Quarterly* (2nd series), VIII (1928), 220.

Surrency, Edwin C. "The Procedure for the Trial of a Pirate," *American Journal of Legal History*, VIII (1957), 251.

"Teach's Light and Teach's Gold Flicker in Bath," *News and Observer* (Raleigh, N.C.), Sept. 10, 1933, sec. 1, p. 3.

The Tryals of Captain John Rackham and Other Pirates. Printed by Robert Baldwin, Jamaica, 1721.

Ubbelohde, Carl W., Jr. "The Vice Admiralty Court of North Carolina," *North Carolina Historical Review*, XXXI (1954), 517.

Upshur, Thomas T. "Eastern-Shore History," *Va. Magazine of History and Biography*, IX (1902), 95.

————. "Eastern-Shore History: Notes," *Va. Magazine of History and Biography*, X (1903), 70–71.

"William Howard the Pirate," *Tyler's Quarterly Historical and Genealogical Magazine*, I (1920), 36–39.

Wood, Leonora W. "Worst Cut-Throat," *Norfolk Virginian-Pilot*, Feb. 4, 1951.

Worth, L. Kinvin. "The Massachusetts Vice Admiralty Court and the Federal Admiralty Jurisdiction," *American Journal of Legal History*, VI (1962), 250.

Unpublished Letters, Manuscripts, and Documents

Letters of Captain Ellis Brand to the Lords of Admiralty, dated Feb. 6, 1718/1719, March 12, 1718/1719, and July 12, 1718/1719. Public Record Office, London, Admiralty 1/1472.

Letter of Captain Brand to Josiah Burchett, Secretary of Lords Commissioners of the Admiralty, dated July 4, 1719. Public Record Office, London, Treasury I, Vol. 223, fols. 7, 7a. A transcript of the letter can be found in N.C. Dept. of Archives, Raleigh.

Letters of Captain George Gordon to the Lords of Admiralty, dated Sept. 14, 1721, and Sept. 17, 1721. Public Record Office, London, Admiralty 1/1826.

Letters of Captain Vincent Pearse to the Lords of Admiralty, dated Feb. 4, 1717/1718, March 4, 1717/1718, June 3, 1718, and Sept. 5, 1718. Public Record Office, London, Admiralty 1/2282.

Letters of Governor Alexander Spotswood to Governor Eden, dated Jan. 28, 1718/1719, Nov. 7, 1718, Dec. 21, 1718. Lee–Ludwell Papers, Archives of the Virginia Historical Society, Richmond, Va.

Letters of James Stanhope to Governor Spotswood, Proclamation of King George I enclosed, dated Nov. 30, 1714. Public Record

Office, London, Colonial Office, Class 5, Vol. 190, p. 116. A copy is in the Library of Congress, Manuscript Division.

Order of Privy Council. Public Record Office, London, Privy Council Register 2187, p. 293.

Records of the trial of Dr. William Howell, Dec. 22, 1721. Public Record Office, London, Colonial Office 23, Vol. 1, Bahamas (1717–1725), pp. 192–97. A photostatic copy may be found in the Library of Congress, Manuscript Division.

Records relating to South Carolina, 1712–1720. Public Record Office, London. Transcript in S.C. Archives Dept., Columbia, S.C.

Royal Instructions from Queen Anne to Governor Eden, dated Jan. 24, 1711. N.C. Dept. of Archives, Raleigh, Council Journal 1712–1718, pp. 84–100.

Royal Instructions and Commission from the Lords Proprietors to Tobias Knight, dated Jan. 24, 1711. N.C. Dept. of Archives, Raleigh, Council Journal 1712–1718.

Royal Instructions from the Lords Proprietors to Governor Spotswood, dated April 15, 1715. Public Record Office, London, Colonial Office 5, Vol. 190, pp. 128–76.

Tyler, John E., "Governor Pollock and Ball-Gra," in "Bertie County's Colonial and State Governors of N.C." Typed manuscript in N.C. Dept. of Archives, Raleigh, 1949.

Index

ML